بسم الله الرحمن الرحيم

شرف أصحاب الحديث

و

نصيحة أهل الحديث

كلاهما

للحافظ أحمد بن علي بن ثابت

المعروف بـ «الخطيب البغدادي»

al-Ḥāfiẓ Abū Bakr Aḥmad Ibn ʿAlī
al-Khaṭīb al-Baghdādī (d.463H)

Disciples of Ḥadīth

being a translation of his
Sharaf al-Aṣḥāb al-Ḥadīth wa Naṣiḥātu Ahlu'l-Ḥadīth

دار السنة

The Messenger of Allāh (ﷺ) said:

"'May Allāh cause a slave to flourish who heard my words and understands them, then he conveys them from me. There may be those who have knowledge but no understanding, and there may be those who convey knowledge to those who may have more understanding of it than they do.'"

[Abū Dāwūd #3660 and Tirmidhī #2656]

Disciples of Ḥadīth

The Noble Guardians

With accompanying notes of the author advising Ahlu'l Ḥadīth

by al-Ḥāfiẓ Abū Bakr Aḥmad Ibn 'Alī
al-Khaṭīb al-Baghdādī (d. 463 H)

Dār as-Sunnah Publishers
BIRMINGHAM

First Published in Great Britain June 2020 / Dhu'l-Qa'dah 1441H
by Dār as-Sunnah Publishers

DĀR AS-SUNNAH PUBLISHERS
P.O. Box 9818, Birmingham, B11 4WA, United Kingdom

W: www.darassunnah.com
E: info@darassunnah.com
E: daar-us-sunnah@mail.com

British Library Cataloguing in publication Data.
A catalogue record for this book is available from the British Library.

Title: Disciples of Ḥadīth
by: al-Ḥāfiẓ Abū Bakr Aḥmad Ibn 'Alī al-Khaṭīb al-Baghdādī
Translated from the original Arabic

ISBN 1-904336-66-3
Paper-back

Published and Typeset by: Dār as-Sunnah Publishers
First Edition, 1441 AH/2020 CE

CONTENT

THE SECOND TREATISE
The Faithful Counsel

FOREWORD

With the Name of Allāh, the All-Merciful, the Most Merciful

All praise and thanks be to Allāh. We praise Him and we ask His Aid and ask for His Forgiveness. And we seek refuge from the evils of ourselves and the wickedness of our deeds. Whomsoever Allāh guides, there is none that can misguide him and whomsoever Allāh sends astray, there is none that can guide him. And I bear witness that none has the right to be worshipped except Allāh, Alone, without partners and I bear witness that Muḥammad is His slave and His Messenger. May the Peace and Blessings of Allāh be upon him and upon his Companions. Allāh, Most High says:

إِنَّا نَحْنُ نَزَّلْنَا ٱلذِّكْرَ وَإِنَّا لَهُۥ لَحَٰفِظُونَ ﴿٩﴾

> "Indeed, it is We who sent down the message [i.e., the Qur'ān], and indeed, We will be its guardian."
>
> [*al-Ḥijr* (15):9]

This is a true promise from Allāh, the Most Glorified, the Most High that He will protect the Reminder in both the Qur'ān and the

Sunnah. As for the Qur'ān, Allāh, Most High has preserved it from alteration or substitution, so no one—whoever he may be—may venture to advance or delay any part of it, alter it, substitute any of it or remove anything from it or write anything in it.

As for the Sunnah, it has been ordained that it should be transmitted by reliable transmitters, impartial narrators and sincere memorisers, who take care to collect them from the hearts of the scholars of ḥadīth and write them down, from the time of the Companions (*raḍiyAllāhu 'anhum*) until our time.

Likewise, He has ordained for it scholars who are knowledgeable concerning weaknesses, who investigate the circumstances of the narrators and who have memorised the sources of those who refute the lies against the Messenger of Allāh (ﷺ) and confirm truthful reports from him.

This group from among the scholars of ḥadīth are the successful ones and the chosen best, of whom the Prophet (ﷺ) informed us in an authentic ḥadīth:

> "A group from among my *ummah* will continue to prevail and they will never be harmed by those who forsake them, until the Hour begins." Narrated by Ibn Mājah

Ibn Al-Madīnī said: 'They are the scholars of ḥadīth.' And Yazīd Ibn Hārūn said: 'If they are not the scholars of ḥadīth, then I do not know who they are.'[1]

And that is the view of many of the scholars.

---

[1] These reports are authentic and I have analysed them in my critique of *'Athar Al-Kitāb'*, each under its subject.

They are the successful group, who adhere to the *Sunan* and they are not harmed by those who abandon them due to their avoidance of religious innovation and they call to the [true] religion of Allāh with knowledge and clear evidence.

So what may be said of people who disparage their importance and seek to diminish their status, while they are a blessing for every Muslim and they have a right upon every believer? Indeed, none attempts to diminish their status except the innovator, who has gone astray or the disbeliever.

This book which is in your hands—my brother and seeker of knowledge—is a reminder from a great Imām, to his brothers among the seekers of knowledge, whose virtue and eminence as students of ḥadīth he acknowledges; and he encourages them in their pursuit of knowledge of ḥadīth and also to act upon them and to spread knowledge of them. Without doubt, he is a thorn in the side of the innovators, who worship Allāh in a heretical manner and depending entirely on their own minds, rejecting aḥadīth of the Prophet (ﷺ) or altering their meanings.

For this reason, I have sought guidance from Allāh (*istikharah*) in the matter of its verification, in order that seekers of knowledge may gain the maximum benefit from it. So I ask Allāh, Most Glorified that this work be purely for the purpose of seeking His Generous Countenance. Verily, He is Able to do all things.

'Amr 'Abdu'l-Mun'im 'Abdu'l-'Alā' Salīm

THE AUTHOR

Ḥāfiẓ Abū Bakr Aḥmad Ibn ʿAlī al-Khaṭīb al-Baghdādī[2]

His Name and Lineage

He is the Imām and Ḥāfiẓ, Aḥmad Ibn ʿAlī Ibn Thābit Ibn Aḥmad Ibn Mahdī, al-Baghdādī, Abū Bakr, better known as Al-Khaṭīb al-Baghdādī. His Father was ʿAlī Ibn Thābit, who was a sermoniser (*Khaṭīb*) in the village of Darzījan. Al-Khaṭīb (may Allāh have Mercy on him) said in the biography of his Father, in *'Tarīkh Baghdād'* (11/359): 'He occupied the position of Khaṭīb at the pulpit in Darzījan for around twenty years.'

His Birth and Upbringing

He was born (may Allāh have mercy on him) in the year 391 AH. He began to acquire knowledge in the bosom of Al-Khaṭīb's family (may Allāh have mercy on him), though his father took great pains with his education, encouraging him to attend ḥadīth

[2] An Abbreviated Version, see his biography in *'al-Siyār'* by Al-Dhāhabī (18/270) and *'Al-Bidayah wa'l-Nihayah'* (12/101).

lectures and to study Islāmic Jurisprudence. He first began attending lectures when he was eleven years of age, then he began to travel in order to acquire knowledge of ḥadīth when he was twenty years old. He travelled to Baṣrah, Nishapur, Al-Sham, Makkah and other places. He travelled around, acquiring [knowledge], listening and accumulating [learning] as he went until he was unequalled and achieved a high status in the eyes of the authoritative people.

His Teachers

As for his teachers, he heard from a very great number of Shaikhs; the most prominent of them included:

- Al-Barqānī
- al-Azharī
- Ibn Bishrān
- Ibn Rizqih
- al-Ḥayrī
- Abū Ḥāzim al-ʿAbdawī
- Al-Khallāl and numerous others

He even narrated from some of his own students, such as Naṣr al-Maqdīsī, Ibn Makūla and al-Ḥumaydī.

Al-Dhahabī (may Allāh have Mercy on him) said: 'This is the way of every Ḥāfiẓ: he narrates from the greater and the lesser [scholars].'

He studied Islāmic Jurisprudence at the hands of Abū'l-Ḥasan Ibn al-Muhamilī and al-Qāḍī Abū'l-Ṭayyib al-Ṭabarī.

Al-Dhahabī said: 'He was one of the foremost Shāfiʿī scholars.'

His Students

Those who transmitted from him included:

- Ibn Makūla
- Al-Ḥumaydī
- Abū'l-Faḍl Ibn Khayrūn
- Al-Mubārak
- Ibn al-Tuyūrī
- A great number of others, including his Shaikh, Al-Barqānī (may Allāh have Mercy on him).

His Belief

As for his beliefs with regard to fundamental principles (*al-usūl*), he was an adherent of the Sunni school and held sound, orthodox beliefs.

Some claimed that he held Ash'arī beliefs, but this is not correct. He wrote a treatise on philosophical discourse (*kalām*) regarding Allāh's Divine Attributes, which proves that he followed the beliefs of *Ahlu'l-Sunnah wa'l-Jama'ah.* And I have previously refuted these claims that he was an Ash'arī.[3]

The Scholars Praise for Him

Ibn Makūla said: "'Abū Bakr was the last prominent scholar that we witnessed who combined such knowledge, memorisation, expertise, precision in the aḥadīth of the Messenger of Allāh (ﷺ), skill regarding their weaknesses and their chains of narrators,

[3] This is a publication which is currently in print and is published by Maktabah Ibn Taimiyyah of Cairo and Al-'Ilm of Jeddah.

knowledge of the authentic, the *gharīb*,[4] the *farḍ*,[5] the *munkar*[5] and the *matrūh*.[7] And Al-Baghdādī was without peer—aside from Abū'l-Ḥasan al-Daraquṭnī. I asked 'Abdullāh al-Sūrī about Al-Khaṭīb and Abū Bakr al-Sajzī, which of them had memorised more aḥadīth? He clearly favoured Al-Khaṭīb.'

Al-Mu'taman al-Sajī said: 'Aside from al-Daraquṭnī, Baghdād has not produced anyone who has memorised more aḥadīth than Abū Bakr al-Khaṭīb.'

Abū'l-'Alī al-Bardanī said: 'It is likely that Al-Khaṭīb never encountered his [own] like.'

Abū Isḥāq al-Shīrazī, the scholar of Islāmic Jurisprudence, said: 'Abū Bakr Al-Khaṭīb resembles al-Daraquṭnī and his peers in his knowledge and memorisation of ḥadīth.'

Abū'l-Fityān al-Ḥāfiẓ said: 'Al-Khaṭīb was the leader in this field; I have neveren countered his like.'

Abū'l-Qāsim al-Nasīb said: 'I heard Al-Khaṭīb saying, 'Abū Bakr al-Barqānī wrote a letter with me to Abū Nu'aym Al-Ḥāfiẓ and in it, he said: 'Our brother, Abū Bakr—may Allāh help him and preserve him—has travelled to you to acquire knowledge and he—all praise and thanks be to Allāh—has an eminent background and a firm

[4] *Gharīb*: A ḥadīth whose chain of narrators contains a particular narrator at any point in its chain who is the only one who reported the ḥadīth.

[5] *Farḍ*: Ibn Hajr held that *gharīb* and *farḍ* are synonyms both linguistically and in ḥadīth terminology, though he explains that scholars of ḥadīth distinguish between the two, according to their usage: so *farḍ* is more commonly applied as meaning *al-farḍ al-mutlaq* (a narration reported by a single Companion), while *gharīb* is more often applied to *al-farḍ al-nisbī* (in which the singular narrator occurs later in the chain).

[6] *Munkar*: A ḥadīth that contradicts what has been authentically reported elsewhere.

[7] *Matrūh*: A ḥadīth that is discarded or rejected.

foundation in this subject. He has journeyed in pursuit of it and gathered knowledge the like of which many of his contemporaries have not acquired. That will be clear to you when you meet him and observe his piety and his reserve, which will impress you."

Al-Ḥāfiẓ Abū Sa'd al-Sam'ānī said: 'Al-Khaṭīb was revered, dignified, trustworthy, analytical, a dependable authority, possessed of a fine hand, extremely precise, eloquent—the Seal of the Huffāẓ.'

Al-Salafī said: "'I asked Shuja' al-Zahlī about Al-Khaṭīb and he said: '[He is] an Imām, author and Ḥāfiẓ, and we do not know anyone of his like.'

His Written Works

As for Al-Khaṭīb's written works, he wrote many. Abū Sa'd al-Sam'ānī said: 'Al-Khaṭīb wrote fifty-six works.'

Al-Dhahabī mentioned a number of them in *'al-Siyār'*, the most well known of them being *'Tarīkh Baghdād'*. It consists of a hundred and six sections and it is without equal. It is greatly beneficial, a reliable source of information regarding the circumstances of many of the inhabitants of Baghdād or those who visited it.

His Death

He died (may Allāh have Mercy on him) in the year 463 AH. Makkī al-Rumaylī said: 'Al-Khaṭīb became ill in the middle of Ramaḍan and his condition worsened on the 1st of Dhū'l-Hijjah; he entrusted the execution of his will to Ibn Khayrūn and he bequeathed his books to him and distributed all of his money in charity and to the scholars of ḥadīth. He died on Monday, the 7th of Dhū'l-Hijjah in the year 463AH. Then on the Tuesday morning, his body was taken out and it was brought to the western quarter [of Baghdād] and it was carried by the judges and the notables of the city. Prayers were conducted over him by Abū'l-Ḥusayn Ibn al-Muhtadī Billāh, who made *takbīr* over him four times, after which he was buried beside the grave of Bishr al-Hāfī.'

Versions Relied on for the Purpose of Verification

For the purpose of verification, I have relied on two versions:

- The first: This is a handwritten version from the manuscripts of Dar Al-Kutub Al-Miṣriyyah, under no. B23736, micro-film no. 25251, which consists of three volumes, from q. 64 to q. 117. This is a good and accurate version, represented by the letter (A).

- The second: This is a Turkish printed version and it is the only printed version of this book. The person who verified it relied on a number of handwritten manuscripts and I have identified them by the letter (B).

THE AUTHOR'S INTRODUCTION

With the Name of Allāh, the All-Merciful, the Most Merciful

We were told by the Shaikh, Imām, scholar and Ḥāfiẓ, Jamāluddīn Abū Muḥammad 'Abdu'l-Qāḍir Ibn 'Abdullāh Al-Rahāwī, the recitation being in his words, while I was present, listening in Al-Mawṣil, on Saturday, the 23rd of Dhū'l-Ḥijjah, in the year 562 AH. He said that he was informed by Shaikh Abū 'Abdullāh Muḥammad Ibn Ḥamzah Ibn Muḥammad Ibn Abū Jamīl al-Qurashī, who said that he was informed by Shaikh Abū Muḥammad Hibatullāh Ibn Aḥmad Al-Akfānī, who said: 'I was told by the Shaikh and Imām, Abū Bakr Aḥmad Ibn 'Alī Ibn Thābit Al-Khaṭīb Al-Baghdādī (may Allāh have mercy on him), with regard to what he had transmitted to us:

All praise and thanks be to Allāh, who chose Islām as a religion for the best of His creation, sent the Messengers whom He chose from among His creation with it and He made us custodians and implementers of His Law (*Sharī'ah*) among the adherents of His religion, to deter from the things that He has made unlawful and to act upon His Sunnah.We praise and thank Him as befits Him and we ask Him to grant us success in following it with integrity and we implore Him to increase His Bounty upon us.

And may the blessings of Allāh be upon the seal of the Messengers, our master, Muḥammad, the most eminent of the Prophets and the finest member in all of Allāh's creation and upon the distinguished Companions and those who follow them with ihsan until the Day of Resurrection.

To proceed: May Allāh grant you success in performing good deeds and may He protect us and you from falling into innovation and doubtful matters. We have stood against the denunciation which you mentioned of the scholars of ḥadīth and *āthār*[8] by the innovators, their maligning of those who involve themselves in learning aḥadīth and memorising traditions, their rejection of authentic narrations transmitted to the Muslim ummah by the truthful Imāms and their mockery of the people of truth, utilising fabrications transmitted to them by the heretics:

ٱللَّهُ يَسْتَهْزِئُ بِهِمْ وَيَمُدُّهُمْ فِي طُغْيَٰنِهِمْ يَعْمَهُونَ ﴿١٥﴾

> "[But] Allāh mocks them and prolongs them in their transgression [while] they wander blindly."
>
> [*al-Baqarah* (2):15]

And this is not surprising from those who follow guidance or from those whom Allāh caused to deviate from the path of guidance. The clearest evidence of their abandonment [of the Sunnah] is their failure to abide by the rulings of the Qur'ān, their failure to abide by the clear evidences contained in its verses, their rejection of the *Sunan* and their reliance on their own opinions when

[8] *Āthār*: Narrations from the Companions (*raḍiyAllāhu 'anhum*).

forming judgements.

Their innovation is intended to cause confusion and man is seduced by philosophical discourse and argument; he has made his religion into something for the purpose of disputation, placed himself in fertile ground for destruction and delivered himself to Satan, repelling truth with doubtful things. When he is shown books of rulings relating to the traditions of our Prophet (ﷺ), he casts them to one side and refuses to look at them, mocking the one who conveys them and the one who transmits them, thereby opposing the religion and maligning the Muslims' Imāms, acting arrogantly towards the common populace by spending his life in learning philosophical discourse, considering that all but he are astray and believing that he alone is saved from blind following, claiming that his words are based on justice and *tawḥīd*, though in fact, his '*tawḥīd*', when it is examined, is actually *shirk* and apostasy. This is because he ascribes partners to Allāh and his '*justice*' is, in fact, a deviation from the path of truth, towards contradiction of the rulings of the Book of Allāh and the Sunnah.

A miserable, wretched person, when he is put to trial by some matter pertaining to his religion, turns toward the scholar of Islāmic Jurisprudence and seeks a ruling from him, then he acts upon what he says and what he narrates, returning to blind following after having fled from it and adhering to its ruling, having previously shunned it. So how can he regard blind following as lawful, when he previously declared it to be unlawful?! And [how can he] minimise the sin of it, having previously attached such great importance to it?! And his rejection of it will not benefit him in this life or the next, for his actions in accordance with the Islāmic Law (*Sharīʿah*) are more appropriate and more worthy.

CHAPTER ONE

The Text

1. We were informed by Abū Sa'īd Muḥammad Ibn Mūsā Ibn al-Faḍl Ibn Shazan al-Ṣayrafī, in Nishapur, who said that Abū'l-'Abbās Muḥammad Ibn Ya'qūb al-Aṣamm told him that he was informed by Muḥammad Ibn Isḥāq al-Saghanī that Isḥāq Ibn 'Isā said: 'I heard Mālik Ibn Anas (*raḍiyAllāhu 'anhu*) censuring argument in matters of religion and he said:

> 'Whenever a man who is more argumentative than another comes to us, he desires us to reject that which Jibrīl (*'alayhis-salām*) brought to the Prophet (ﷺ).''[9]

[9] Its chain of narrators is authentic.

The tradition was narrated by Al-Lalaka'ī in *'Sharḥ Usūl al-I'tiqād'* (#293) by way of Al-Ḥasan Ibn 'Alī al-Ḥalwanī, on the authority of Isḥāq Ibn 'Isā. He also narrated it from another source on the authority of Mālik. A different narration was authentically reported on Imām Mālik's authority regarding the censure of disputation and argumentativeness in religious matters: It was reported on the authority of Ma'n Ibn 'Isā that he said: "Mālik Ibn Anas (*raḍiyAllāhu 'anhu*) was once returning from the masjid, leaning on my arm, when a man called Abū'l-Ḥuwayriyah who was accused of irja' caught up with him. He said. 'O slave of Allāh! Listen to something I have to say and debate with me and let me tell you my opinion.' Mālik said: 'And what if you overcome me?' The man replied, 'If I defeat you, you follow me.' Mālik asked, 'And what if another man comes =

2. We were informed by Abū'l-Qāsim 'Abdu'l-Raḥmān Ibn Muḥammad Ibn 'Abdullāh al-Siraj, in Nishapur that he said that he was informed by Bishr Ibn Aḥmad al-Asfarayīnī, who said that Ja'far Ibn Muḥammad al-Firyabī told him: 'I was informed by Bishr Ibn Al-Walīd, who said: 'I heard Abū Yūsuf saying, 'It used to be said that whoever seeks [knowledge of] the religion through philosophical discourse is a *zindīq*[10];whoever seeks the *gharīb* among ḥadīth is a liar and whoever seeks wealth through alchemy will become bankrupt."[11]

=
and defeats us (both)?' He replied, 'Then we follow him.' To this, Mālik replied, 'O slave of Allāh! Allāh sent Muḥammad (ﷺ) with a single religion, but I see you moving from religion to religion. 'Umar Ibn 'Abdu'l-'Azīz said: 'Whoever makes his religion the object of argumentation will frequently change it."' (Narrated by Al-Ajurī in *'Al-Shariah'*, p. 56, with an authentic chain of narrators). And many traditions have been authentically reported on the authority of the Salaf regarding the censure of argument and disputation in religious matters. I have referred to them in other places and they are narrated in the full version of the book *'Al-Sharī'ah'* by Al-Ajurī, authenticated by us.

[10] *Zindīq*: A *zindīq* is a person who acknowledges the Prophethood of the Messenger of Allāh (ﷺ) and accepts the principle tenets of Islām, but at the same time adheres to beliefs which are unanimously branded as *kufr* (disbelief) in the Sharī'ah.According to this definition the term *zindīq* will apply to all persons who proclaim themselves to be Muslims while at the same time adhering to *kufr* beliefs.

There is no objection to its *isnād* (chain of narrators). In it is Bishr Ibn Al-Walīd Al-Kindī; scholars hold conflicting opinions regarding him: Al-Daraqutni declared him to be trustworthy, while Sāliḥ Jazarah said of him, "He is honest, but he was not rational, having become senile in his dotage." Al-Sulaymānī said: "His ḥadīth is *munkar*." Al-Ajurī said: "I asked Abū Dāwūd: 'Is Bishr Ibn Al-Walīd trustworthy?' He replied, 'No'."

[11] I say: Some of the scholars of ḥadīth refrained from commenting on his status at the end of his life due to the conflicting reports about him, as is made plain by the words of Sāliḥ Jazarah, who was among those who learnt Islāmic Jurisprudence from Abū Yūsuf and so his narration from him is likely correct, due to the shortness of the chain of narrators and the fact that he accompanied him for a lengthy period. And tolerance in the matter of *āthār* is more acceptable than in the matter of traditions with asaneed (chains of narrators) and aḥadīth; and the Shaikh of the author is trustworthy and a jurist, who has a biography in *'Al-Muntakhab Min Al-Ṣiyāq'* by Al-Ṣayrafīnī (#995) and *'Al-'Ibār'* by Al-Dhahabī (2/235). The athar was narrated by Al-Lalakā'ī (#305), Abū'l-Qāsim Al-Asbahānī in *'Al-Hujjah fi Bayān Al-Mahajjah'* (1/105) by way of Bishr Ibn Al-Walīd.

3. We were informed by Abū Manṣūr Muḥammad Ibn ʿIsā Ibn ʿAbdu'l-ʿAzīz al-Bazzār in Ḥamadhān that he said that he was told by ʿUbaydullāh Ibn Saʿīd al-Qāḍī in Burūjad that he said that he was informed by ʿAbdullāh Ibn Wahb Al-Ḥāfiẓ al-Daynūrī, who said that Sufyān al-Thawrī said:

> "The religion is only through traditions, not through opinion; the religion is only through traditions, not through opinion; the religion is only through traditions, not through opinion."[12]

4. We were informed by Abū'l-Ḥasan ʿAlī Ibn Aḥmad Ibn Muḥammad Ibn Bakrān Al-Fuwwī in Al-Baṣrah, that he said that Abū ʿAlī Al-Ḥasan Ibn Muḥammad Ibn ʿUthmān Al-Fasawī said that he was informed by Yaʿqūb Ibn Sufyān, who said that Al-Faḍl Ibn Ziyād said: "I asked Abū ʿAbdullāh [Aḥmad Ibn Ḥanbal] about Al-Karabīsī and what he has proclaimed and he frowned and said:

> "Their trial has only come from the books that they fabricated; they have abandoned the traditions of the Messenger of Allāh (ﷺ) and his Companions (*raḍiyAllāhu ʿanhum*) and they have devoted themselves to these books."[13]

---

[12] Its chain of narrators is extremely weak.

In it is ʿAbdullāh Ibn Muḥammad Ibn Wahb al-Daynūrī; Al-Dāraquṭnī said: "[He is] abandoned." And in another narration, it was reported that he said: "He fabricates aḥadīth." He was suspected by Ibn ʿUqdah [of being untruthful] and ʿUmar Ibn Sahl called him a liar. It was narrated by Ibn ʿAbdu'l-Barr in *'Jāmiʿ Bayān Al-ʿIlm'* (2/137) from another source, on the authority of Ibn Al-Mubārak, who reported on the authority of Sufyān, but its chain contains someone whom I do not know.

[13] Its chain of narrators is weak.

I have not taken a position on what has been said regarding the author's Shaikh, with respect to critique and praise (*al-Jarḥ wat-Taʿdīl*), except to mention what Al-Samaʿanī said of him in *'Al-Ansab'* (4/410): He mentioned his narration on the authority of Al-Fasawī =

5. We were informed by Abū'l-Ḥasan Muḥammad Ibn 'Ubaydullāh Ibn Muḥammad al-Ḥannā'ī, who said that he was informed [by Abū Bakr][14] Aḥmad Ibn Salmān al-Najjād, who said that he was informed by 'Abdullāh Ibn Aḥmad Ibn Ḥanbal that he said: "My father told me that he was informed by 'Abdu'l-Raḥmān Ibn Mahdī, who said: 'I heard Mālik Ibn Anas (*raḍiyAllāhu*

=

and the narration of Al-Khaṭīb on his authority, though Imām Aḥmad (may Allāh have Mercy on him) that criticised the claim that any writings can be attributed to him. In *'Masa'il Isḥāq Ibn Ibrāhim Ibn Hānī' al-Naysabūrī'* (#1908), it was reported from him that he said: "I heard Abū 'Abdullāh saying, 'Nothing impresses me from the books [of opinions] and whoever wrote anything from the books is an innovator'." He also said (#1912), "Every writing that is innovated is a heresy."

And this harshness on the part of Imām Aḥmad was for two reasons:

The first is that it was not confirmed to him that anyone from among the Companions of the Prophet (ﷺ) or the *Tabi'ūn* wrote a book; in *'Al-Masa'il'* (#1911) he said: "I was listening to Abū 'Abdullāh and a man from Ardabīl asked him about a man known as 'Abdu'l-Raḥmān, did he write a book? Abū 'Abdullāh said: "Say to him: 'Did anyone from among the Companions of the Messenger of Allāh (ﷺ) do this? Or did any of the Tabi'oon?" And he was angry and severe regarding this matter and forbade it, saying, "Forbid the people from doing it and adhere to the ḥadīth."

The second is his fear that such books as these and the opinions of men that they contain would divert people away from the fundamental source, which is the Book [of Allāh] and the Sunnah.

Likewise, 'Uthmān Ibn Sa'īd al-Darimī transmitted from him that he said: "Do not look at the books of Abū 'Ubayd, nor anything written by Isḥāq, nor Sufyān, nor Al-Shafi'ī, nor Mālik; [instead] it is incumbent upon you to go back to the fundamental source [i.e. the Qur'ān and Sunnah]."

And it has been authentically reported from him that he permitted the writing down of that which does not contain opinion.

He said: "Every innovated book is a heresy," or "Every book that is a novelty is a heresy. As for that which contains debate, in which a man informs the reader of the knowledge that he has and what he has heard from formal legal opinions, I do not see any objection to that."

Al-Khaṭīb spoke at length about this matter and he cited its evidences in his book *'Taqyīd Al-'Ilm'*.

As for his words regarding Al-Karabīsī, it has been confirmed from him in *'Masa'il Isḥāq'* (#1865), where he said: "I heard him saying, 'May Allāh humiliate Al-Karabīsī; none should sit with him, nor repeat his words, nor copy his books and nor should we sit with those who sit with him." And he spoke a great deal about him.

[14] This addition is from manuscript (B).

'anhu) say:

> 'The Messenger of Allāh (ﷺ) and those appointed to authority after him established Sunan and adopting them is affirmation of the Book [of Allāh, the Almighty, the All-Powerful],[15] implementation of the requirement to obey Allāh, strengthening of Allāh's Religion; whoever acts upon it is rightly guided and whoever supports it will be victorious, while whoever opposes it has followed something other than the path of the Believers and Allāh will hold him responsible for that for which he undertook responsibility."[16]

6. Abū Sa'īd Muḥammad Ibn Mūsā al-Ṣayrafī informed us that Abū'l-'Abbās Muḥammad Ya'qūb al-Aṣamm told him that Al-'Abbās Ibn Al-Walīd Ibn Mazīd Al-Bayrūtī informed him that he heard Al-Awzā'ī saying:

> "It is incumbent upon you to adhere to the traditions of those who came before, even if the people reject you. And I warn you against the opinions of men, even if they embellish them with fine words, for the matter is clear and you are following the straight path."[17]

[15] This addition is from manuscript (B).

[16] Its chain of narrators is authentic.

It was reported from another source, narrated by Al-Ājurī in *'Al-Sharī'ah'* (p. 48): Al-Firyābī informed us that Al-Ḥasan Ibn 'Alī Al-Ḥalwānī in Tarsus told him in the year 233 AH.: "I heard Mutrif Ibn 'Abdullāh saying, 'I heard Mālik Ibn Anas (*raḍiyAllāhu 'anhu*) saying, when those who deviate from the religion were mentioned in his presence, "Umar Ibn 'Abdu'l- 'Azīz (*raḍiyAllāhu 'anhu*) said...' and he quoted the narration'."

And its chain is authentic.

It was narrated by Al-Lalakā'ī in *'Sharh Usūl Al-I'tiqād'* (134) by way of Rushdayn Ibn Sa'd, who said that 'Uqayl informed him on the authority of Shihāb, on the authority of 'Umar Ibn 'Abdu'l-'Azīz.

But its *isnād* is weak, due to the weakness of Rushdayn.

[17] Its chain of narrators is authentic.

It was narrated by Al-Ājurī in *'Al-Sharī'ah'* (p. 58).

7. We were informed by Al-Ḥasan Ibn Abū Bakr, who said that 'Abdullāh Ibn Isḥāq Ibn Ibrāhīm al-Baghawī told him that he was informed by Al-Ḥasan Ibn 'Ulayl that he was told by Aḥmad Ibn Al-Ḥusayn, the companion of Al-Qawha, who said: "I heard Yazīd Ibn Zurai' (may Allāh have mercy on him) saying,

> 'The people of opinion are the enemies of the Sunnah'."[18]

He [Abū Bakr][19] said:

If any of the people who hold reprehensible opinions was to occupy himself with knowledge that benefits him and studied the *Sunan* of the Messenger of the Lord of the worlds and followed the path of jurists and scholars of ḥadīth, he would find therein that which would render him needless of anything else and he would suffice himself with the path and eschew his [baseless] opinion. This is because the ḥadīth comprises knowledge of the principles of *tawḥīd* and an explanation of the promise [of Paradise for the believers] and the threat [of punishment for the disbelievers] and the Divine Attributes of the Lord of the worlds, rather than the sayings of the heretics. There is also information concerning characteristics of Paradise and of the Fire and what Allāh has prepared therein for the pious and for the profligate, and the wonderful miracles and great signs that He has created,

---

Al-Firyābī informed us, saying, 'Al-'Abbās told us... up to the words...'
And its isnād is also authentic.

[18] Its *isnād* is weak.
In its chain of narrators is 'Abdullāh Ibn Isḥāq Ibn Ibrāhīm, who is the son of 'Abdu'l-'Azīz al-Marzaban al-Baghawī; he has a biography in *'Tārīkh Baghdād'* (9/4144). Al-Daraquṭnī said: "He is lenient (i.e. not strict). As for Al-Ḥasan Ibn 'Ulayl, I have not found any biography for him.

[19] This is from manuscript (B).

in addition to accounts pertaining to the angels who are near to Allāh and descriptions of those who stand in rows [in prayer] and those who glorify [Allāh].

And in the ḥadīth there are stories of the Prophets, reports concerning the ascetics and those close to Allāh, exhortations of the eloquent, speeches of the jurists, biographies of the Arab and non-Arab kings, the stories of the early generations, explanations of the battles fought by the Messenger of Allāh (ﷺ),[20] his military expeditions, collections of his rulings and judgements, his sermons and admonitions, his signs and his miracles, the number of his wives, his children, his in-laws and his Companions (*raḍiyAllāhu ʿanhum*) and a description of their virtues and their deeds and explanations of their stories and their exploits, the range of their ages and an explanation of their lineages.

In them there is also *tafsīr* of the Noble Qur'ān and the tidings and wise reminders contained therein, along with the sayings of the Companions (*raḍiyAllāhu ʿanhum*) regarding rulings that were memorised from them and the identification of those Imāms and jurists who endorsed the sayings of each one of them. Allāh, Most High appointed his family members as pillars of the *Sharīʿah* and destroyed through them every repugnant innovation. They were the trusted ones of Allāh from among Allāh's creation and the intermediaries between the Prophet (ﷺ) and his people and they were those who strove to preserve his religion. Their light is brilliant, their virtues are everlasting, their signs are dazzling, their beliefs are clear and [their evidences][21] are irresistible.

And every group that turns towards heretical belief will return

[20] This is from manuscript (B).

[21] In manuscript (A) it says, "their evidence".

to it, or they will deem an opinion goodand they will adhere to it—except for the people of ḥadīth, for the Book [of Allāh] is their preparedness, the Sunnah is their evidence, the Messenger (ﷺ) is their party and their allegiance is to him; they do not deviate towards heresy, nor do they pay any attention to opinions. They accept what they have narrated from the Messenger of Allāh (ﷺ) and they are the trustworthy and impartial [bearers of his message]. They are the preservers and treasurers of the religion and the vessels and bearers of knowledge. When there is any disagreement in matters of ḥadīth, reference is made to them, so whatever their judgement is, it is listened to and accepted. Every scholar of Islāmic Jurisprudence and Imām among them reveres his Prophet (ﷺ) is abstemious, distinguished in virtue, skilful in [Qur'ān] recitation and a master sermoniser.

They are the great majority and their path is the Straight Path; every innovation is clear to them and they do not deviate from their mazhab. Those who conspire against them, Allāh will shatter them and those who stubbornly oppose them, Allāh will humiliate them—and he whom He humiliates will not harm them,[22] nor will those whom He isolates be successful.

8. Abū Bakr Aḥmad Ibn ʿUmar al-Dallāl informed us that he was informed by [Abū Muḥammad][23] Jaʿfar Ibn Muḥammad Ibn Naṣīr al-Khaldī that Khalaf Ibn ʿAmr Al-ʿAkbārī told him that Saʿīd Ibn Manṣūr said that he was informed by ʿAbdu'l-Raḥmān Ibn Ziyād that Shuʿbah told him, on the authority of Muʿāwiyah Ibn Qurrah, who reported from the Prophet (ﷺ) that he said:

"Some people (*anās*)[24] from my *ummah* will continue to

[22] In manuscript (B) it says, *"those whom He humiliates"*.

[23] This is from manuscript (B).

[24] In manuscript (B) it says (*nās*) (There is no difference in the meaning).

> be helped [by Allāh] and those whofor sake them will not harm them until the Hour is established."[25]

9. Muḥammad Ibn Aḥmad Rizq Al-Bazzār informed us that he was told by Muḥammad Ibn Al-'Abbās al-'Aṣimī that Abū Isḥāq Aḥmad Ibn Muḥammad Ibn Yāsīn[26] Al-Harawī told him, "I was informed by 'Uthmān Ibn Sa'īd al-Dārimī that he said: "Alī Ibn Al-Madanī said regarding the ḥadīth of the Prophet (ﷺ):

> "A group from among my *ummah* will continue to adhere to the truth and those who oppose them will not harm them.'"[27]

"They are the people of ḥadīth (*Ahl Al-ḥadīth*), who adhere to

---

[25] This is an authentic narration.

It was narrated by Imām Aḥmad (5/34), Ibn Abū 'Aṣim (2/333), Al-Ṭayālisī (#1076), Tirmidhi (#2192), Ibn Mājah (#6), Ibn Ḥibbān (*Mawārid*: #2313) and Al-Khaṭīb (8/417-418 and 10/182)—both of them with the first part sharing the same complete wording that will be mentioned, by way of Shu'bah Ibn Al-Ḥajjāj, with an authentic chain of narrators.

The complete wording is: "When the inhabitants of Al-Shām become corrupt, then there will be no good in you. There will never cease to be a group in my *ummah* who will be helped [by Allāh], they will not be harmed by those who forsake them until the Hour is established."

There is another source for it on the authority of Mu'āwiyah, from the narration of his son, Iyas, which was narrated by Abū Nu'aym in *'Al-Ḥilyah'* (7/230), which contains the first portion of the ḥadīth.

[26] In manuscripts (A) and (B) it says Yūnus, but the correct name is the one we have given.

[27] Its chain of narrators is weak, though the text of the ḥadīth is correct.

In it [the chain] is Abū Isḥāq Aḥmad Ibn Muḥammad Ibn Yāsīn al-Harawī; he was declared a liar by al-Dāraquṭnī and he said of him, "He is *matrūk* (abandoned)." Al-Khalīlī said: "He is not strong; he narrates things that do not conform [to what has been authentically reported].

But the text of the ḥadīth is confirmed on the authority of Ibn Al-Madanī.

It was narrated by Tirmidhī, following the narrations of the previous ḥadīth (4/485) and he said: "Muḥammad Ibn Isma'īl (i.e. Al-Bukhārī) said: "Alī Ibn Al-Madanī said: 'They are the people of ḥadīth'."

the ways of the Messenger (ﷺ) and they defend the knowledge. Were it not for them, you would not find anything of the Sunan with the Mu'tazilites, the Rafidhites, the Jahmites, the followers of Al-Irja' and opinion."

[Abū Bakr said][28]:

The Lord of the worlds made the victorious group the protectors of the religion and He turned away from them the plots of the stubborn and wilful, in order that they might hold fast to the Sharī'ah and follow in the footsteps of the Companions (*raḍiyAllāhu 'anhum*) and the *Tābi'ūn*. Their stance is one of preserving the traditions, crossing deserts and wastelands, riding across land and sea in order to acquire [knowledge] of what the Messenger, Al-Mustafa (ﷺ) legislated and they do not turn against it, in favour of opinion or heretical views.

They accepted his Sharī'ah both in word and in deed and they guarded his Sunnah, by preserving it and transmitting it until they had confirmed its source. They were the most qualified regarding it and its adherents. And how many are the heretics who desire to adulterate the Sharī'ah with things that are not from it. But Allāh, Most High protects the people of ḥadīth from them and they are the preservers of its pillars and they are the ones who carry out its commands and are responsible for it. And when people turn away from defending it, it is they who protect it.

أُوْلَٰٓئِكَ حِزْبُ ٱللَّهِۚ أَلَآ إِنَّ حِزْبَ ٱللَّهِ هُمُ ٱلْمُفْلِحُونَ ﴿٢٢﴾

"Those are the party of Allāh. Unquestionably, the party of Allāh—they are the successful."

[28] This is from manuscript (B).

[*al-Mujadilah* (58): 22]

10. Abū'l-Ḥusayn Muḥammad Ibn Al-Ḥasan Ibn Aḥmad Al-Ahwāzī[29] informed us that he was told by Al-Ḥasan Ibn ʿAbdullāh Ibn Saʿīd Al-ʿAskarī that he was informed by ʿAbdān—ʿAbdullāh Ibn Aḥmad Ibn Mūsā—that he was informed by Zayd Ibn Al-Ḥarīsh, who was informed by ʿAbdullāh Ibn Kharrāsh, on the authority of al-ʿAwwam Ibn Ḥawshab, who reported on the authority of Shahr Ibn Ḥawshab: It was reported on the authority of Muʿādh Ibn Jabal (*raḍiyAllāhu ʿanhu*) from the Prophet (ﷺ) something similar to the preceding ḥadīth, saying:

> "This knowledge will be carried by the trustworthy people of every successive generation, refuting the corruption of extremists, the distortions of falsifiers, and the interpretations of the ignorant."[30]

11. Al-Ḥasan Ibn Abū Ṭālib told me that he was informed by Abū ʿUmar Muḥammad Ibn Al-ʿAbbās al-Khazzāz that Abū Bakr Ibn Abū Dāwūd told him: 'I was told by Aḥmad Ibn Sinān that he reported on the authority of a man whom he mentioned, that he saw the Prophet (ﷺ) in a dream and he was standing in the Masjid, between two circles [i.e. gatherings]; in one of them was Aḥmad Ibn Ḥanbal and in the other was Ibn Abū Dāwūd and the Prophet (ﷺ) said:

---

[29] In manuscript (A) it says Abū'l-Ḥasan, but the correct name is that which we have confirmed.

[30] With this chain of narrators, it is fabricated.

The Shaikh of Al-Khaṭīb was accused of lying; indeed, he used to steal and fabricate [narrations]. In addition, ʿAbdullāh Ibn Kharrāsh was reported as being similar to him. Also, Zayd Ibn Al-Ḥarīsh is not strict and is described as being of unknown status. As for his lack of strictness, Ibn Ḥibbān said of him in *'Al-Thiqāt'* (8/251), "It may be that he made mistakes." As for his unknown status, when Al-Ḥāfiẓ [Ibn Ḥajr] reported on him in *'Al-Lisān'* (2/620), he reported from Ibn Al-Qaṭṭān that he said: 'His status is unknown.'

> "If these (people) disbelieve in it," and he (ﷺ) pointed to Ibn Abū Dāwūd and his companions: 'then we have entrusted it to a people who do not disbelieve in it,' and he pointed (ﷺ) to Aḥmad Ibn Ḥanbal and his companions.'[31]

[Abū Bakr] said[32]:

Abū Muḥammad 'Abdullāh Ibn Muslim Ibn Qutaybah spoke in his book *'Ta'wīl Mukhtalif Al-Ḥadīth'* about the people of *bid'ah* and their disparagement of the people of ḥadīth, then he spoke of the corruption of the people of *bid'ah* in a manner that is convincing to those whom Allāh has blessed with guidance and right intentions. And I will mention in this book of mine what has been narrated from the Messenger of Allāh (ﷺ) regarding the encouragement to convey [guidance] from him and the virtue of transmitting what has been heard from him, then what has been narrated from the Companions (*raḍiyAllāhu 'anhum*) and the *Tābi'ūn* and those scholars who came after them, regarding the honourableness of the people of ḥadīth and their virtue, elevated status and nobility, in addition to their aforementioned merits and their distinguishing characteristics.

We ask Allāh that He benefit us with love of them, cause us to live upon their Sunnah and to die upon their beliefs, that He gather us among their group, for verily, He is All-Knowing and All-Seeing of us and He is Most Able to do all things.

---

[31] Its chain of narrators is authentic up to Aḥmad Ibn Sinan.
And Al-Ḥasan Ibn Abū Ṭālib is Al-Ḥasan Ibn Muḥammad al-Khallāl,

[32] This is from manuscript (B).

CHAPTER TWO

What Has Been Narrated from the Messenger of Allāh (ﷺ) Regarding the Encouragement to Convey His Message and Preserve His Words—may the blessings and peace of Allāh be upon Him:[33] *"Convey from me, even one verse of the Qur'ān and relate from me, and do not lie against me."*[34]

12. We were informed by Abū Nu'aym Aḥmad Ibn 'Abdullāh Ibn Aḥmad Ibn Isḥāq Al-Ḥāfiẓ, in Aṣbahān that he said that 'Abdullāh Ibn Ja'far Ibn Aḥmad Ibn Fāris said that he was told by Abū Mas'ūd Aḥmad Ibn al-Furāt al-Rāzī that Ibn Numayr 'Abdullāh informed[35] him.

---

[33] In manuscript (B) it says: (ﷺ).

[34] This is an authentic ḥadīth.

It was narrated by 'Abdu'l-Razzāq (#10157), by Imām Aḥmad (2/159, 202 and 214), by Al-Bukhārī (2/258), Tirmidhī (5/40), Al-Dārimī (#542), Al-Ṭahāwī, in *'Sharḥ Ma'ānī Al-Āthar'* (4/128), Al-Qadhā'ī, in *'Al-Shihāb'* (#162), Abū Nu'aym, in *'Al-Ḥilyah'* (6/78) and the author, in *'Tārīkh Baghdād'* (13/157) from a number of sources, on the authority of Al-Awzā'ī.

[35] In manuscript (A) it says: "*(anbā'nā)* imparted to us".

And we were informed by Abū Sa'īd Muḥammad Ibn Mūsā Ibn Al-Faḍl al-Sayrāfī, in Nishapur, that he said that he was told by Abū Ḥāmid Aḥmad Ibn Muḥammad Ibn Shu'ayb, that he was told by Sahl Ibn 'Ammār Al-'Aṭkī, that he was told by Muḥammad Ibn Al-Qāsim—Al-Asadi.

And we were informed by Abū'l-Ḥusayn Muḥammad Ibn Al-Ḥusayn Ibn Muḥammad Ibn Al-Faḍl Al-Qaṭṭān, who said that he was informed by 'Abdullāh Ibn Ja'far Ibn Darastawayh Al-Nahwī, who said that he was told by Ya'qūb Ibn Sufyān.

And we were informed by Abū'l-Ḥasan[36] 'Alī Ibn Aḥmad Ibn 'Umar Al-Muqrī', who said that he was told by Ḥabīb Ibn Al-Ḥasan Al-Qazzāz, who said that he was told by Abū Muslim Ibrāhīm Ibn 'Abdullāh Al-Baṣrī, who said that they were told by Abū 'Aṣim.

And we were informed by Abū'l-Qāsim 'Alī Ibn Muḥammad Ibn 'Alī Al-'Iyāḍī, who said that he was informed[37] by Aḥmad Ibn Yūsuf Ibn Khallād Al-'Aṭṭār, who said that he was told by Al-Hārith Ibn Muḥammad Al-Tamīmī, who said that he was told by 'Aṣim Ibn 'Alī, who said that his brother told him: Al-Ḥasan Ibn 'Alī.

And we were informed by Al-Qāḍī Abū'l-'Ala' Muḥammad Ibn 'Alī Ibn Ya'qūb Al-Wasiṭī, who said that he was informed by Aḥmad Ibn Ja'far Ibn Hamdān, who said that he was told by Bishr[38] Ibn Mūsā, who said that he was told by Mu'āwiyah Ibn 'Amr, who reported on the authority of Abū Isḥāq—Al-Fazārī.

[36] In manuscript (B) it says: Abū'l-Ḥusayn, but the correct name is that which we have confirmed.

[37] In manuscript (B) it says: "(*anbā'nā*) imparted to us".

[38] In manuscript (B) it says: Bashīr.

All of them on the authority of Al-Awzāʿī.

And we were informed by Abū'l-Ḥusayn ʿAlī Ibn Muḥammad Ibn ʿAbdullāh Ibn Bishrān Al-Mu'addal, who said that he was informed by Abū Bakr Muḥammad Ibn Jaʿfar Ibn Muḥammad Al-Adamī Al-Qārī,[39] who said that he was told by Ibn al-Ṭabba', who said that he was told by Muḥammad Ibn Muṣʿab.

And we were informed by ʿAlī Ibn ʿAlī Al-Mu'addal, who said that he was informed by[40] Al-Ḥasan Ibn Jaʿfar Ibn Muḥammad Al-Samsar, who said that he was told by Abū Shuʿayb Al-Ḥarānī, who said that he was told by Yaḥyā Ibn ʿAbdullāh.

And we were informed by Muḥammad Ibn ʿAlī Ibn Al-Fatḥ Al-Ḥarbī [the wording of the tradition is his], who said that he was informed by[41] ʿUmar Ibn Ibrāhīm Al-Muqrīʿ, who said that he was informed by[42] ʿAbdullāh Ibn Muḥammad Ibn ʿAbdu'l-ʿAzīz, who said that he was told by Abū Khaythamah, who said that he was told by Al-Walīd Ibn Muslim, who said that they were told by Al-Awzāʿī, that he was told by Ḥassān Ibn ʿAṭiyyah, who said that he was told by Abū Kabshah that ʿAbdullāh Ibn ʿAmr told him that he heard the Messenger of Allāh (ﷺ) saying:

> "Convey from me, even if it is only a single verses from the Qur'ān and transmit from Banu Isra'īl—and there is no objection [to that]—but whoever deliberately lied against me, let him prepare his place in the Fire."

And their wordings in the text of the ḥadīth are the same.

---

[39] In manuscript (B) it says: Al-Qārī Al-Adamī.

[40] In manuscript (B) it says: "(*anbā'nā*) imparted to us".

[41] In manuscript (B) it says: "(*anbā'nā*) imparted to us".

[42] In manuscript (B) it says: "(*anbā'nā*) imparted to us".

Abū Bakr said[43]:

And this[44] was narrated by 'Abdu'l-Raḥmān Ibn Thābit Ibn Thawbān, on the authority of Ḥassān Ibn 'Aṭiyyah.

13. We were informed by Abū Muḥammad Al-Ḥasan Ibn 'Alī Ibn Aḥmad Ibn Bashshār An-Naysabūrī, in Al-Baṣrah, who said that he was told by Abū Bakr Muḥammad Ibn Aḥmad Ibn Mahmawayh Al-'Askarī, who said that he was told by Muḥammad Ibn Ibrāhīm Ibn Kathīr As-Suwarī, who said that he was told by Al-Firyābī, who reported on the authority of Ibn Thawbān, who reported on the authority of Ḥassān Ibn 'Aṭiyyah, who reported on the authority of Abū Kabshah As-Salūlī, who reported on the authority of 'Abdullāh Ibn 'Amr Ibn Al-'Aṣ, who said: "The Messenger of Allāh (ﷺ) said:

> "Convey from me, even if it is a single verse of the Qur'ān and transmit from Banu Isra'īl—and there is no objection to that—but whoever deliberately lied against me, let him prepare his place in the Fire."[45]

14. We were informed by Al-Qāḍī Abū Bakr Aḥmad Ibn Al-Ḥasan Ibn Aḥmad Al-Ḥarashi, in Nishapur, who said that he was told by Abū'l-'Abbās Muḥammad Ibn Ya'qūb Al-Aṣamm, who said that he was informed by[46] Al-Rabī' Ibn Sulaymān, who said that he was informed by Al-Shāfi'ī,[47] who said that he was informed by

[43] This is from manuscript (B).

[44] In manuscript (B) it says: "in this way".

[45] Its chain of narrators is weak, but the ḥadīth is authentic.

This is because 'Abdu'l-Raḥmān Ibn Thābit is weak; he related munkar narrations, though he was followed by Al-Awzā'ī.

The tradition from this source was narrated by Tirmidhī (#2669): Muḥammad Yaḥyā told us that he was told by Muḥammad Ibn Yūsuf, on the authority of Ibn Thawbān.

[46] In manuscript (B) it says: "(*anbā'nā*) imparted to us".

[47] In manuscript (B) it says: "(*anbā'nā*) imparted to us".

Sufyān, who reported on the authority of Muḥammad Ibn ʻAmr, who reported on the authority of Abū Salāmah, who reported on the authority of Abū Hurayrah (*raḍiyAllāhu ʻanhu*) that the Messenger of Allāh (ﷺ) said:

> "Transmit from Banu Isra'īl—and there is no objection to that—and transmit from me, but do not lie against me."[48]

[48] This ḥadīth is ḥasan.

It was narrated by Imām Aḥmad (2/474 and 502), Al-Ḥumaydī (#1165), Abū Dāwūd (#3662), Ibn Mājah (#34). Ibn Ḥibbān (*'Mawārid'*: #109) from a number of sources: on the authority of Muḥammad Ibn ʻAmr Ibn ʻAlqamah, on the authority of Abū Salāmah, on the authority of Abū Hurayrah (*raḍiyAllāhu ʻanhu*).

I say: In the narration of Muḥammad Ibn ʻAmr, on the authority of Abū Salāmah is considered weak, though numerous narrators reported it from him in a single form, which proves that this narrations has been accurately reported, especially since other narrations from the aforementioned ḥadīth of Ibn ʻAmr have been reported that confirm it.

CHAPTER THREE

The Saying of the Prophet (ﷺ): "It is incumbent on those who are present to inform those who are absent."

15. We were informed by Abū'l-Ḥasan Aḥmad Ibn Muḥammad Ibn Aḥmad Ibn Mūsā Ibn Hārūn Ibn al-Ṣalt Al-Ahwāzī that he was told by Al-Qāḍī [Abū 'Abdullāh][49] Al-Ḥusayn Ibn Isma'īl Al-Muḥāmilī, who said that he was told by Yūsuf Ibn Mūsā, who said that he was told by Hawzah, who said that he was told by 'Abdullāh Ibn 'Awn.[50]

And we were informed by 'Alī Ibn Muḥammad Al-Mālikī, who said that he was informed by[51] Aḥmad Ibn Yūsuf Al-'Aṭṭār, who said that he was told by Al-Ḥārith Ibn Muḥammad, who said that he was told by Ḥawzah.

[49] This is from manuscript (B).

[50] This is an authentic ḥadīth.

[51] In manuscript (B) it says: "(*anbā'nā*) imparted to us"..

And we were informed by Abū Bakr Aḥmad Ibn 'Alī Ibn Muḥammad Al-Yazdī Al-Ḥāfiẓ, in Nishapur, who said that he was informed by[52] Zāhir Ibn Aḥmad, who said that he was informed by[53] Ibrāhīm Ibn 'Abdullāh Al-Zaynabī, who said that he was told by Muḥammad [i.e. Ibn 'Abdu'l- 'Alā' Al-Sana'ānī], who said that he was told by Bishr Ibn Al-Mufaḍḍal, who said that they were told by Ibn 'Awn, who reported on the authority of Muḥammad Ibn Sīrīn, who reported on the authority of 'Abdu'l-Raḥmān Ibn Abū Bakrah.

And we were informed by 'Alī Ibn Muḥammad Ibn 'Abdullāh Ibn Bishrān, who said that he was informed by Abū Ja'far Muḥammad Ibn 'Amr Ibn Al-Bakhtarī Al-Razzāz, who said that he was told by Muḥammad Ibn Aḥmad Ibn Abū'l-'Awwām and 'Abdu'l- Mālik Ibn Muḥammad, who said that they were told by Abū 'Amir.

And we were informed byAbū'l-Ḥasan 'Alī Ibn Aḥmad Ibn Muḥammad Ibn Dāwūd Al-Razzāz, who said that he was told by Aḥmad Ibn Salmān Al-Najjād, who said that he was told by 'Abdu'l-Mālik Ibn Muḥammad, who said that he was told by 'Abdu'l-Mālik Ibn 'Amr Abū 'Amir Al-'Aqdī, who said that he was told by Qurrah Ibn Khālid, on the authority of Muḥammad Ibn Sīrīn, who said that he was told by 'Abdu'l-Raḥmān Ibn Abū Bakrah and a man who, in my opinion, is better than 'Abdu'l-Raḥmān [i.e. Ḥumayd Ibn 'Abdu'l-Raḥmān], on the authority of Abū Bakrah, who said: "The Messenger of Allāh (ﷺ) said:

> "So it is incumbent upon those who are present to convey it (this information) to those who are absent because the informed one might comprehend it (what I have said) better than the one who hears (it)."

[52] In manuscript (B) it says: "(*anbā'nā*) imparted to us".

[53] In manuscript (B) it says: "(*anbā'nā*) imparted to us".

The wording is that of the ḥadīth of Qurrah.

16. We were informed by Al-Qāḍī Abū Bakr Aḥmad Ibn Al-Ḥasan Al-Ḥayrī, in Nishapur, who said that he was informed by Abū 'Alī Muḥammad Ibn Aḥmad Ibn Muḥammad Ibn Ma'qal Al-Maidani, who said that he was told by Abū 'Abdullāh Muḥammad Ibn Yaḥya [Al-Zahlī], who said that he was told by 'Abdu'l-Razzāq, who reported on the authority of Ma'mar, who reported on the authority of Ayyūb, who reported on the authority of Ibn Sīrīn, who reported on the authority of 'Abdu'l-Raḥmān Ibn Abū Bakrah, who reported on the authority of his Father, that the Prophet (ﷺ) said during the Farewell Pilgrimage:

> "It is incumbent upon those who are present to convey it (this information) to those who are absent because the informed one might comprehend it [what I have said] better than the one who hears [it]."[54]

17. We were informed by 'Alī Ibn Muḥammad Ibn 'Alī Al-'Iyāḍī,

[54] This is an authentic ḥadīth.

However, there is disagreement regarding Ayyūb; Ibn 'Aliyyah reported it in (the narrations of) Aḥmad (5/39), Abū Dāwūd (#1947), Nasā'i (7/127), on the authority of Ayyūb, who reported on the authority of Ibn Sīrīn, who reported on the authority of Abū Bakrah, in a *mursal* form.

Ibn 'Aliyyah disagreed: Ḥammād Ibn Zayd, 'Abdu'l-Wahhāb Al-Thaqafī in the narration of Al-Bukhārī and Ma'mar in the narration of the author. They reported it in a mawsool form and that is correct.

And Al-Qadhā'ī narrated it in *'Al-Shihāb'* (1418) by way of Yazīd Ibn Ibrāhīm Al-Tustarī, on the authority of Ibn Sīrīn, who reported on the authority Abū Bakrah.

And in the chain to Yazīd there is someone whom I do not know and I do not consider it to be *maḥfūẓ* (i.e. something reliably reported) on his authority. If it was *maḥfūẓ* on his authority, it would be *shaẓ* (a ḥadīth that is opposite in meaning to what has been reliably reported elsewhere) on the authority of Ibn Sīrīn, due to the agreement of the trustworthy reporters regarding its narration by way of Ibn Sīrīn, on the authority of Abū Bakrah in Wasiṭah.

who said that he was informed by Aḥmad Ibn Yūsuf Ibn Khallād, who said that he was told by Al-Ḥārith Ibn Muḥammad, who said that he was told by Dāwūd Ibn Al-Muḥabbar, who said that he was told by 'Abdu'l-Ḥamīd Ibn Bahram, who reported on the authority of Shahr, who said that he was told by Asmā' Bint Yazīd, who said that the Messenger of Allāh (ﷺ) said:

> "It is incumbent upon those who are present to convey it [this information] to those who are absent."[55]

Abū Bakr said: "I abbreviated it."

18. We were informed by Abū Bakr Muḥammad Ibn 'Abdullāh Ibn Ṣāliḥ Al-'Aṭṭār, in Aṣbahān, who said that he was informed by Abū Muḥammad 'Abdullāh Ibn Muḥammad Ibn Ja'far Ibn Ḥayyān, who said that he was told by his maternal uncle, who reported on the authority of Abū Ḥātim Al-Razī that he said:

> "Spreading knowledge gives life to it and conveying from the Messenger of Allāh (ﷺ) is a mercy. Every believer holds fast to it and it will be a proof against every obstinate rejecter and heretic."[56]

Al-Awzā'ī said: "If innovations become prevalent and the scholars do not reject them, they will looked upon as the Sunnah."

---

[55] Its chain of narrators is extremely weak.

In it is Dāwūd Ibn Al-Muḥabbar, who is accused [of lying] and whose ḥadīth is abandoned (*matrūk*).

[56] I have not found any biography for the Shaikh of the author; and the maternal uncle of the Shaikh of Ibn Ḥayyān is 'Abdullāh Ibn Maḥmūd Ibn Al-Faraj; he has a biography in *'Ṭabaqāt Al-Muḥaddithīn'*, by the Shaikh's father (4/350), but I do not know if he heard from Abū Ḥātim Al-Razī or not. He was not mentioned among the students of Al-Razī and Al-Razī was not mentioned among his Shaikhs.

CHAPTER FOUR

The saying of the Prophet (ﷺ): "May Allāh cause a man to flourish who hears a ḥadīth from us, memorises it by heart and conveys it (to others)."

19. We were informed by Al-Qāḍī Abū Bakr Aḥmad Ibn Al-Ḥasan Al-Ḥarshī, who said that he was told by Abū'l-'Abbās Muḥammad Ibn Ya'qūb Al-Aṣamm, who said that he was told by Abū 'Utbah Aḥmad Ibn Al-Faraj, who said that he was told by Baqiyyah.

We were informed by Abū Nu'aym Aḥmad Ibn 'Abdullāh Al-Ḥāfiẓ, who said that he was told by 'Abdullāh Ibn Ja'far Ibn Aḥmad Ibn Fāris, who said that he was told by Yūnus Ibn Ḥabīb, who said that he was told by Abū Dāwūd.

They both said that they were told by Shu'bah, who reported on the authority of 'Umar Ibn Sulaymān Ibn 'Aṣim Ibn 'Umar Ibn Al-Khaṭṭāb, who reported on the authority of 'Abdu'l-Raḥmān

Ibn Abān Ibn ʿUthmān, who reported on the authority of his Father, who reported on the authority of Zayd Ibn Thābit, who said: "The Messenger of Allāh (ﷺ) said:

> "May Allāh cause a man to flourish who hears a ḥadīth from us, memorises it by heart and conveys it as he heard it. It could be that a bearer of knowledge conveys it to one who has more understanding than he; and it could be that a bearer of knowledge has no understanding [of it]."

And this is the wording of the ḥadīth of Baqiyyah.[57]

20. We were informed by Al-Ḥasan Ibn Abū Bakr, who said that he was told by ʿAlī Ibn Muḥammad Ibn Al-Zubayr Al-Qurashī Al-Kūfī, who said that he was told by Ibrāhīm Ibn Isḥāq Ibn Abū'l-ʿAnbas Al-Qāḍī Al-Zuhrī, who reported on the authority of Muḥammad Ibn Jubayr Ibn Mutʿim, who reported on the authority of his Father that he said: "The Messenger of Allāh (ﷺ) stood among us at Al-Khayf, near Mina and said:

> 'May Allāh cause a slave to flourish who heard my words and understands them, then he conveys them from me. There may be those who have knowledge but no understanding, and there may be those who convey knowledge to those who may have more understanding of it than they do.'"[58]

---

[57] This is an authentic ḥadīth.

It was narrated by Imām Aḥmad (5/183), by Abū Dāwūd (#3660), by Tirmidhī (#2656), Nasāʾī in *'Al-Kubra'*, by Ibn Ḥibbān (*Mawārid*: #72 and #73) by way of Shuʿbah.

I say: This chain of narrators is authentic; some of them narrated it in a longer form than this.

It has another source reported by Ibn Mājah (#230), but in it is Layth Ibn Abū Salīm, who is weak.

[58] Its chain of narrators is extremely weak. =

21. I was told by Abū Ṭālib Yaḥya Ibn ʻAlī Ibn Al-Ṭayyib Ad-Daskarī, in Ḥalwan, who said that he was told by Abū Bakr Muḥammad Ibn Ibrāhīm Ibn Al-Muqrī', in Aṣbahān.

And we were informed by Abū Jaʻfar Muḥammad Ibn Jaʻfar Ibn ʻAllan[59] Al-Warraq—and the wording is his—he said that he was informed by[60] Muḥammad Ibn Al-Ḥusayn Al-Azdī al-Ḥāfiẓ, who both said that they were told by Abū Yaʻlā Aḥmad Ibn ʻAlī, who said that he was told by ʻAbdullāh Ibn Muḥammad Ibn Sālim Al-Maflūj, who said that he was told by ʻUbaydah Ibn Al-Aswad, who reported on the authority of Al-Qāsim Ibn Al-Walīd Al-Hamdanī, who reported on the authority of Al-Ḥārith, who reported on the authority of Al-Ḥārith, who reported on the authority of Ibrāhīm,

=

Ibn Isḥaq is a *mudallis* (one who practices *tadlīs* to conceal weaknesses in a ḥadīth) and he has narrated it through *al-ʻan'anah* (narrating a chain by saying, "On the authority of so-and-so, who reported on the authority of so-and so...").

It was narrated by Ibn Mājah (#231) by way of Ibn Numayr, on the authority of Muḥammad Ibn Isḥāq, who reported on the authority of ʻAbdu'l-Salām, who reported on the authority of Az-Zuhrī, with his chain of narrators.

ʻAbdu'l-Salām—who is Ibn Abū'l-Junūb—added something that proves that he resorted to tadlees to cover up a chain that was deficient.

In addition, ʻAbdu'l-Salām is extremely weak; Ibn Al-Madīnī said: "He reports *munkar* narrations." Abū Ḥātim said: "He is an abandoned Shaikh." He was also declared weak by more than one scholar. He was alone in reporting ḥadīth on the authority of Al-Zuhrī, which proves the *munkar* nature of its chain from this source. And Allāh knows better.

And Imām Aḥmad narrated it in his *'Musnad'* (4/82): We were told by Yaʻqūb that he said that he was told by his Father, who reported on the authority of Abū Isḥāq... then he quoted it on the authority of in an abbreviated form.

He said: "And it was reported on the authority of Ibn Isḥāq that he said: 'I was told by ʻAmr Ibn Abū ʻAmr, the freed slave of Al-Muṭṭālib, who reported on the authority of ʻAbdu'l-Raḥmān Ibn Al-Huwayrith, on the authority of Muḥammad Ibn Jubayr Ibn Mut'im, who reported it on the authority of his Father'."

I say: ʻAmr Ibn Abū ʻAmr is weak and Ibn Isḥāq, it is not thought that there are many chains of narrators on his authority. And Allāh knows better.

[59] In manuscript (A) it says (*ghaylān*), but the correct thing is what we have confirmed.

[60] In manuscript (B) it says, "(*anbā'nā*) imparted to us".

who reported on the authority of Al-Aswad, who reported on the authority of ʿAbdullāh Ibn Masʿūd (*raḍiyAllāhu ʿanhu*) that he said: "The Messenger of Allāh (ﷺ) said:

> "May Allāh cause to flourish a person who hears my words and understands them, then he conveys them from me. There are those who have knowledge but no understanding, and there may be those who convey knowledge to those who may have more understanding of it than they do."[61]

22. I was told by someone who heard from ʿAbdu'l- Ghani Ibn Saʿīd Al-Miṣrī Al-Ḥāfiẓ, who said: "The most authentic ḥadīth narrated on this subject is this ḥadīth of ʿUbaydah Ibn Al-Aswad.[62]

23. We were told by Abū Ḥāzim ʿUmar Ibn Aḥmad Ibn Ibrāhīm Al-ʿAbdī Al-Ḥāfiẓ, in Nishapur, who said that he heard Naṣr Ibn Muḥammad Ibn Yaʿqūb saying that he was told by Ibrāhīm Ibn Al-Muwallad, who said that he was told by Aḥmad Ibn Marwān, who said that he was told by Muḥammad Ibn Ismaʿīl Ibn Sālim, who said that he was told by Al-Ḥumaydī that he said: "I heard

[61] Its chain of narrators is ḥasan and the ḥadīth is authentic.

In its chain of narrators is ʿUbaydah Ibn Al-Aswad; Abū Ḥātim said: "There is no objection to his ḥadīth." And Ibn Ḥibbān mentioned him in *'Al-Thiqāt'*, saying, "His ḥadīth is respected when it is clear that he heard (the ḥadīth) and the person from whom he heard and the one to whom he transmitted are trustworthy."

It has another source on the authority of Ibn Masʿūd, from the narration of his son, ʿAbdu'l-Raḥmān.

It was narrated by Imām Aḥmad (1/437), by Tirmidhī (#2657 and #2658), by Ibn Mājah (#232) and Abū Nuʿaym (7/331).

I say: This chain of narrators is authentic; there is disagreement regarding whether or ʿAbdu'l-Raḥmān heard from his father, but a number of the scholars have confirmed that he heard from his father.

[62] Its chain of narrators is *munqatiʿ* (i.e. the link in the chain of narrators is broken due to a missing narrator or due to one of the narrators not having met the person he is supposed to have heard from).

Sufyān Ibn 'Uyaynah saying:

> "There is no one who seeks the ḥadīth except that in his face is there is a glow; this is based on the saying of the Prophet (ﷺ): "May Allāh cause to flourish a person who hears something from us and communicates it to others."[63]

[63] Its chain of narrators is weak.

In it is Ibrāhīm Ibn Al-Muwallad, who is one of the Shaikhs of the Ṣūfis and I have not found anything that proves his status, though he has been described as devout and pious; however, that is one thing, but accuracy is another. In addition, Aḥmad Ibn Marwān, who is Al-Daynūri was declared weak by Al-Daraquṭnī.

CHAPTER FIVE

The saying of the Prophet (ﷺ): "Whoever memorised for my *Ummah* forty narrations..."

24. We were informed by Abū Nuʿaym Al-Ḥāfiẓ that he said that he was told by ʿAbdullāh Ibn Jaʿfar Ibn Aḥmad Ibn Fāris, who said that he was told by Muḥammad Ibn ʿUmar Ibn Yazīd, the brother of Rustah, who said that he was told by Muḥammad Ibn Abān, who said that he was told by Ma'la (i.e. Ibn Hilāl), who reported on the authority of Abān, who reported on the authority of Anas (*raḍiyAllāhu ʿanhu*) that he said: "The Messenger of Allāh (ﷺ) said:

> "Whoever memorised for my *ummah* forty aḥadīth concerning matters of this religion, Allāh will resurrect him on the Day of Resurrection as a jurist and (religious) scholar."[64]

[64] This ḥadīth is a fabrication.

In its chain of narrators is Abān Ibn Abū ʿAyyāsh, who is abandoned. It also contains Mu'alla Ibn Hilāl, whose dishonesty is agreed upon by scholars.

25. We were informed by Abū Sa'd Aḥmad Ibn Muḥammad Ibn Aḥmad Al-Malīnī that he said that he was informed by[65] 'Alī Ibn 'Isā Ibn Al-Muthnī Al-Malīnī, who said that he was informed by[66] Al-Ḥasan Ibn Sufyān, who said that he was told by Ḥumayd Ibn Zanjawayh, who said that he was told by Al-Ḥajjāj Ibn Naṣīr, who said that he was told by Ḥafs Ibn Jamī', who reported on the authority of Anas Ibn Mālik (*raḍiyAllāhu 'anhu*), who said: "The Messenger of Allāh (ﷺ) said:

> "If anyone memorised forty *aḥādīth* from the [knowledge] that they require of *ḥalāl* [lawful] and *ḥarām* [unlawful], Allāh will record him as a jurist and a (religious) scholar."[67]

26. We were informed by Abū Sa'd Al-Malīnī, who said that he was informed by 'Alī Ibn 'Isā Ibn Al-Muthnī, who said that he was informed by Al-Ḥasan Ibn Sufyān, who said that he was informed by 'Alī Ibn Hujr Al-Sa'dī, who said that he was told by Isḥāq Ibn Najīḥ, who reported on the authority of Ibn Jurayj, who reported on the authority of 'Aṭā', who reported on the authority of Ibn 'Abbās (*raḍiyAllāhu 'anhumā*) that he said: "The Messenger of Allāh (ﷺ) said:

> "Whoever memorised for my *ummah* forty *aḥādīth* pertaining to the Sunnah, I will be an intercessor for him

---

[65] In manuscript (B) "it says "(*anbā'nā*) imparted to us".

[66] In manuscript (B) it says "(*anbā'nā*) imparted to us".

[67] This ḥadīth is fabricated.

In its chain of narrators is Abān, of whom we have spoken previously. In addition, Ḥafs Ibn Jamī' is weak; he reported munkar narrations. Al-Ḥajjāj Ibn Nasīr is similar to him, except that he used to gather (transmissions) and people would receive from him; so it could be that he collected this ḥadīth with this sanad on the authority of Abān, for the weakness in it, in my opinion is from Mu'alla Ibn Hilāl.

And the ḥadīth from this source was narrated by Ibn Al-Jawzī in *'Al-'Ilal'* (1/125).

on the Day of Resurrection."[68]

27. I was informed by Muḥammad Ibn Ja'far Ibn 'Allan Al-Shurūtī, who said that he was told by Sa'd Ibn Muḥammad Ibn Isḥāq Al-Ṣayrafi, who said that he was told by Muḥammad Ibn 'Uthmān Ibn Abū Shaybah, who said that he was told by Muḥammad Ibn Ḥafs Al-Ḥuzamī[69]—who is from Kūfa—that he was told by Daḥīm Ibn Muḥammad Al-Ṣaydawī Al-Naḥḥās, who said that he was told by Abū Bakr Ibn 'Ayyāsh, who reported on the authority of 'Āṣim, who reported on the authority of Zirr, who reported on the authority of 'Abdullāh (*raḍiyAllāhu 'anhu*), who said: "The Messenger of Allāh (ﷺ) said:

> "Whoever memorised for my *ummah* forty *aḥādīth*, Allāh will benefit those people by them and it will be said to him: "Enter Paradise by any gate that you wish."[70]

---

[68] This is a fabricated ḥadīth.

In its chain of narrators is Isḥāq Ibn Najīḥ, who is a liar who fabricated aḥadīth. Al-Khaṭīb attributed this ḥadīth to him in his biography in *'Tarikh Baghdād'* (6/322) and he transmitted on the authority of Ṣāliḥ Ibn Muḥammad his saying: "This ḥadīth is false." And he cited as this man, Isḥāq as the reason for its weakness.

The ḥadīth from this source was narrated by Al-Ḥasan Ibn Sufyān in his 'Musnad' and in *'Al-Arba'īn'* and in *'Al-Talkhīs Al-Ḥabīr'* (3/93).

And among its chains is that cited by Ibn 'Adiyy in *'Al-Kamil'* (3/889), by Ibn 'Āsakir in *'Al-Arba'īn Al-Buldaniyah'* (#3), by Ibn Al-Jawzī in *'Al-'Ilal'* (1/123): "We were told by 'Alī Ibn Ḥujr, who said that he was told by Isḥāq Ibn Najīḥ Al-Maltī..."

[69] In manuscript (A) it says Al-Ḥarāmī, but the correct version is the one we have confirmed.

[70] This ḥadīth is fabricated.

The weakness in it is from Muḥammad Ibn Ḥafs Al-Ḥuzamī, or from his Shaikh, Daḥīm, whose name is 'Abdu'l-Raḥmān Ibn Muḥammad Al-Ṣaydawī—and both of them are unknown. Al-Dhahabī reported this ḥadīth in the biography of Daḥīm in *'Al-Mīzan'* (2/588) and he said: "This ḥadīth is false. It was only reported by Hafs Ibn Al-Ḥuzamī."

And in the biography of Al-Ḥuzamī, he said: "(3/526): "He or his Shaikh is the weakness."

The ḥadīth was also narrated by Abū Nu'aym in *'Al-Ḥilyah'* (4/189), by Ibn 'Āsakir in *'Al-Arba'īn'* (#4) and by Ibn Al-Jawzī (1/19) by way of Al-Ḥuzamī.

CHAPTER SIX

The Advice of the Prophet (ﷺ) to Honour the Scholars of Ḥadīth

28. We were informed by Abū ʿUmar Muḥammad Ibn Muḥammad Ibn ʿAlī Ibn Ḥubaysh Al-Tammār, who said that he was told by Abū ʿAlī Isma'īl Ibn Muḥammad Al-Ṣaffār by way of dictation and he said that he was told by Muḥammad Ibn ʿAlī Al-Sarkhasī, who said that he was told by ʿAlī Ibn ʿĀṣim.

And we were informed by ʿAlī Ibn Muḥammad Ibn ʿAbdullāh Ibn Basharān Al-Mu'addal, who said that he was told by Abū ʿAmr ʿUthmān Ibn Aḥmad Al-Daqqāq by way of dictation and he said that he was told by Abū Bakr Yaḥyā Ibn Jaʿfar Al-Wāsiṭī, who said that he was informed by[71] ʿAlī Ibn ʿĀṣim, who said that he was informed by Abū Hārūn Al-ʿAbdī, who said: "Whenever we went to Abū Saʿīd al-Khudrī (*raḍiyAllāhu ʿanhu*), he said: "I welcome you with the advice of the Messenger of Allāh (ﷺ)." He said: "And what is the advice of the Messenger of Allāh (ﷺ)?" He said: "The

[71] In manuscript (B) it says "(*anbā'nā*) imparted to us".

Messenger of Allāh (ﷺ) said:

> "After me there will come a people who will ask you about ḥadīth from me. So if they come to you, treat them with kindness and speak with them."[72]

It is the wording of Ibn Basharān.

29. I was informed by Abū'l-Ḥusayn Muḥammad Ibn Al-Ḥusayn Ibn Al-Faḍl Al-Qaṭṭān that he said that he was informed by Muḥammad Ibn Al-Ḥasan Ibn Ziyād Al-Muqrī', who said that he was told by Abū 'Abdu'l-Raḥmān Muḥammad Ibn Makkī Ibn

---

[72] This is a fabricated ḥadīth.

In its chain of narrators is Abū Hārūn Al-'Abdī, whose name is 'Umarah Ibn Jawīn and he is abandoned; he was declared to be a liar by more than one scholar, including Ibn 'Aliyyah, Ḥammād Ibn Zayd, Ibn Ma'īn and others—and he was alone in narrating it on the authority of Abū Sa'īd (*raḍiyAllāhu 'anhu*).

The ḥadīth was also narrated by Tirmidhī (#2650 and #2651), by Ibn Mājah (#247), by Al-Ramhurmuzī in *'Al-Muḥaddith Al-Fāṣil'* (#22), by Ibn Khayr Al-Ashbīlī in his *'Fihris'* (p. 8) from various sources on the authority of Abū Hārūn.

And Tirmidhī said: "We do not know this ḥadīth except from the ḥadīth of Abū Hārūn, who reported on the authority of Abū Sa'īd (*raḍiyAllāhu 'anhu*)."

He also narrated something similar from the ḥadīth of Abū Hurayrah (*raḍiyAllāhu 'anhu*).

Ibn Mājah narrated it (#248) by way of Mu'allā Ibn Hilāl, who reported on the authority of Ismā'īl, who said: "We entered the presence of Al-Ḥasan to inquire after him until we filled the house. He tucked up his legs, then he (Al-Ḥasan) said: 'We visited Abū Hurayrah (*raḍiyAllāhu 'anhu*) to inquire after him until we filled the house. He tucked up his legs and said: 'We visited the Messenger of Allāh (ﷺ) until we filled the house. He was lying on his side, but when he saw us, he tucked up his legs then he said: 'After I am gone, there will come to you people seeking knowledge. Welcome them, greet them and teach them'."

Al-Būṣayrī said in *'Miṣbāh Al-Zujājah'* (1/81):

"This chain of narrators is weak; in it is Al-Mu'allā Ibn Hilāl, who was declared to be a liar by Aḥmad , Ibn Ma'īn and others. More than one (scholar) attributed the fabrication of the ḥadīth to him. Ismā'īl is Ibn Muslim and scholars are in agreement that he is weak.

I say: It was narrated from another source on the authority of Abān, who reported on the authority of Anas (*raḍiyAllāhu 'anhu*), as we mentioned earlier (#24).

Jamīl Ibn Ziyād, who said that he was told by 'Alī Ibn Ḥajr, who said that he was told by Ar-Rabī' Ibn Badr, who reported on the authority of Abū Hārūn Al-'Abdī, who reported on the authority of Abū Sa'īd Al-Khudrī (*raḍiyAllāhu 'anhu*), from the Prophet (ﷺ) that he said:

> "Young men will come to you from [all] countries of the earth seeking ḥadīth; so if they come to you, make a point of treating them well."[73]

30. We were informed by Ibn Al-Faḍl, who said that he was told by Abū Sahl Aḥmad Ibn Muḥammad Ibn 'Abdullāh Ibn Ziyād Al-Qaṭṭān, who said that he was told by Muḥammad Ibn Al-Jahm Al-Samrī, who said that he was told by Al-Haytham Ibn Khālid Al-Muqrī', who said that he was told by Yaḥyā Ibn Al-Mutawakkil Al-Bāhilī, who said that he was told by Muḥammad Ibn Zakwān Al-Azdī, who said that he was told by Abū Hārūn Al-'Abdī, who reported on the authority of Abū Sa'īd Al-Khudrī (*raḍiyAllāhu 'anhu*) that when he saw young men, he would say, "I welcome you with the advice of the Messenger of Allāh (ﷺ):

> "The Messenger of Allāh (ﷺ) advised us to make room for you in the gathering and to instruct you in ḥadīth, for you are our successors and the people of ḥadīth after us."[74]

---

[73] This ḥadīth is fabricated.

Al-Rabī' Ibn Badr is abandoned in matters of ḥadīth.

See what preceded.

[74] This ḥadīth is fabricated.

Muḥammad Ibn Zakwān and Yaḥyā Ibn Al-Mutawakkil are both weak, in addition to its fundamental defect.

The ḥadīth was narrated from another source, on the authority of Abū Sa'īd (*raḍiyAllāhu 'anhu*) and it was cited by Ibn Abū Ḥātim in *'Al-Jarḥ wal-Ta'dīl'* (1/1/12), by Al-Ramhurmuzī (#21), by Al-Ḥākim (1/88) and by Tamām in *'Al-Fawā'id'* (*Al-Rawḍh*

=

31. We were informed by Abū'l-Ḥasan Muḥammad Ibn Aḥmad Ibn Muḥammad Ibn Aḥmad Ibn Rizq Al-Bazzār , who said that he was informed by Muḥammad Ibn Al-Ḥasan Ibn Ziyād An-Naqqāsh, who said that he was told by Muḥammad Ibn Ja'far Al-Qattāt, in Al-Kūfah, who said that he was told by Ja'far Ibn Muslim, who said: "We crowded around Ḥusayn Al-Ju'fī and we broke his shoe strap; he was angry and he quoted a ḥadīth with

=

Al-Bassām: #93) by way of Sa'īd Ibn Sulaymān, who said that he was told by 'Abbād Ibn Al-'Awwām, who said that he was told by Al-Jarīrī, who reported on the authority of Abū Naḍhrah, who reported on the authority of Abū Sa'īd Al-Khudrī (*raḍiyAllāhu 'anhu*) that he said: "I welcome you with the advice of the Messenger of Allāh (ﷺ): The Messenger of Allāh (ﷺ) used to advise us regarding you."

I say: This chain of narrators is *shāzz* (i.e. it is narrated by a trustworthy narrator, but contradicts what has been authentically reported by someone more reliable elsewhere). It is believed that the person responsible for that is Al-Jarīrī, for he used to confuse things. The ḥadīth is known from the narration of Abū Hārūn Al-'Abdī, as confirmed by Tirmidhī in what we previously transmitted from him. And Imām Aḥmad declared this narration to be weak.

In *'Al-Muntakhab'* by Ibn Qudāmah—as mentioned in *'Al-Ṣaḥīḥah'* (1/504) by Al-Albānī (may Allāh mercy on him) it says: Muhanna said: "I asked Aḥmad about the ḥadīth of Sa'īd Ibn Sulaymān..." and he quoted the ḥadīth with its chain of narrators. Imām Aḥmad said: "Allāh did not create anything of this. This is the ḥadīth of Abū Hārūn, on the authority of Abū Sa'īd."

I say: It was reported by a large number of narrators on the authority of Abū Hārūn Al-'Abdī and the ḥadīth is well known from his narration, as indicated by Aḥmad (may Allāh have mercy on him).

However, it has another source collected by Al-Rāmhurmuzī (#23) from the narration of Al-Ḥamānī, who reported on the authority of Ibn Al-Fasīl, who reported on the authority of Abū Khālid, the freed slave of Ibn Al-Ṣabah, who reported on the authority of Abū Sa'īd (*raḍiyAllāhu 'anhu*).

But Al-Ḥamānī is accused of stealing *aḥādīth*, while Ibn Al-Fasīl and Abū Khālid are unknown.

It has a fourth source, which is not *maḥfūz* (a form of acceptable ḥadīth, narrated by a more trustworthy narrator, as opposed to a less trustworthy narrator, due to more accuracy on his part or other reasons) from the narration of 'Ubaydullāh Ibn Zahr, who reported on the authority of Layth Ibn Abū Sulaym, who reported on the authority of Shahr Ibn Ḥawshab, who reported on the authority of Abū Sa'īd (*raḍiyAllāhu 'anhu*).

It was narrated by Al-Khaṭīb in *'Al-Jāmi' li-Akhlāq Al-Rāwi wa Ādāb Al-Sāmi'* (#357). But its chain of narrators is weak, due to the weakness of Ibn Zahr and Layth.

its *isnād* to us, saying,

> 'Whoever sought a ḥadīth in order that people should talk about him, he will not find [even] the breath of Paradise'."He [the narrator] said: "When he had calmed his anger, he quoted a ḥadīth with its chain of narrators to us, in which he said: 'Towards the end of time, a people will come seeking knowledge and ḥadīth; if they come to you, inform them, honour them and convey the ḥadīth to them."[75]

[75] Its chain of narrators is extremely weak.

In it is Muḥammad Ibn Al-Ḥasan Ibn Muḥammad Ibn Ziyād Al-Naqqāsh Al-Muqrī'. Al-Khaṭīb cited evidence in his biography in *'Tārīkh Baghdād'* that proves his weakness; and Ṭalḥah Ibn Muḥammad Al-Shahid declared him to be a liar, while Al-Barqānī said: "Every ḥadīth of Al-Naqqāsh is *munkar*." In addition, Muḥammad Ibn Ja'far Al-Qattāt was declared weak by Al-Khaṭīb (2/129); I do not know him. It is only narrated from Al-Ḥusayn Al-Ju'fī: Ja'far Ibn Muḥammad Ibn 'Imrān; and it is most likely in my opinion that it is from among the confused narrations of Al-Naqqāsh, for he suffered from this weakness, as elaborated in his biography.

CHAPTER SEVEN

The saying of the Prophet (ﷺ): "Islām began as something strange and will go back to being something strange, so glad tidings to the strangers."

32. We were informed by Abū'l-Ḥasan ʿAlī Ibn Aḥmad Ibn ʿUmar Al-Muqrī' and Abū'l-Qāsim ʿAbdu'l-Mālik Ibn Muḥammad Ibn ʿAbdullāh Al-Wāʿiẓ, who both said that they were informed by Abū Bakr Muḥammad Ibn Al-Ḥusayn Al-Ājurī, in Makkah, who said that he was told by Abū Aḥmad Hārūn Ibn Yūsuf Al-Tājir, who said that he was told by Muḥammad Ibn Abū ʿUmar Al-ʿAdnī, who said that he was told by Marwān Ibn Muʿāwiyah Al-Fazārī, who reported on the authority of Yazīd Ibn Kaisan, who reported on the authority of Abū Hāzim, who reported on the authority of Abū Hurayrah (*raḍiyAllāhu ʿanhu*) that he said: "The Messenger of Allāh (ﷺ) said:

> "Verily, Islām began as something strange (*gharīb*) and it will go back to being something strange (*gharīb*) , so

glad tidings to the strangers. (*ghurabā'*)"[76]

33. We were informed by Abū Muḥammad 'Abdullāh Ibn Aḥmad Ibn 'Abdullāh Ibn Ibrāhīm Al-Aṣbahānī, who said that he was told by Abū Sulaymān Muḥammad Ibn Al-Ḥusayn Al-Ḥaranī, who said that he was told by Al-Nu'mān Ibn Mudrik, who said that he was told by Ja'far Ibn Al-Faḍīl, who said that he was informed by[77] Isḥāq Ibn Ibrāhīm Al-Ḥunaynī, who reported on the authority of Kathīr Ibn 'Abdullāh, who reported on the authority of his father, who reported on the authority of grandfather that he said: "The Messenger of Allāh (ﷺ) said:

> "Verily, Islām began as something strange and it will go back to being something strange, so glad tidings to the strangers." It was said: "O Messenger of Allāh! Who are the strangers?" He (ﷺ) replied: "[They are] those who keep alive my Sunnah after me and teach it to the slaves of Allāh."[78]

34. We were informed by Muḥammad Ibn Al-Ḥasan Ibn Abū 'Alī Al-Aṣbahānī, who said that he was told by Abū Ḥakīm Aḥmad

---

[76] This is an authentic ḥadīth.

It was narrated by Muslim (1/130), by Ibn Mājah (#3986), by Al-Ājurī in *'Al-Ghurabā'* (#4) and by the author in *'Tarīkh Baghdād'* (11/307). In his version is an addition that is *mawqūf* (i.e. it emanates from the Companion who narrated it) to Abū Hurayrah (*raḍiyAllāhu 'anhu*). All of them reported it by way of Yazīd Ibn Kaysan. See English translation of Al-Ājurī's *'Al-Ghurabā'*—The Journey of The Strangers—accompanying a treatise by Ibn Rajab published by Dār as-Sunnah Publishers, Birmingham, United Kingdom, 1st ed., 2009.

[77] In manuscript (B) it says "told by".

[78] Its chain of narrators is extremely weak.

In it is Kathīr Ibn 'Abdullāh Ibn 'Amr Ibn 'Awf, who is weak; indeed, more than one scholar declared him to be a liar. In addition, Al-Ḥunaynī is extremely weak. The ḥadīth was narrated by Al-Bazzār in his *'Musnad'* (*Kashf Al-Astar* #3287), by Al-Qaḍā'ī in *'Al-Shihāb'* (#1052 and #1053), by Ibn 'Abr Al-Barfi in *'Jāmi' Bayān Al-'Ilm wa Faḍlihi'* (2/120) by way of Isḥāq Ibn Ibrāhīm Al-Ḥunaynī.

It was narrated by Tirmidhī and others from the ḥadīth of Ismā'īl Ibn Abū Uways,

Ibn Muḥammad Al-Subai'ī, in Al-Ahwāz, who said that he was told by 'Abdān Al-Qāḍī, who said that he was told by Abū Bakr Ibn Abū Shaybah, who said that he was told by Ḥafṣ Ibn Ghiyāth, who reported on the authority of Al-A'mash, who reported on the authority of Abū Isḥāq, who reported on the authority of Abū'l-Aḥwaṣ, who reported on the authority of 'Abdullāh (*raḍiyAllāhu 'anhu*) that he said: "The Messenger of Allāh (ﷺ) said:

> "Verily, Islām began as something strange and it will come back to being something strange, just as it began." It was said: "O Messenger of Allāh! Who are the *ghurabā'*?" He (ﷺ) replied, "The strangers from among the tribes (*qabā'il*)."[79]

'Abdān said: "They are the scholars of ḥadīth (*aṣḥāb al-ḥadīth*) from the early generations."

---

on the authority of Kathīr, in a longer version than this.

[79] It was narrated by Imām Aḥmad and his son, 'Abdullāh in *'Zawā'id 'Alal-Musnad'* (1/398), by Al-Ājurī's *'Al-Ghurabā'* (2), by Ibn Wadhdhah in *'Al-Bid'āh wal-nahy 'anha'* (169) (which has been checked for authenticity by us), by Al-Khaṭṭābī in *'Gharīb Al-Ḥadīth'* (1/174), by way of Ibn Abū Shaybah.

The men in this chain of narrators are trustworthy, though Al-Subā'ī is a *mudallis* and he has narrated it through *al-'an'anah*. To me, he is a person whose ḥadīth cannot be cited as proof, unless he makes it clear that he heard directly from the narrator, or another evidence proves that he did not commit *tadlīs* in his narration.

CHAPTER EIGHT

The saying of the Prophet (ﷺ): "My *Ummah* will Split into More Than Seventy Sects..."

35. We were informed by Al-Ḥasan Ibn Aḥmad Ibn Ibrāhīm Al-Bazzār, who said that he was told by[80] Aḥmad Ibn Isḥāq Ibn Nīkhab Al-Ṭayyibī, who said that he was told by Isḥāq Ibn Ibrāhīm Ibn Bahram Al-Rayhanī, in Ḥamazān, who said that he was told by Al-Ḥajjāj Ibn Yūsuf Ibn Qutaybah Ibn Muslim Al-Aṣbahānī, who said that he was told by Bishr Ibn Al-Ḥusayn, who reported on the authority of[81] Al-Zubayr Ibn 'Adiyy, who reported on the authority of Anas (*raḍiyAllāhu 'anhu*) that the Messenger of Allāh (ﷺ) said:

> "Banu Isra'īl split into seventy-one sects, the Christians split into seventy-two sects and my *ummah* will split into seventy-three sects—all of them will be in the Fire except one."[82]

[80] In manuscript (B) it says "told by".
[81] In manuscript (B) it says "told by".

36. We were informed by Abū Nuʿaym Al-Ḥāfiẓ, who said that he was told by Sulaymān Ibn Aḥmad Ibn Ayyūb Al-Ṭabāranī, who said that he was told by Aḥmad Ibn Muḥammad Ibn Hashim Al-Baʿlbakī, who said that he was told by ʿAbdu'l- Mālik Ibn Al-Aṣbagh Al-Baʿlbakī, who said that he was told by Al-Walīd Ibn Muslim, who said that he was informed by[83] Al-Awzāʿī, who said that he was told by Qatādah, who reported on the authority of Anas Ibn Mālik (*raḍiyAllāhu ʿanhu*), who said: "The Messenger of Allāh (ﷺ) said:

> "Verily, Banu Isra'īl split into seventy-one sects and verily, my *ummah* will split into seventy-two sects and all of them will be in the Fire except one—and that is the *jamāʿah*."[84]

37. I was told by ʿAbdullāh Ibn Aḥmad Ibn ʿAlī As-Sūzarjanī, in

[82] Its chain of narrators is extremely weak and it is not inconceivable that from this source, it is fabricated.

In it is Bishr Ibn Al-Ḥusayn Al-Hilālī; Al-Bukhārī was suspicious of him, saying, "There is some doubt in him." Abū Ḥātim said: "He lies regarding Al-Zubayr." Ad-Daraquṭnī said: "He is abandoned."

I say: It is not inconceivable that he stole this ḥadīth and narrated it on the authority of Al-Zubayr, for it is only well known from the narration of Yazīd Ibn Abān Al-Raqashī, who reported on the authority of as will be shown shortly, if Allāh, Most High wills.

[83] In manuscript (B) it says: "told by".

[84] Its chain of narrators is *shāẓẓ*.

It was collected by Ibn Abū ʿĀṣim in *'As-Sunnah'* (#64), by Ibn Mājah (#3993): We were told by Hisham Ibn ʿAmmar, who said that he was told by Al-Walīd...

Al-Būṣayrī said in *'Miṣbāh Al-Zujājah'* (2/96), "This isnād is authentic and its narrators are all trustworthy."

I say: In fact, it is defective; it was narrated by more than one of them: Muʿāwiyah Ibn Ṣāliḥ, ʿIsā Ibn Yūnus, Fuḍayl Ibn ʿIyāḍ, Abū Isḥāq Al-Fazarī, who reported on the authority of Al-Awzāʿī, who said that he was told by Yazīd Al-Raqashī, who reported on the authority of Anas (*raḍiyAllāhu ʿanhu*).

It was collected by Abū'l-Qāsim Al-Aṣbahānī in *'Al-Ḥujjah'* (1/108).But the more correct version is the narration of the majority, and Al-Raqashī is weak.

It is strengthened by the authentic ḥadīth of Muʿāwiyah Ibn Abū Sufyān (*raḍiyAllāhu ʿanhu*) which was mentioned in my commentary of the book *'Al-Mudhakkir al-Tadhkīr*
=

Aṣbahān, that he said that he heard ʻAbdullāh Ibn Abū'l-Qāsim, who said that he heard from Aḥmad Ibn Muḥammad Ibn Rawah,[85] who said that he was informed by[86] Ibrāhīm Ibn Muḥammad Ibn Al-Ḥasan,[87] that he said that he was told on the authority of Aḥmad Ibn Ḥanbal—and he mentioned the ḥadīth of the Prophet (ﷺ):

> "The *ummah* will split into more than seventy sects and all of them will be in the Fire except one sect (*firqah*). He (ﷺ) added, "If they are not the people of ḥadīth, then I do not know who they are."[88]

38. I was told by Muḥammad Ibn Abū'l-Ḥasan, who said that he was informed by Abū'l-Qāsim Ibn Sakhtawayh, who said that he heard Abū'l-Ḥasan Muḥammad Ibn ʻAbdullāh Ibn Bishr, in Fasā,[89] who said:

> "I saw the Prophet (ﷺ) in a dream and I said: 'Who are the saved sect (*al-firqah al-nājiḥa*) from among the seventy-three sects?' He (ﷺ) replied, 'You! O people of ḥadīth (*aṣḥāb al-ḥadīth*).'"[90]

=

wal-Zhikr', by Ibn Abū ʻĀṣim (p. 38). And the majority of the *aḥādīth* in the chapter have been mentioned in my commentary of *'Al-Sharīʻah'*, by Al-Ājurī.

[85] In manuscript (B) it says "*Wawah*".

[86] In manuscript (B) it says "told us".

[87] In manuscript (A) it says "Al-Ḥusayn".

[88] Its chain of narrators is *munqati'* (interrupted). It was collected by Al-Ḥākim in *'Maʻrifah Al-Ḥadīth'* (p. 3): "I heard Abū ʻAbdullāh Muḥammad Ibn ʻAbdu'l- Ḥameed Al-Aadami, in Makkah, who said that he heard Mūsā Ibn Hārūn say that he heard Aḥmad Ibn Ḥanbal say, when he was asked about this ḥadīth, 'If this successful group is not the people of ḥadīth, then I do not know who they are'." And Al-Ḥāfiẓ (Ibn Ḥajr) declared its chain of narrators authentic in *'Al-Fatḥ'* (13/306).

[89] Fasā: A city in Persia.

[90] In its chain of narrators there is someone whom I do not know.

CHAPTER NINE

The Saying of the Prophet (*ʿalayhis-salām*)[91]: "A group from among my *Ummah* will continue to adhere to the truth and those who abandon them will not harm them."

39. We were informed by Abū Nuʿaym Al-Ḥāfiẓ, who said that he was told by ʿAbdullāh Ibn Jaʿfar, who said that he was told by Yūnus Ibn Ḥabīb, who said that he was told by Abū Dāwūd, who said that he was told by Shuʿbah, who said that he was informed by Muʿāwiyah Ibn Qurrah, who reported on the authority of his Father that he said: "The Prophet (ﷺ) said:

> "A group (*ṭā'ifah*) from among my *ummah* will continue to adhere to the truth and those who abandon them will not harm them until the Hour is established."[92]

---

[91] In manuscript (B) it says (ﷺ).

[92] This is an authentic ḥadīth.

40. We were informed by Muḥammad Ibn Ṭalḥah Al-Na'alī, who said that he was told by Muḥammad Ibn Al-Ḥasan Ibn Kawthar, who said that he was told by Muḥammad Ibn Yūnus, who said that he was told by Abū Zayd Saʿīd Ibn [Zayd Ibn][93] Al-Rabīʿ, who said that he was informed by[94] Shuʿbah, who said that he was informed by Muʿāwiyah Ibn Qurrah, who reported on the authority of his Father that he said: "The Messenger of Allāh (ﷺ) said:

> "A group (*tā'ifah*) from among my *ummah* will continue to adhere to the truth and those who abandon them will not harm them until the Hour is established."[95]

41. I was informed by Muḥammad Ibn Al-Ḥasan Al-Ahwāzī, who said that he was told by Muḥammad Ibn Isḥāq Ibn Ibrāhīm Al-Qāḍī, in Al-Ahwāz, who said that he was told by Yazīd Ibn Hārūn, who reported on the authority of Ḥammād Ibn Salāmah, who reported on the authority of Qatādah, who reported on the authority of Muṭrif, who reported on the authority of ʿImrān Ibn Ḥusayn that he said:

> "My *ummah* will continue to fight in the cause of truth

=

It was narrated by Imām Aḥmad (3/436 and 5/34 and 35), by Ibn Abū ʿĀṣim in *'Al-Āhad wal-Mathanī'* (2/233). By Ibn Abū Shaybah in *'Al-Muṣannaf'* (6/409), by Tirmidhī (#9192), by Ibn Mājah (#6), by Al-Ṭabāranī in *'Al-Muʿjam Al-Kabīr'* (19/27) and by Al-Ḥākim in *'Maʿrifah ʿUlūm Al-Ḥadīth'* (p. 2)—from different sources, all on the authority of Shuʿbah.

Some of them added to the beginning of the ḥadīth the words: "If the people of Ash-Sham become corrupt, there will be no good in you."

Some of them narrated it in the first half, while others narrated it in the second half.

Tirmidhī added the comment: "Muḥammad Ibn Ismāʿīl said that ʿAlī Ibn Al-Madīnī said: 'They are the people of ḥadīth'."

And it has previously been mentioned with the no. 8.

[93] From manuscript (A).

[94] This is from manuscript (A).

[95] This is an authentic ḥadīth.

See what was mentioned previously.

until the Hour is established."

Yazīd Ibn Hārūn said: "If they are not the people of ḥadīth (*aṣḥāb al-ḥadīth*), then I do not know who they are."[96]

42. I was informed by 'Ubaydullāh Ibn Abū'l-Fatḥ and Al-Ḥasan Ibn Abū Ṭālib, who both said that they were told by Muḥammad Ibn Al-'Abbās Abū 'Umar Al-Khazzāz, who said that he was

[96] This is authentic, but *mawqūf.*

In its chain of narrators is Ḥammād Ibn Salāmah, and while he was trustworthy, he was alone in narrating this ḥadīth on the authority of Qatādah, without the remainder of his trustworthy and reliable companions, such as Shu'bah, Hisham Al-Dastawa'ī, Sa'īd Ibn Abū 'Urūbah.

This kind of *tafarrud* (being alone in narrating from someone)impairs it; the *tafarrud* of a trustworthy person on the authority of the Ḥāfiẓ in the narration, without the remainder of his companions is one of the things that impairs the narration, as pointed out by Imām Muslim in the foreword of his *'Ṣaḥīḥ'*. So how then, if there is a contradiction in the isnād of this ḥadīth? For it was narrated by Imām Aḥmad (4/434) as follows: We were told by Ismā'īl, who said that he was informed by Al-Jarīrī, who reported on the authority of Abū'l-'Alā' Ibn Al-Shakhīr, who reported on the authority of Muṭrif that he said: "'Imrān said to me, 'I will tell you of a ḥadīth today by which Allāh, the Almighty, the All-Powerful will benefit you after today: 'The best of Allāh, Most Blessed, Most High's slaves on the Day of Resurrection will be those who praise (Allāh). And know that a group from among the people of Islām will continue to fight for the truth and to be victorious over those who oppose them, until they fight the Dajjal...'"

I say: This chain of narrators is authentic; Ismā'īl is Ibn 'Aliyyah and his hearing it from Al-Jarīrī was before his confusion.

And the ḥadīth was narrated by Imām Aḥmad (4/429 and 437), by Abū Dāwūd (#2484), by Al-Ḥākim (4/450) and Al-Lalāka'ī in *'Sharh Usūl Al-I'tiqād'* (#168 and #169) from various sources on the authority of Ḥammād Ibn Salāmah.

As for the saying of Yazīd Ibn Hārūn: "If they are not the people of ḥadīth..." it is not confirmed with the isnād of the author, for it contains Al-Ḥasan Ibn 'Uthmān Al-Tustarī, who was declared a liar by Ibn 'Adiyy.

It was narrated from this source by Ar-Ramhurmuzi in *'Al-Muhaddith Al-Fāsil'* (#27): "We were told by Al-Ḥasan Ibn 'Uthmān At-Tustarī..."

But *Qiwām Al-Sunnah* (Abū'l-Qāsim Ismā'īl Ibn Muḥammad Al-Taymī Al-Asbahānī) reported it from another source in *'Al-Hujjah'* (1/247) and he said: 'Abū Muḥammad Ibn Ḥayyān said: 'Mūsā Ibn 'Abdu'l-Raḥmān that he was told by 'Abdullāh Al-Muqrī, who said that he was told by Aḥmad Ibn Abū Khalaf, who reported on the authority Yazīd.

told by Abū Bakr Ibn Abū Dāwūd that he said that he was told by his father, who reported on the authority of Sa'īd Ibn Ya'qūb Al-Ṭāliqānī or another, who said that Ibn Al-Mubārak mentioned the ḥadīth of the Prophet (ﷺ):

> "A group (*ṭā'ifah*) from among my *ummah* will continue to support the truth and those who oppose them will not harm them until the Hour is established."[97]

Ibn Al-Mubārak said: "In my opinion, they are the people of ḥadīth."

43. We were informed by Abū Nu'aym Al-Ḥāfiẓ that he said that he was told by Muḥammad Ibn Ja'far Al-Mu'addib that he said that he was told by 'Abdullāh Ibn Muḥammad Ibn Al-Khalīl that he said that he heard Al-Faḍl Ibn Ziyād saying, "I heard Aḥmad Ibn Ḥanbal..." and he mentioned the ḥadīth:

> "A group (*ṭā'ifah*) from among my *ummah* will continue to support the truth..." and he said: "If they are not the people of ḥadīth, then I do not know who they are."[98]

44. We were also informed by Abū Nu'aym, who said that he was told by 'Abdullāh Ibn Muḥammad Ibn Ja'far, who said that he was told by Muḥammad Ibn Al-Faḍl Ibn Al-Khaṭṭāb, who said that he was told by Abū Ḥātim, who said that he heard Aḥmad Ibn Sinan... and he mentioned the ḥadīth:

---

[97] Its chain of narrators is authentic—if it is from the narration of Al-Ṭāliqānī; if not, then that is only the situation of its narrator on the authority of Ibn Al-Mubārak.

[98] Its chain of narrators is weak, but the text (of the ḥadīth) is correct.

In it is Muḥammad Ibn Ja'far Al-Mu'addib; he was mentioned by Al-Dhahabī in *'Al-Mīzān'* (3/510); he said: "Ibn Abū'l-Fawāris said that he is *mutasaḥil* (not strict), though someone else said that there is no objection to him."

We have previously given its *takhrīj* with an authentic chain of narrators (no. 37).

> "A group (*ṭā'ifah*) from among my *ummah* will continue to adhere to the truth..." and he said: "They are the people of knowledge and the people of the traditions."[99]

45. We were informed by Abū Ya'lā Aḥmad Ibn 'Abdu'l-Wāḥid Al-Wakīl, who said that he was informed by Al-Ḥasan Ibn Muḥammad Ibn Shu'bah Al-Marwazī, who was said that he was told by Muḥammad Ibn Aḥmad Ibn Maḥbūb, who said that he was told by Abū 'Isā Tirmidhī—and he mentioned the ḥadīth of Mu'āwiyah Ibn Qurrah, who reported on the authority of his father that he said: "The Messenger of Allāh (ﷺ) said:

> "A group (*ṭā'ifah*) from among my *ummah* will continue to be helped (by Allāh) and those who oppose them will not harm them."[100]

Abū 'Isā said: "Muḥammad Ibn Ismā'īl said: "'Alī Ibn Al-Madīnī said: 'They are the people of ḥadīth'."

46. We were informed by Abū Nu'aym Al-Ḥāfiẓ that he said that he was told by Abū Muḥammad Ibn Ḥayyān, who said that he was told by Isḥāq Ibn Aḥmad, who said that he was told by Muḥammad Ibn Ismā'īl Al-Bukhārī... and he mentioned the ḥadīth of Mūsā Ibn 'Uqbah, who reported on the authority of Abū Al-Zubayr, who reported on the authority of Jabir (*raḍiyAllāhu 'anhu*), who reported from the Prophet (ﷺ) that he said[101]:

---

[99] Its chain of narrators is authentic.

Muḥammad Ibn Al-Faḍl Ibn Al-Khaṭṭāb was declared trustworthy by Abū Ash-Shaikh, in *'Ṭabaqāt Al-Muḥaddithīn bi-Aṣbāhan'* (4/323) and the Shaikh of Abū Nu'aym is Abū Al-Shaikh Ibn Ḥayyān.

The tradition was narrated by *Qiwām Al-Sunnah* in *'Al-Hujjah'* (1/246) by way of Abū Ash-Shaikh.

[100] This is an authentic ḥadīth.

It was set forth and its *takhrīj* given in no. 39.

> "A group (*ṭā'ifah*) from among my *ummah* will continue..."[102]

Al-Bukhārī said: "It means the people of ḥadīth."

[101] This is from manuscript (A).

[102] Isḥāq Ibn Aḥmad is Ibn Khalaf Al-Ḥāfiẓ, or Ibn Zayrak Al-Fārisī and I have found no biography for the latter. The remainder of the narrators in the chain are trustworthy.

CHAPTER TEN

The Saying of the Prophet (ﷺ): "This Knowledge is borne in Every Generation by its Just People."

47. We were informed by Al-Qāḍī Abū Muḥammad Al-Ḥasan Ibn Al-Ḥusayn Ibn Ramīn Al-Astarabazī that he said that he was told by Abū Aḥmad 'Abdullāh Ibn 'Adiyy Al-Jurjanī Al-Ḥāfiẓ, who said that he was told by Abū Qudahī Ismā'īl Ibn Muḥammad Ibn Isḥāq Al-'Azrī, in Damascus, that he said that he was told by Sulaymān Ibn 'Abdu'l-Raḥmān Al-Dimashqī, who said that he was told by Maslamah [i.e. Ibn 'Ulayy], who said that he was told by 'Abdu'l-Raḥmān Ibn Yazīd Al-Sulamī, who reported on the authority of 'Alī Ibn Muslim Al-Bakrī, who reported on the authority of Abū Ṣāliḥ Al-Ash'arī, who reported on the authority of Abū Hurayrah (*raḍiyAllāhu 'anhu*) that he said: "The Messenger of Allāh (ﷺ) said:

> "This knowledge will be borne in every generation by its just people; they refute the corruptions of extremists, the distortionsof the falsifiers and the [false] interpreta-

tions of the ignorant."[103]

48. Abū'l-Ḥusayn Aḥmad Ibn 'Umar Ibn 'Alī Al-Qāḍī in Darzījan informed me that he was informed by Aḥmad Ibn 'Alī Ibn Muḥammad Ibn Al-Jahm Al-Kātib (the scribe), that he said

[103] Its chain of narrators is weak.

In it is Maslamah Ibn 'Alī Al-Khushnī and he is *matrūk* (abandoned) in matters of ḥadīth. Al-Bukhārī and Abū Zur'ah said that his ḥadīth is *munkar* (rejected), while Ibn Ma'īn said: "He is nothing." Nasā'ī said: "He is not trustworthy." And more than one scholar declared him to be weak. His Shaikh, 'Abdu'l-Raḥmān Ibn Yazīd Al-Sulamī is extremely weak.

The ḥadīth was narrated by Ibn 'Adiyy in *'Al-Kāmil'* (1/153).

It was also narrated by the author in *'Al-Jami'* (#134) from various sources: Al-Ṭabāranī said that he was told by Aḥmad Ibn Al-Mu'alla Al-Dimashqī, who said that he was told by Sulaymān Ibn 'Abdu'l-Raḥmān Al-Dimashqī.

It also has another source on the authority of Abū Hurayrah (*raḍiyAllāhu 'anhu*), from the narration of Khālid Ibn 'Amr Al-Qurashī, who reported on the authority of Al-Layth Ibn Sa'd, who reported on the authority of Yazīd Ibn Abū Ḥabīb, who reported on the authority of Abū Qabīl, who reported on the authority of Abū Hurayrah (*raḍiyAllāhu 'anhu*) and 'Abdu'l-Raḥmān Ibn 'Umar (*raḍiyAllāhu 'anhu*).

It was also narrated by Al-Bazzār (*Kashf*: #143).

And it was also narrated by Ibn 'Adiyy (1/152) and by Tamam Al-Razī in *'Al-Fawā'id'* (*Al-Rawḍh Al-Bassam*: #80), from the ḥadīth of Ibn 'Umar (*raḍiyAllāhu 'anhu*) alone; but he said: "It was reported on the authority of Yazīd, who reported on the authority Sālim, who reported on the authority of Ibn 'Umar (*raḍiyAllāhu 'anhu*)..."

Al-Bazzār said: "The ḥadīth of Khālid Ibn 'Amr is *munkar*; he reported aḥādīth that do not conform (to what has been authentically reported)—and this is one of them."

I say: His situation is even worse than that, for a group from among the scholars have declared him to be weak and Ibn Ma'īn said that he was a liar, while Ibn 'Adiyy accused him of fabricating aḥādīth.

The ḥadīth was reported from another source collected by Ibn 'Adiyy (1/152) from the narration of Dāwūd Ibn Sulaymān Al-Ghassānī: We were told by Marwān Al-Fazarī, who reported on the authority of Yazīd Ibn Kaysan, who reported it on the authority of Abū Hurayrah (*raḍiyAllāhu 'anhu*).

Ibn 'Adiyy said: "I have not seen this ḥadīth of Marwān Al-Fazarī with this isnād except from this source."

It appears from this that he was indicating that it is *munkar*. In addition, it is not correct that Abū Hāzim heard from Abū Hurayrah (*raḍiyAllāhu 'anhu*).

The *takhrīj* of some of those who reported from the Companions (*raḍiyAllāhu 'anhu*) can be found in the chapter, whole others may be found in my verification of the book *'Al-Sharī'ah'* (no. 1).

that he was told by Muḥammad Ibn Jarīr Al-Ṭabarī, who said that he was told by ʿUthmān Ibn Yaḥya, who said that he was told by ʿAmr Ibn Hashim Al-Bayrūtī, who reported on the authority of Muḥammad Ibn Sulaymān [i.e. Ibn Abū Karīmah], who reported on the authority of Maʿān Ibn Rifāʿah Al-Salāmī, who reported on the authority of Abū ʿUthmān Al-Nahdī, who reported on the authority of Usāmah Ibn Zayd (*raḍiyAllāhu ʿanhu*) that he said: "The Messenger of Allāh (ﷺ) said:

> "This knowledge will be borne in every generation by its just people; they refute the corruptions and the distortions of the falsifiers."[104]

We were informed by ʿUbaydullāh Ibn Aḥmad Ibn ʿUthmān Al-Ṣayrafī, who said that he was told by Muḥammad Ibn Al-Muẓaffar Al-Ḥāfiẓ, who said that he was told by Aḥmad Ibn Yaḥya Ibn Zukayr, who said that he was told by Muḥammad Ibn Maymūn Ibn Kāmil Al-Hamrāwī, who said that he was told by Abū Ṣāliḥ, who said that he was told by Al-Layth Ibn Saʿd, who reported on the authority of Yaḥya Ibn Saʿīd, who reported on the authority of Saʿīd Ibn Al-Musayyib, who reported on the authority of ʿAbdullāh Ibn Masʿūd (*raḍiyAllāhu ʿanhu*) that he said: "The Messenger of Allāh (ﷺ) said:

> "This knowledge will be inherited in every generation by its just people."[105]

[104] Its chain of narrators is extremely weak. In it is Muḥammad Ibn Sulaymān Ibn Abū Karīmah; he was reported to be weak by Abū Ḥātim in *'Al-Jarḥ wal-Taʿdīl'* (2/3/268). Al-ʿUqaylī said: "He narrated on the authority of Hashim Bawatīl." In addition, the report is known to be the narration of Maʿān Ibn Rifāʿah, who reported on the authority of Ibrāhim Al-ʿAzrī, of whom we shall speak in no. 50.

[105] Its chain of narrators is munkar.

In it are Aḥmad Ibn Yaḥya Ibn Zukayr and Muḥammad Ibn Maymūn Ibn Kāmil, both of whom were declared weak by Al-Daraquṭnī, as reported in *'Lisān Al-Mīzān'* (by Ibn =

50. We were informed by Muḥammad Ibn Aḥmad Ibn Rizq Al-Bazzāz, who said that he was told by ʿUmar Ibn Jaʿfar Ibn Salm, who said that he was told by ʿAlī Ibn Muḥammad Ibn ʿAbdu'l-Mālik Ibn Abū Al-Shawaryb and Yaʿqūb Ibn Yūsuf Al-Muṭawiʿī, who both said that they were told by Abū Al-Rabīʿ, who said that he was told by Ḥammād Ibn Zayd, who said that he was told by Baqiyyah Ibn Al-Walīd, who said that he was told by Maʿān Ibn Rifāʿah, who reported on the authority of Ibrāhim Ibn ʿAbdu'l-Raḥmān Al-ʿAzrī, who said: "The Messenger of Allāh (ﷺ) said:

> "This knowledge will be borne in every generation by its just people (*ʿadūl*); they refute the corruptions of the extremists (*tawīl al-ghālīn*), the distortions of the falsifiers (*intiḥāl al-mubṭalīn*) and the [false] interpretations of the ignorant (*taḥʿrīf al-jāhilīn*)."[106]

=

Ḥajr) (1/356). At the first mention, he said: "He is nothing in ḥadīth," then he said: "Aḥmad is not satisfactory in ḥadīth." He was alone in narrating this ḥadīth and I did not find anyone who concurred with them."

[106] Its chain of narrators is weak. In it are Maʿān Ibn Rifāʿah—who is *layyin* (lenient, not strict) in ḥadīth—and Ibrāhim Al-ʿAzrī, of whom Al-Dhahabī said in *'Al-Mīzān'* (1/45), "He is a Tābiʿī who has few narrations and those which I know of are weak."

So his narration from the Prophet (ﷺ) is *mursal.*

The ḥadīth was narrated by Ibn Abū Ḥātim in the foreword of *'Al-Jarḥ wa'l-Taʿdīl'* (p. 17), by Ibn ʿAdiyy in *'Al-Kāmil'* (1/153), by Al-ʿUqaylī (4/256), by Al-Bayhaqī in *'Al-Kubrā'* (10/209) and *'Dalāʿil Al-Nubuwwah'* (1/37) and by Ibn Wadhdhah in *'Al-Bidʿāh wal-Nahi ʿAnha'* (1) from a number of sources on the authority of Maʿān.

I also found it after that in *'Al-Sharīʿah'* by Al-Ājurī (the complete version) (2/*al-Sulaymaiyyah*) from sources on the authority of Maʿān.

The surprising thing is that the verifier of the book, Shaikh Ḥāmid Al-Faqī (may Allāh have mercy on him and forgive him) indicated that there is a blank space after the name of Maʿān and he completed it with another sanad and text, which is the ḥadīth: "Allāh will cause a man to flourish..." and he indicated that this was from the deeds of Shaikh Muḥammad ʿAbdu'l-Razzāq Ḥamzah (may Allāh have mercy on him), but this is based on surmise. For this reason, this insertion of something that is not from the text, the attempt to make it appear authentic by referring to the books of the Sunnah, without knowledge of the science of *takhrīj* and the contradictions in the chains of narrators and the texts is a huge mistake—and the printed version, sadly, is filled with such examples, in addition to advancement and delaying of things from their proper places in many instances, to say nothing of the omissions—especially in the final section of =

51. It was related on the authority of ʿAbdu'l-ʿAzīz Ibn Jaʿfar Al-Faqīh that he said that he was told by Abū Bakr Al-Khallāl that he read to Zuhayr Ibn Ṣāliḥ Ibn Aḥmad, who said that he was informed by Mahna—Ibn Yaḥyā—who said: "I asked Aḥmad —Ibn Ḥanbal—about the ḥadīth of Maʿān Ibn Rifāʿah, on the authority of Ibrāhīm Ibn ʿAbdu'l-Raḥmān Al-ʿAzrī and he said that the Messenger of Allāh (ﷺ) said:

> "This knowledge will be borne in every generation by its just people (*ʿadūl*); they refute the [false] interpretations of the ignorant (*taḥʿrīf al-jāhilīn*), the distortions of the falsifiers (*intiḥāl al-mubṭalīn*) and the corruptions of the extremists (*tawīl al-ghālīn*)."

I said to Aḥmad, 'It appears as if it is fabricated speech!' He replied, 'It is authentic.' So I said [to him],[107] 'From whom did you hear it?' He said: 'From more than one [person].' I asked, 'Who are they?' He replied, 'I was told of it by Miskīn, except that he said [it was from] Maʿān, on the authority of Al-Qāsim Ibn ʿAbdu'l-Raḥmān.' Aḥmad added, '[As for] Maʿān Ibn Rifāʿah, there is no objection to him'."[108]

=

it, which accounts for more than half of the manuscript. All praise and thanks be to Allāh, I have completed the verification of the first volume on this great journey and may Allāh make it easy for me to verify the remainder of the volumes, for verily, He is the Protecting Friend of that and the Ability is His.

[107] This is from manuscript (A).

[108] The men in the chain of narrators are trustworthy. Zuhayr Ibn Ṣāliḥ Ibn Al-Imām Aḥmad has a biography in *'Tarīkh Baghdād'* (8/486) and he was declared trustworthy by Al-Darāquṭnī. But I do not know if this speech can be reliably attributed to Imām Aḥmad or not, because his great knowledge (of ḥadīth) and his firm grounding in it make it unlikely that he would have declared a weak ḥadīth to be authentic. So it would seem likely that the weakness in it is from the one from whom Al-Khaṭīb heard it.

After I had written the above statement, I read the words of Al-'Irāqī in *'Al-Taqyīd wal-Īḍāḥ'* (p. 139) regarding this information to Al-Khallāl in *'Al-ʿIlal'*. So there is no way to declare this chain of narrators weak or to discredit it due to the unknown status of the intermediary between Al-Khaṭīb and ʿAbdu'l-ʿAzīz Ibn Jaʿfar. In fact, it is without

=

52. I was informed by 'Ubaydullāh Ibn Abū'l-Fatḥ Al-Fārisī, who said that he was informed by 'Abdu'l-Raḥmān Ibn 'Umar Al-Khallāl, who said that Muḥammad Ibn Aḥmad Ibn Ya'qūb Ibn Shaybah said: "I saw a man who sent forth a man to Ismā'īl Ibn Isḥāq Al-Qāḍī and he made some claims to him which he rejected, asking him, 'Do you have any proof?' He replied, 'Yes, So-and-so and So-and-so.' He replied, 'As for the first person [you have mentioned], he is one of my witnesses, while as for the second person [you mentioned], he is not one of my witnesses.' He asked, 'Does Al-Qāḍī know him?' He replied, 'Yes.' He asked, 'And from what?' He said: 'I know him from the books of ḥadīth.' He asked, 'And what do you know of him from the books of ḥadīth?' He said: 'I know nothing of him except good.' He added, 'The Prophet (ﷺ) said:

> "This knowledge will be borne in every generation by its just people (*'adūl*)."[109]

'So he whom the Messenger of Allāh (ﷺ) declared to be just is more deserving than one whom you declare to be just.' He said: 'So stand forth and give it to me, for I have accepted his testimony.'"

=

doubt authentic and it is proof of the confusion of Ma'an'. It is possible that what Imām Aḥmad meant when he described it as being authentic was that it could be confirmed in a mursal form—and therefore it does not necessitate confirming that it is an authentic ḥadīth. Ibn Al-Qaṭṭān commented on Imām Aḥmad's assertion that Ma'an was a just narrator in his book *'Bayān al-Wahm wal-Īhām'*, saying, "What was known to others about him was unknown to Aḥmad."

[109] Its chain of narrators is authentic. The author's Shaikh is 'Ubaydullāh Ibn Abū'l-Fatḥ Aḥmad Ibn 'Uthmān Ibn Al-Faraj Al-Ṣayrafī, whose biography was given by Al-Khaṭīb in his *'Tārīkh'* (10/385) and he said: "He was one of those who wrote and heard numerous aḥādīth, was painstaking and meticulous (regarding their authenticity) and in collecting them, as well as being honest, trustworthy, credible, upright, orthodox, having correct beliefs and constantly studying the Qur'ān."

CHAPTER ELEVEN

The People of Ḥadīth are the Successors of the Messenger of Allāh (ﷺ) in Conveying His Message

53. I was informed by Muḥammad Ibn Abū ʿAlī Al-Aṣbāhanī, who said that he was told by Aḥmad Ibn Maḥmūd Al-Qāḍī, Ibn Al-Ahwāz, who said that it was recited to Abū'l-Ḥusayn Muḥammad Ibn Al-Ḥusayn that Aḥmad Ibn ʿIsā Ibn ʿAbdullāh Al-ʿAlawī informed them...

We were informed by ʿAlī Ibn Abū ʿAlī Al-Baṣrī, who said that he was told by Abū'l-Qāsim ʿUbaydullāh Ibn Al-Ḥusayn Ibn Jaʿfar Ibn Abū Mūsā Al-Qāḍī Al-Mawsilī, who said that he was told by Saʿīd Ibn ʿAlī Ibn Al-Khalīl, who said that he was told by ʿAbdu'l-Salām Ibn ʿUbayd, who said that they were told by Ibn Abū Fudayk, who reported on the authority of Hishām Ibn Saʿd, who reported on the authority of Zayd Ibn Aslam, who reported on the authority of ʿAṭā' Ibn Yasār, who reported on the authority of Ibn ʿAbbās (*raḍiyAllāhu ʿanhumā*) that he said: "I heard ʿAlī Ibn

Abū Ṭālib (*raḍiyAllāhu 'anhu*) saying:

> "The Messenger of Allāh (ﷺ) came out to us and he said: 'O Allāh! Show Mercy to my successors.' He ('Alī) said: 'We asked, 'O Messenger of Allāh! Who are your successors?' He replied, '(They are) those who come after me and narrate my *aḥādīth* and my Sunnah and teaches them to the people.'''

And in the ḥadīth of Al-'Alawī, he said: "I heard 'Alī (*raḍiyAllāhu 'anhu*) saying: 'The Prophet (ﷺ) came out (to us)[110] and said: 'O Allāh! Show Mercy to my successors.' We said: 'O Messenger of Allāh...' and the rest of the ḥadīth is the same.[111]

I was informed of it by 'Alī Ibn Aḥmad Ibn Muḥammad Al-Razzāz, who said that he was informed by 'Alī Ibn Ibrāhīm.

54. I was informed by Abū Bakr Ibn Ḥammād Al-Qāḍī Al-Azdī, who said that he was told by Abū Ḥusayn Al-Qāḍī, who said that he was told by Aḥmad Ibn 'Isā Ibn 'Abdullāh... and he narrated something similar, except that he said that it was on the authority

---

[110] This is from manuscript (A).

[111] (This ḥadīth is) fabricated.

In the first chain is Aḥmad Ibn 'Isā Ibn 'Abdullāh Al-'Alawī, of whom Al-Darāquṭnī said: "(He is) a liar. For this reason, Al-Dhahabī said in *'Al-Mīzān'* (1/127) after setting forth this ḥadīth, "(It is) false."

In the second chain is 'Abdu'l-Salām Ibn 'Ubayd, of whom Ibn Ḥibbān said: "He used to steal aḥādīth and narrate fabrications," while Al-Awzā'ī said: "His aḥādīth should not be written."

The ḥadīth from the first source was narrated by Al-Ramāhurmuzī in *'Al-Muḥaddith Al-Fāsil'* (p. 163), by Al-Ṭabāranī in *'Al-Awsaṭ'* and in *'Al-Majmā''* (1/126), by Abū Nu'aym in *'Akhbār Aṣbāhan'* (1/81), and by Al-Qāḍī 'Iyāḍ in *'Al-Ilma''* (p. 17).

The second source was ascribed in *'Takhrīj Al-Iḥyā''* by Al-'Irāqī, to Ibn 'Asakir, (who cited it) in *'Al-Amalī'* as mentioned in *'Ittiḥāf Al-Sādah Al-Muttaqīn'* (1/117).

Something similar was narrated on the authority of Al-Ḥasan in a *mursal* form and I have cited it in my book *'Ṣawn Al-Shar' al-Ḥanīf'*.

of 'Aṭā' Ibn Abū Rabah, who reported on the authority of Ibn 'Abbās (*raḍiyAllāhu 'anhumā*).

[Abū Bakr said][112]: "The first is closer to the truth. And Allāh knows better."

54. I was informed by Abū Bakr 'Abdullāh Ibn Muḥammad Ibn Aḥmad Ibn Al-Fallū Al-Kātib, who said that he was informed by Abū Bakr Aḥmad Ibn 'Abdu'l-Raḥmān Al-Daqqāq—who is better known as Al-Waliyy—who said that he was told by Abū Ja'far Al-Ḥasan Ibn 'Alī Ibn Al-Walīd Ibn Al-Nu'mān Al-Fārisī Al-Fasawī Al-Karabīsī, who said that he was told by Khalaf Ibn 'Abdu'l-Ḥamīd Ibn Abū'l-Ḥasnā', who said that he was told by Abū'l-Ṣabāh 'Abdu'l-Ghafūr, who reported on the authority of Abū Hishām Al-Rummānī, who reported on the authority of Zādhān, who reported on the authority of 'Alī (*raḍiyAllāhu 'anhu*), who reported from the Prophet (ﷺ) that he said:

> "Shall I not guide you to a sign of the successors among my Companions and from among the Prophets who came before me? They are the bearers of the Qur'ān and the *aḥādīth* from me and from them in Allāh's Cause and for [the sake of] Allāh, the Almighty, the All-Powerful."[113]

55. We were informed by Muḥammad Ibn Ḥayyān, who was

[112] This is from manuscript (B).

[113] (This ḥadīth is) fabricated.

In it is 'Abdu'l-Ghafūr Abū'l-Ṣabāh Al-Wāsiṭī, of whom Ibn Ma'īn said: "His ḥadīth his nothing," while Ibn Ḥibbān said: "He was one of those who fabricate aḥādīth." Al-Bukhārī said: "They (the scholars of ḥadīth) abandoned him," while Ibn 'Adiyy said: "(He is) weak and his ḥadīth is *munkar*."

The ḥadīth was narrated by Abū Nu'aym in *'Akhbār Aṣbāhan'* (2/134) and by Al-Sahmī in *'Tārīkh Jurjān'* (p. 372), by way of 'Abdu'l-Ghafūr.

told by Muḥammad Ibn Al-Faḍl, who said that he was told by Abū Ḥātim, who said that he heard Isḥāq Ibn Mūsā Al-Khaṭṭābī saying:

> "No authority has been granted to anyone in this *ummah* like the authority that has been granted to the people of ḥadīth, because Allāh, the Almighty, the All-Powerful says in His Book:
>
> وَلَيُمَكِّنَنَّ لَهُمْ دِينَهُمُ ٱلَّذِى ٱرْتَضَىٰ لَهُمْ
>
> "He will surely establish for them [therein] their religion which He has preferred for them."
>
> [*al-Nūr* (24): 55]

So that which Allāh has chosen, He has given authority to its adherents to practise—and He has not given authority to the people of heresy, that He might accept a single ḥadīth on the authority of the Companions of the Prophet (ﷺ), while the aḥādīth of the Messenger of Allāh (ﷺ) and his Companions are accepted from the people of ḥadīth. And if there is any man among them who commits innovations, his aḥādīth are rejected, even though he might be among the most truthful of people."[114]

[114] Muḥammad Ibn Al-Faḍl is the son of Khaṭṭāb Al-'Anbarī. His biography was given by ('Abdullāh Ibn Muḥammad) Abū Al-Shaikh in '*Ṭābaqāt Aṣbāhan*' (4/323) and he said: "(He is) a trustworthy Shaikh and one of the fine people of Usūl. (He narrated) many *aḥādīth*."

CHAPTER TWELVE

The Description Given by the Messenger of Allāh (ﷺ) of the Faith of the People of Ḥadīth

56. We were informed by Abū 'Umar 'Abdu'l-Wāḥid Ibn Muḥammad Ibn 'Abdullāh Ibn Mahdī Al-Dībajī, by Abū'l-Ḥusayn Muḥammad Ibn Al-Ḥusayn Ibn Al-Faḍl Al-Qaṭṭān, by Abū Muḥammad Ibn Yaḥyā Ibn 'Abdu'l-Jabbār Al-Sukkarī and by Abū'l-Ḥasan Muḥammad Ibn Muḥammad Ibn Muḥammad Ibn Ibrāhīm Ibn Mukhallad Al-Bazzār, who said that they were informed by Abū 'Alī Ismā'īl Ibn Muḥammad Al-Ṣaffār, who said that he was told by Al-Ḥasan Ibn 'Urfah, who said that he was told by Ismā'īl Ibn 'Ayyāsh Al-Ḥimṣī, who reported on the authority of Al-Mughīrah Ibn Qays Al-Tamīmī, who reported on the authority of 'Amr Ibn Shu'ayb, who reported on the authority of his father, who reported on the authority of his grandfather that he said: "The Messenger of Allāh (ﷺ) said:

"Which creation is more amazing to you in faith?" They

said: "The angels." He (ﷺ) said: "And why would they not have faith, when they are with their Lord?" They said: "[It is] we." He (ﷺ) replied, "And why would you not have faith, when I am among you?" He added: "Verily, the most amazing creation to me in faith are a people who will come after you and they will find manuscripts in which there are writings; and they will believe in what is contained therein."[115]

57. We were told by Abū Ṭālib Yaḥyā Ibn ʿAlī Al-Daskarī, in Ḥalwān, who said that he was told by Abū Bakr Ibn Al-Muqrī', in Aṣbāhan, who said that he was informed by Abū Yaʿlā Aḥmad Ibn ʿAlī Ibn Al-Muthannā Al-Mawsilī, who said that he was told by Mūsā Ibn Muḥammad Ibn Ḥayyān, who said that he was told by Muḥammad Ibn Abū ʿAdiyy, who said that he was told by Muḥammad Ibn Abū Ḥamīd, who reported on the authority of Zayd Ibn Aslam, who reported on the authority of his father, who reported on the authority of ʿUmar Ibn Al-Khaṭṭāb (*raḍiyAllāhu ʿanhu*) that he said: "I heard the Messenger of Allāh (ﷺ) saying to us:

"Inform me of the best of the people of faith." We said: "O Messenger of Allāh! [They are] the angels." He (ﷺ) said: "They are so and it is right that they should be so; and what would prevent them, when Allāh has [certainly][116] granted them the status that He has

[115] Its chain of narrators is *munkar.*

In it is Al-Mughīrah Ibn Qays Al-Baṣrī, of whom Abū Ḥātim said: "He is *munkar* in ḥadīth." In addition, the narration of Ismāʿīl Ibn ʿAyyāsh on the authority of the people of Al-Sham is weak, for Al-Mughīrah is from Baṣrah.

The ḥadīth was narrated by Al-Ḥasan Ibn ʿUrfah in his *'Juz'* (#19), with the aforementioned chain of narrators.

And from the same source, it was narrated by Qiwam Al-Sunnah in *'Al-Targhīb wa'l-Tarhīb'* (#48).

[116] This is from manuscript (B).

granted them? Nay, it is a people other than them." We said: "O Messenger of Allāh! Then [they are] the Prophets whom Allāh has honoured with Prophecy and Messages."[117] He (ﷺ) said: "They are so and it is right that they should be so; [and what would prevent them, when Allāh has certainly honoured them with Prophecy and Messages]?"[118] We said: "O Messenger of Allāh! [They are] the martyrs whom Allāh has honoured with martyrdom with the Prophets." He (ﷺ) said: "They are so and it is right that they should be so; and what would prevent them from being so, when Allāh has certainly honoured them with martyrdom? Nay, it is a people other than them." We said: "O Messenger of Allāh! Then who?" He (ﷺ) said: "[They are] a people from the loins of men who will come after me and they will have faith in me without having seen me and believe in me without having seen me. They will see the annotated document and they will act upon what is written in it."[119]

---

[117] This is from manuscript (A).

[118] This is from manuscript (B).

[119] [This ḥadīth is] *munkar.*

In its chain of narrators is Muḥammad Ibn Abū Ḥamīd—whose nickname was Ḥammād—and of whom Al-Bukhārī said: "(He is) *munkar* in ḥadīth," while Nasā'ī said: "He is not trustworthy." And more than one scholar has declared him to be weak. In addition there something *munkar* in the text (of the ḥadīth).

The ḥadīth was attributed to Abū Ya'lā by Al-Haythamī in *'Al-Majma"* (10/65).

I say: It was narrated by Abū Ya'lā in *'Al-Musnad'* (1/147/no. 160) and by Al-Bazzār in his *'Musnad'—'Al-Baḥr Al-Zakhkhār'* (1/412/no. 288) by way of Muḥammad Ibn Abū Ḥamīd.

It was also narrated by Al-Bazzār (289), by Al-'Uqaylī in *'Al-Ḍhu'afā"* (4/238) by way of Al-Minhāl Ibn Baḥr, who said that he was told by Hisham Al-Dastawā'ī , who reported on the authority of Yaḥyā Ibn Abū Kathīr, who reported on the authority of Zayd Ibn Aslam, who reported on the authority of his father, who reported something similar on the authority of 'Umar (*raḍiyAllāhu 'anhu*),

Al-'Uqaylī said: "This ḥadīth is only known from Muḥammad Ibn Abū Ḥamīd, on

=

[Shaikh][120] Abū Bakr [Al-Ḥāfiẓ][121] said: "And the people most deserving of this description are the people of ḥadīth and those who follow them."

=
the authority of Zayd Ibn Aslam, but it is not memorised from the ḥadīth of Yaḥyā Ibn Abū Kathīr and no one accepts (the ḥadīth of) Minhāl."

Al-Bazzār declared it weak, referring to the same weakness that Al-ʿUqaylī pointed out.

They attributed the weakness to Al-Minhāl, whom Al-Bazzār had declared weak. He said: "He is not strong." Ibn ʿAdiyy also said that he was not strict, while Al-ʿUqaylī said: "There is doubt in his ḥadīth." As for Abū Ḥātim Al-Razī, he declared him to be trustworthy; but it is possible that his status, while clear to others, was not apparent to him.

120 This is from manuscript (A).

121 This is from manuscript (A).

CHAPTER THIRTEEN

The Fact that the People of Ḥadīth are the Most Deserving of the Messenger of Allāh (ﷺ) due to the Continual Sending of Prayers on Him (ﷺ)[122]

58. We were informed by Al-Qāḍī Abū Bakr Aḥmad Ibn Al-Ḥasan Ibn Aḥmad Al-Ḥarashī, who said that he was told by Abū'l-ʿAbbās Muḥammad Ibn Yaʿqūb Al-Aṣamm, who said that he was told by Muḥammad Al-Dawrī, who said that he was told by Khālid Al-Qaṭwanī.

We were informed by Abū'l-Qāsim Ṭalḥah Ibn ʿAlī Ibn Al-Ṣaqr Al-Katani, who said that he was told by Muḥammad Ibn ʿAbdullāh Ibn Ibrāhīm Al-Shāfiʿī, who said that he was told by Muḥammad Ibn ʿAbdullāh Marba', who said that he was told by Yaḥyā Ibn Maʿīn.

We were informed by Abū Nuʿaym Al-Ḥāfiẓ, whose wording it is,

[122] This is from manuscript (B).

that he was told by Abū Bakr ʿAbdullāh Ibn Yaḥyā Al-Talhī, who was told by Ibn Ghannām, who said that he was told by Abū Bakr Ibn Abū Shaybah, who both said that they were told by Khālid Ibn Mukhallad, who said that he was told by Mūsā Ibn Yaʿqūb Al-Zamaʿī, who said that he was told by ʿAbdullāh Ibn Kaysan, who said that he was informed by ʿAbdullāh Ibn Shidād Ibn Al-Hād, who reported on the authority of his father, who reported on the authority of ʿAbdullāh Ibn Masʿūd (*raḍiyAllāhu ʿanhu*), who said: "The Messenger of Allāh (ﷺ) said:

> "Verily, the people most deserving of me on the Day of Resurrection will be those who most frequently sent prayers on me."[123]

---

[123] Its chain of narrators is *munkar* and there is *iḍṭirāb* (contradiction) in it.

ʿAbdullāh Ibn Kaysān was alone in narrating it on the authority of Ibn Masʿūd (*raḍiyAllāhu ʿanhu*) and his status is unknown; no one declared him to be trustworthy except Ibn Ḥibbān.

This ḥadīth was narrated in contradictory forms, as mentioned by Al-Bukhārī in *'Al-Tārīkh Al-Kabīr'*. Also Khālid Ibn Mukhallad narrated aḥadīth that are *munkarah* and furthermore, there is a weak narrator in the chain.

Mūsā Ibn Yaʿqūb Al-Zamaʿī was declared trustworthy by Ibn Maʿīn and Ibn Al-Qaṭṭān, while Ibn ʿAdiyy said: "There is no objection to him."

As for Imām Aḥmad, he said: "His aḥādīth do not impress me," while Ibn Al-Madīnī said: "(He is) weak in ḥadīth and he narrates aḥādīth that are munkarah." Nasāʾī said: "He is not strong."

The ḥadīth was narrated by Al-Bukhārī in *'Al-Tārīkh Al-Kabīr'* (1/3/177), by Ibn Ḥibbān (*Mawārid* #2389), by Ibn ʿAdiyy in *'Al-Kāmil'* (3/906) and by the author in *'Al-Jāmiʿ'* (#1304).

It was also narrated by Tirmidhī (#484)—and from Al-Baghawī's source in *'Sharḥ Al-Sunnah'* (2/284):

We were told by Muḥammad Ibn Bashshār, who reported on the authority of Muḥammad Ibn Khālid Ibn ʿUthmah, who was told by Mūsā Ibn Yaʿqūb... and he quoted the ḥadīth without the words "on the authority of his father".

Tirmidhī said: "(It is) ḥasan *al-gharīb* (A gharīb narration is one in which there is some kind of uniqueness. There are a number of kinds of uniqueness, the most important of which are two: (i) Absolute uniqueness, which is where a particular narrator—at any stage of the *isnād*—is the only one who narrated the ḥadīth, and no one else narrated it alongside him. So in this case the *gharīb* narration is one which is only known to be

=

[Shaikh][124] Abū Bakr said to us:

> This is a noble trait to which the narrators and transmitters of traditions can lay special claim, because it is not known that any group from among the scholars send prayers on the Messenger of Allāh (ﷺ) more than this group, both in writing and in speech.

59. I was informed by Abū'l-Qāsim Al-Azharī, who said that he was informed by 'Alī Ibn 'Umar Ibn Aḥmad Al-Ḥāfiẓ, who said that he was told by Muḥammad Ibn Al-Qāsim Ibn Zakariyya Al-Muḥāribī who said that he was told by 'Abbād Ibn Ya'qūb, who said that he was informed by Abū Dāwūd Al-Nakha'ī, Sulaymān Ibn 'Amr, who reported on the authority of Ayyūb Ibn Mūsā, who reported on the authority of Al-Qāsim Ibn Muḥammad, who reported on the authority of his father—and I believe that he reported on the authority of his grandfather—Abū Bakr Al-Ṣiddīq (*raḍiyAllāhu 'anhu*) that he said: "The Messenger of Allāh (ﷺ) said:

> "Whoever wrote knowledge from me and wrote with it prayers upon me, he will continue to be rewarded for as long as that book is read."[125]

=

narrated from the Prophet (ﷺ) with one isnād. (ii) Relative uniqueness, which means that one of the narrators of a particular ḥadīth was the only one to narrate it from his Shaikh, even though the ḥadīth was narrated via a number of chains, but only one of his students narrated it from him).

[124] This is from manuscript (A).

[125] (This is) fabricated.

In its (chain of narrators) is Abū Dāwūd Al-Nakha'ī Sulaymān Ibn 'Amr, of whom Imām Aḥmad said: "He used to fabricate aḥādīth," while Ibn Ma'īn said: "He is well known as a fabricator of ḥadīth." And Qutaybah Ibn Sa'īd and Ibn Rahawayh declared him to be a liar.

The ḥadīth was narrated by Ibn 'Adiyy in *'Al-Kāmil'* (3/1100)—and from Ibn Al-Jawzī's source in *'Al-Mawḍū'āt'* (1/228)—and by the author in *'Al-Jāmi''* (#564), by way of 'Abbād

=

60. I was informed by Abū Ṭālib Makkī Ibn ʻAlī Ibn ʻAbdu'l-Razzāq Al-Ḥarīrī, who said that he was told by Ibrāhīm Ibn Maḥmūd Al-Muqrī', who said that he was told by Muḥammad Ibn Mahrān Al-Naysabūrī, who said that he was told by Muḥammad Ibn ʻAbdullāh Ibn Ḥamīd Al-Naṣrī, in Makkah, who said that he was told by Bishr Ibn ʻUbayd, who said that he was told by Ḥāzim Ibn Bakr, Abū ʻAlī, who said that he was told by Yazīd Ibn ʻIyāḍ, who reported on the authority of ʻAbdu'l-Raḥmān Al-ʻAraj, who reported on the authority of Abū Hurayrah (*raḍiyAllāhu ʻanhu*) that he said: "The Messenger of Allāh (ﷺ) said:

> "Whoever sent prayers on me in a book, the angels will continue to seek forgiveness for him for as long as my name is [read] in that book."[126]

61. We were informed by Muḥammad Ibn ʻAlī Ibn Al-Fatḥ, who said that he was told by ʻUmar Ibn Ibrāhīm Al-Muqrī', who said that he was told by Abū Bakr ʻUmar Ibn Aḥmad Ibn Abū Maʻmar

---

=

Ibn Yaʻqūb, whom Ibn ʻAdiyy adjudged to be guilty of fabricating aḥādīth—and Ibn Al-Jawzī concurred with this view.

[126] (It is) fabricated.

In it(s chain of narrators) is Yazīd Ibn ʻIyāḍ, who is described as *'ṭalif'* (bad, broken, damaged). Al-Bukhārī said: "(He is) *munkar* in ḥadīth," while Yaḥyā said: "He is not trustworthy," and in another narration, "He used to tell lies." Mālik Ibn Anas (*raḍiyAllāhu ʻanhu*) was asked about Ibn Samʻan and he said: "(He is) a liar." He asked, "And (what about) Yazīd Ibn ʻIyāḍ?" He replied, "A worse liar." And Bishr Ibn ʻUbayd was declared to be a liar by Al-Azdī, while Ibn ʻAdiyy said: "He is *munkar* in ḥadīth from the Imāms."

The ḥadīth from this source was narrated by Al-Ṭabārānī in *'Al-Awsaṭ'* as in *'Al-Majma'* (1/137) and by Ibn Al-Jawzī in *'Al-Mawḍū'āt'* (1/228).

It has another source from the narration of Muḥammad Ibn Ibrāhīm Ibn Umayyah Al-Qurashī Al-Madīnī, who reported on the authority of ʻAbdu'l-Raḥmān Ibn ʻAbdullāh Al-Aʻraj, who reported it on the authority of Abū Hurayrah (*raḍiyAllāhu ʻanhu*).

It was narrated by Abū'l-Qāsim Al-Aṣbāhanī in *'Al-Targhīb wa'l-Tarhīb'* (#1697).

I say: 'I have not found any biography for Abdu'l-Raḥmān and I believe that Muḥammad Ibn Ibrāhīm is most likely Al-Qurashī whose biography is given in *'Al-Lisan'* (5/27) and he is unknown.

Al-Saffar, who said that he was told by Abū Ja'far Muḥammad Ibn Yaḥyā Al-Halwānī—this is how it was written in the book of Ibn Al-Fatḥ, but the correct name is Aḥmad Ibn Yaḥyā—who said that he heard Aḥmad Ibn Yoonus saying, "I heard Sufyān Al-Thawri saying:

> "Even if there was no benefit for the scholar of ḥadīth except the prayers that he sends on the Messenger of Allāh (ﷺ) [it would be enough for him] that prayers would continue to be sent on him for as long as the book (is read)."[127]

62. I was told directly by 'Abdu'l-'Azīz Ibn Abū'l-Ḥasan Al-Qarmīsīnī, who said that he was told through recitation by 'Alī Ibn Al-Ḥasan Ibn 'Alī Ibn Muṭrif Al-Qāḍī, who said that Muḥammad Ibn 'Abdu'l-Raḥīm Al-Aṣbāhani, who said that he was told by 'Abdullāh Ibn Muḥammad Ibn Sinan Al-Baṣrī, who said that he was told by Muḥammad Ibn Abū Sulaymān that he said: "I saw my father in a dream and I said to him, "O my father! What did Allāh do to you?" He said: "He forgave me." I said: "Due to what?" He said:

> "Due my having written prayers upon the Prophet (ﷺ) in every ḥadīth."[128]

63. I was told by Abū Ṣāliḥ Aḥmad Ibn 'Abdu'l-Mālik Al-Naysabūrī that he said that he heard Abū 'Abdullāh Al-Ḥusayn

[127] Its chain of narrators is weak.

In it is 'Umar Ibn Aḥmad Ibn Abū Ma'mar, whose biography was given by Al-Khaṭīb in *'Tārīkh Baghdād'* (11/42) and neither criticism or praise was reported of him.

[128] Its chain of narrators is extremely weak and it is quite possible that it is fabricated.

In it(s chain of narrators) is 'Abdullāh Ibn Muḥammad Ibn Sinān Al-Baṣrī, of whom Al-Darāquṭnī said: "(He is) *matrūk* (abandoned)," while Abū Nu'aym Al-Ḥāfiẓ said: "He fabricates ḥadīth." And Al-Barqānī said: "He is not trustworthy."

Ibn Muḥammad Ibn Aḥmad Al-Halabī, in Damascus, say that he heard Abū 'Abdullāh Aḥmad Ibn 'Aṭā' Al-Rawzabarī say that he heard Abū'l-Qāsim 'Abdullāh Al-Mirwazī saying, "My father and I were meeting [at night][129] to discuss ḥadīth and in the place where we were meeting, a column of light was seen which reached to the clouds in the sky and it was said: "What is this light?" Someone replied,

> "It is the prayers that they send on the Messenger of Allāh (ﷺ) when they meet."[130]

[129] This is from manuscript (B).

[130] In it(s chain of narrators) is Aḥmad Ibn 'Aṭā' Al-Rawzabarī, whose biography was given by Al-Khaṭīb in *'Tārīkh Baghdād'* (4/336) and he mentioned information that proved the weakness of the narration—and this is the case with many of the righteous and the devout.

CHAPTER FOURTEEN

The Glad Tidings given by the Prophet (ﷺ) to His Companions (*raḍiyAllāhu ʿanhum*) regarding the Seekers of Knowledge after Him being a Connection via the *Isnād* between Them and Him

64. We were told via recitation by Abū'l-Ḥasan Muḥammad Ibn Aḥmad Ibn Rizq Al-Bazzāz, who said that he was told by ʿUthmān Ibn Aḥmad Al-Daqqāq, who said that he was told by Aḥmad Ibn ʿAlī Al-Khazzāz, who said that he was told by Muḥammad Ibn ʿImrān Ibn Muḥammad Ibn Abū Laylā, who was told by his father, who was told by Ibn Abū Laylā, who reported on the authority of ʿIsā, who reported on the authority of ʿAbdu'l-Raḥmān Ibn Abū Laylā, who reported on the authority of Thābit Ibn Qays, who said: "The Messenger of Allāh (ﷺ) said:

> "You hear, you are heard from, those people hear from those who heard from you, then after that, a corpulent

> people who love fatness will give testimony before they are asked [for it].”[131]

65. We were informed by Abū Bakr Aḥmad Ibn ʿAlī Ibn Yazdadh Al-Qarīʿ, who said that he was informed by ʿAbdullāh Ibn Muḥammad Ibn Jaʿfar Al-Aṣbāhanī, who was told by Muḥammad Ibn Yaḥyā (i.e.)[132] Ibn Mindah, who said that he was told by Muḥammad Ibn ʿIsam, who reported on the authority of his Father, who reported on the authority of Sufyān, who reported on the authority of Al-Aʿmash, who reported on the authority of ʿAbdullāh Ibn ʿAbdullāh, who reported on the authority of Saʿīd Ibn Jubayr, who reported on the authority of Ibn ʿAbbās (*raḍiyAllāhu ʿanhu*), who said: “The Messenger of Allāh (ﷺ) said:

> “You hear [from me] and others will hear from you; and people will hear from those who heard from you.”[133]

66. We were informed by Ibrāhīm Ibn Muḥammad Ibn Sulaymān Al-Mu'addib, in Aṣbāhan, who said that he was informed by Abū Bakr Ibn Al-Muqrī', who said that he was told by Salāmah Ibn

[131] Its chain of narrators is weak and it is *munqaṭiʿ* (broken).

In its (chain of narrators) is Muḥammad Ibn ʿAbdu'l-Raḥmān Ibn Abū Layla, who is weak, while the status of his son is unknown.

The ḥadīth from this source was narrated by Al-Ṭabāranī in *'Al-Kabīr'* (2/321), by Al-Bazzār in his *'Musnad'* (*Kashf*: 146), by Al-Ramāhurmuzī in *'Al-Muḥaddith Al-Fāsil'* (#91).

Al-Haythamī said in *'Al-Majma''* (1/137):

“ʿAbdu'l-Raḥmān Ibn Abū Layla did not hear from Thābit Ibn Qays.”

I say: This is another weakness.

[132] This is from manuscript (B).

[133] Its narrators are trustworthy.

It was narrated by Imām Aḥmad (1/321), by Abū Dāwūd (#3659), by Ibn Ḥibbān (*Mawārid*: #77), by Al-Haythamī in *'Al-Kubra'* (10/1250), by Al-Ḥākim (1/95), by Al-Ramāhurmuzī (#92) and by Ibn Khayr in his *'Fiḥris'* (p. 10 and 13), by way of Al-Aʿmash.

I say: The men of this chain of narrators are trustworthy, but there is the *'anʿanah* of Al-Aʿmash in it, in addition to which, he is a *mudallis*.

Maḥmūd Al-Qaysī, who said that he was told by Muḥammad Ibn Khalaf, who was told by Aḥmad Ibn Shabābah that he said that Isḥāq Ibn Rāhawayh said:

> "Every matter narrated on the authority of three [persons] is an athar [tradition], according to the saying of the Prophet (ﷺ): "You hear [from me] and others will hear from you; and people will hear from them who heard from you."[134]

67. We were informed by Abū Nuʿaym Al-Ḥāfiẓ, who said that he was told by ʿAbdullāh Ibn Jaʿfar Ibn Aḥmad Ibn Fāris, who was told by Ismāʿīl Ibn ʿAbdullāh Ibn Masʿūd Al-ʿAbdī, who said that he was told by ʿAbdullāh Ibn Ṣāliḥ, who said that he was told by Ibn Lahīʿah, who reported on the authority of Qays Ibn Rāfiʿ, who reported on the authority of Shafiyy Al-Aṣbāhī, who said:

> "The treasuries of everything will be opened to this *ummah*, until the treasuries of ḥadīth are opened to them."[135]

---

[134] There is someone whom I do not know in the chain of narrators.

[135] Qays Ibn Rāfiʿ is *mastūr* (screened, i.e. no prominent person narrated from him); no one declared him trustworthy except Ibn Ḥibbān. In addition, Ibn Lahīʿah used to get things mixed up after his books were burnt, and he was also described as being a *mudallis* and he committed *ʿanʿanah* in the chain of narrators.

Also, there is weakness in ʿAbdullāh Ibn Ṣāliḥ, with regard to his memory.

CHAPTER FIFTEEN

Clear Evidence of the Virtue of the *Isnād* and that it is One of Things with Which Allāh has Favoured this *Ummah*

68. We were informed by Muḥammad Ibn Aḥmad Ibn Rizq, who said that he was informed by Muḥammad Ibn Al-Ḥasan Ibn Ziyād Al-Naqqāsh, who said that he was told by Abū Isḥāq Al-ʿAṭṭār, who reported on the authority of Aḥmad Ibn Bishr Al-Ḥalabī, who reported on the authority of Yazīd Ibn Mawhab, who reported on the authority of Ḍhamrah.

We were told by Muḥammad Ibn Yūsuf Al-Naysabūrī Al-Qaṭṭān, who said that he was informed by Muḥammad Ibn ʿAbdullāh Al-Sabiyy, who said that he was informed by Aḥmad Ibn Muḥammad Al-ʿAnazī, who said that he was told by ʿUthmān Ibn Saʿīd, who said that he was told by Yazīd Ibn Mawhab, who said that he was told by Ḍhamrah Ibn Ḥabīb, who reported on the authority of Shawzab, who reported on the authority of Maṭar, that he said regarding the Words of Allāh, Most High:

أَوْ أَثَـٰرَةٍ مِّنْ عِلْمٍ

"a [remaining] trace of knowledge."
[*al-Aḥqāf* (46): 4]

"(It means) the *isnād* of the ḥadīth."[136]

69. We were informed by 'Alī Ibn Aḥmad Al-Razzāz, who said that he was told by Al-Qāḍī Abū Bakr Muḥammad Ibn 'Umar Ibn Al-Ja'abī, who said that he was told by 'Abdullāh Ibn Muḥammad Ibn Bishr Ibn Ṣāliḥ, who said that he was told by Sa'īd Ibn 'Amr Ibn Abū Salāmah, who said that he was told by his father, who reported on the authority of Mālik that he said regarding the Words of Allāh, Most High:

وَإِنَّهُۥ لَذِكْرٌ لَّكَ وَلِقَوْمِكَ

"And indeed, it is a remembrance for you and your people."
[*al-Zukhruf* (44):43]

"[It means] the saying of a man: "I was told by my father, who reported on the authority of my grandfather..."[137]

[136] In the first chain of narrators is Muḥammad Ibn Al-Ḥasan Al-Naqqāsh and he is accused (of being dishonest); we discussed him previously.

The second chain of narrators is authentic up to 'Uthmān Ibn Sa'īd Al-Dārimī. Muḥammad Ibn 'Abdullāh Al-Ḍhabbī is Abū 'Abdullāh Al-Ḥākim, and I have not found any biography for Yazīd Ibn Mawhab; he is not the one mentioned in Ibn Ḥibbān's *'Thiqāt'*—that person narrated on the authority of Mālik Ibn Yukhamir. Likewise, Ḍhamrah Ibn Ḥabīb is unknown to me; he is not Al-Ḥimsī. Ḍhamrah Ibn Rabī'ah only narrates on the authority of Ibn Shawzab; it is possible that he is Ḍhamrah Ibn Ḥabīb Al-Maqdisī, who is mentioned in *'Al-Tahẓīb'*.

The tradition was narrated by Al-Ramāhurmuzī (#98) by way of Aḥmad Ibn Bishr Al-Raqqī, who said that he was told by Yazīd Ibn Mawhab...

[137] Its chain of narrators is weak.

The author's Shaikh has a biography in *'Tārīkh Baghdād'* (1/235) and he is personally =

70. We were informed by Muḥammad Ibn 'Isā Ibn 'Abdu'l- 'Azīz Al-Bazzāz, in Hamazān, who said that he was told by Ṣāliḥ Ibn Aḥmad Al-Ḥāfiẓ, who said that he heard Abū Bakr Muḥammad Ibn Aḥmad saying:

> "It was conveyed to me that Allāh favoured this *ummah* with three things that He did not give to anyone before it: (i) the *isnād* [chain of narrators], (ii) the lineages and (iii) [Arabic] grammar."[138]

71. I was informed by Abū Bakr Muḥammad Ibn Al-Muzaffar Ibn 'Alī Al-Daynūrī Al-Muqrī', who said that he was told by Ibrāhīm Ibn Muḥammad Ibn Yaḥyā Al-Muzakkī, who said that he heard Abū'l-'Abbās Muḥammad Ibn 'Abdu'l-Raḥmān Al-Daghūlī Al-Sarkhasī, who said that he heard Muḥammad Ibn Ḥātim Ibn Al-Muẓaffar saying:

> "Verily, Allāh has honoured, ennobled and favoured this Ummah with the isnād [chain of narrators]—and none of the former or the latter nations has it. They [what they have] are only manuscripts in their hands, and they have mixed together their books [i.e. Revelations] with their [own] stories, so that they are unable to distinguish between what was revealed in the Torah and the Injīl given to them by their Prophets and the stories that they themselves have added to them and which they acquired from untrustworthy sources.

This *ummah*, however, only conveys the ḥadīth from a trustwor-

=

truthful, though a son of his used to interfere with his books and he would claim to have heard things that he did not hear. In addition, there is weakness in 'Amr Ibn Abū Salāmah and I have not found anyone who mentions either criticism or praise of him. As for Al-Ja'abī, there is (negative) talk about him.

[138] Its chain of narrators is authentic.

thy source, who is known in his own time and is renowned for his truthfulness and his trustworthiness, narrating from another of similar characteristics, so that their information attains a high degree of reliability. Then they research exhaustively, until they learn who is the best in memorisation, the most painstaking and those who sit for longest with those who are above them [in learning] and shortest with those who are below them.

Then they record the ḥadīth from twenty or more sources, so that they can remove mistakes and errors from it, correct its letters and prepare it [for inclusion in their books].

This is the greatest blessing from Allāh, Most High upon this *ummah* and we send thanks to Allāh for this Blessing and ask him to make us firm, grant us success in attaining what causes us to advance and draw near to Him and keep us obedient to Him. Verily, He is a Most Praiseworthy Protector.

There is none from among the people of ḥadīth who shows partiality towards his father, his brother or his son in the matter of ḥadīth."

'Alī Ibn 'Abdullāh Al-Madīnī was the Imām of ḥadīth in his time; not a single letter was narrated from him in support of his Father; on the contrary, the opposite was narrated from him.

All praise and thanks be to Allāh for those matters in which He has granted us success.

CHAPTER SIXTEEN

Clarification that the *Asanīd* are the Path to Knowing the Rulings of the *Sharīʿah*

72. We were informed by Abū Bakr Muḥammad Ibn ʿUmar Ibn Jaʿfar Al-Ḥarqī, who said that he was informed by Aḥmad Ibn Jaʿfar Al-Khatlī, who said that he was told by Aḥmad Ibn ʿAlī Al-Ubār, who said that he was told by Abū Bakr Al-Ṭāliqānī Saʿīd Ibn Yaʿqūb, who said: "ʿAbdullāh Ibn Al-Mubārak said:

"The isnād is part of the Religion (*dīn*)."[140]

73. And we were told by Al-Ḥasan Ibn Abū Ṭālib, who said that he was told by ʿUmar Ibn Aḥmad Al-Wā'iẓ (Al-Muqrī'),[141] who

[139] This is in manuscript (A), while in manuscript (B) it says: Al-Kharqī.

[140] Its chain of narrators is ḥasan up to Al-Ṭāliqānī.

I do not know whether it is correct that he heard from Ibn Al-Mubārak or not. Scholars have only mentioned that he narrated from him.

The author cited a biography for his Shaikh in his *'Tārīkh'* and he said: "We wrote from him and he was truthful."

[141] This is from manuscript (B).

said that he was told by Muḥammad Ibn Ḥamdawayh Al-Mirwazī, who said that he was told by Abū'l-Muwajjih, who said that he was informed by 'Abdān, who said: "I heard 'Abdullāh —Ibn Al-Mubārak—saying:

> "The isnād in my opinion is a part of the Religion and were it not for the isnād, anyone who wished would have said whatever he wanted."[142]

74. I was informed by Muḥammad Ibn Al-Muẓaffar Al-Daynūrī that he said that he was told by Ibrāhim Ibn Muḥammad Ibn Yaḥyā Al-Muzakkī, who said that he was told by Imām Abū Bakr Muḥammad Ibn Isḥāq Ibn Khuzaymah that he said that he heard Aḥmad Ibn Naṣr Al-Muqrī', who said that he heard Ibrāhim Ibn Ma'dān say that Ibn Al-Mubārak said:

> "The likeness of one who seeks knowledge of his Religion without a chain of narrators is as one who seeks to ascend to the roof without a stair."[143]

75. We were informed by Abū'l-Ḥusayn Muḥammad Ibn Al-Ḥusayn Ibn Al-Faḍl Al-Qaṭṭān, who said that he was told by Abū 'Isā Aḥmad Ibn Yaḥyā Ibn Muḥammad Ibn Shāzān Al-Jawharī, who said that he was told by[144] his grandfather, who said: "I asked

[142] (This is) authentic.

It was narrated by Muslim in the foreword of his *'Ṣaḥīḥ'* (1/15), by Tirmidhī in *'Al-'Ilal Al-Ṣaghīr'* (5/340), by Ibn Abū Ḥātim in *'Al-Jarḥ wa'l-Ta'dīl'* (1/1/16), by Al-Ḥākim in *'Ma'rifah 'Ulūm al-Ḥadīth'* (p. 8) and by Al-Sam'ānī in *'Adab Al-Imlā' wa'l-Istimlā''* (p. 6-7) from sources on the authority of 'Abdān—and its chain of narrators is authentic.

It was also narrated by Al-Ramāhurmuzī (#96) by way of 'Alī Ibn Al-Ḥasan, who said that he heard Ibn Al-Mubārak... and he quoted the narration.

[143] I have not found any biography for those who narrated on the authority of Ibn Al-Mubārak.

The tradition was narrated by Abū Sa'd Al-Sam'ānī in *'Adab Al-Imlā' wa'l-Istimlā''* (p. 6) from another source on the authority of Ibn Khuzaymah.

[144] In manuscript (B) it says "I was told," as opposed to "We were told."

ʿAlī Ibn Al-Madīnī about the *isnād* of a ḥadīth that I came across and he said: "Do you know what Abū Saʿīd Al-Ḥaddād said? He said:

> "The isnād is like a stair and if the foot of the one who is ascending slips on the stair, he will fall. And opinion is like a wave [on the sea]."[145]

76. We were told by Muḥammad Ibn Yūsuf Al-Naysabūrī, who said that he was informed by Muḥammad Ibn ʿAbdullāh Al-Ḍhabbī, who said that he was informed by Muḥammad Ibn Yaʿqūb Al-Muqrī', who said that he was told by Muḥammad Ibn ʿAbdu'l-Raḥmān Al-Faqīh Abū'l-ʿAbbās, who said that he was told by Al-Ḥusayn Ibn Al-Faraj, who said that he was told by ʿAbdu'l-Ṣamad Ibn Ḥassān, who said that he heard Sufyān al-Thawrī saying:

> "The isnād is the weapon of the believer; and if he had no weapon, then with what would he fight?"[146]

[145] Its chain of narrators is ḥasan.

A biography was cited by the author for Aḥmad Ibn Yaḥyā Ibn Muḥammad Ibn Shazān in his *'Tārīkh'* (5/216) and he said: "...on the authority of his grand Father, Muḥammad Ibn Shazān correct aḥādīth were reported."

[146] It is extremely weak.

In it is Al-Ḥusayn Ibn Al-Faraj, of whom Ibn Maʿīn said: "He is a liar, a drunkard and a scoundrel." Abū Zurʿah said: "(He is) nothing; I do not report from him." He was also declared weak by more than one of the scholars.

The tradition was narrated by Al-Samʿānī in *'Adab Al-Imlā' wa'l-Istimlā'"* (p. 8) by way of Al-Ḥusayn Ibn Al-Faraj...

And there he is incorrectly recorded as Sulh Ibn Al-Ḥusayn Ibn Al-Faraj.

CHAPTER SEVENTEEN

The People of Ḥadīth are the Representatives of the Messenger of Allāh (ﷺ) due to their Preservation of the *Sunan* and their Distinction in doing so

77. We were informed by Abū ʿUbayd Muḥammad Ibn Abū Naṣr Al-Naysabūrī, who said that he heard from Abū'l-Ḥasan Muḥammad Ibn ʿAlī Al-ʿAlawī Al-Ḥasanī, who said that he heard from Al-Qāsim Ibn Al-Bandār, who said that he heard from Abū Ḥātim Al-Rāzī, who said:

> "There has never been an *ummah* from among the *umam*[147] since Allāh created mankind representatives who preserved and protected the traditions of the Messenger of Allāh (ﷺ) except in this *ummah*." A man said to him, "O Abū Ḥātim! It might be that they narrate a ḥadīth that has no basis and is not authentic?" He replied, "Their scholars know the authentic from the

[147] *Umam*: Plural of *Ummah* (i.e. nations).

> weak and their narrations are based on their knowledge, which allows those who come after them to distinguish the traditions and to preserve them." Then he said: "May Allāh have Mercy on Abū Zur'ah; by Allāh, he was diligent in preservation and protection of the traditions of the Messenger of Allāh (ﷺ)."[148]

78. We were informed by Muḥammad Ibn 'Abdullāh Ibn Muḥammad Ibn Ṣāliḥ Al-'Aṭṭār, who said that he was informed by Abū Muḥammad Ibn Hayyān, who said that he was told by Muḥammad Ibn Yaḥyā Al-Sulamī, who said that he heard Muḥammad Ibn Al-Khalīl saying that he was informed by 'Abdu'l-Raḥmān that he heard 'Abdullāh Ibn Dāwūd Al-Kharībī, who said:

> "I heard from our Imāms and those above us that the people of ḥadīth and the bearers of knowledge are the ones trusted by Allāh to preserve His Religion, the protectors of the Sunnah of His Prophet (ﷺ), which they know and practise."[149]

79. We were informed by Abū 'Ubayd Al-Naysābūrī, who said that he heard Muḥammad Ibn 'Alī Al-'Alawī saying that he heard Abū Aḥmad Al-Dallāl say that he heard Kahmas Al-Hamdānī saying:

> "Anyone who does not acknowledge that the people of

[148] Its chain of narrators is weak.

Al-Khaṭīb gave Al-'Alawī's biography in his *'Tārīkh'* (3/90) and he did not mention any criticism or praise of him; he ended his biography of him by saying, "It was said of him that he was vague in his narrations towards the end of his life."

Al-Zurqānī attributed the report in *'Sharḥ Al-Mawāhib Al-Ladunniyyah'*, as did Al-Laknawī (p. 24) in *'Al-Ajwibah Al-Fāḍilah'* to Ibn 'Asākir in *'Tārīkh Dimashq'*.

[149] Its chain of narrators is weak.

'Abdu'l-Raḥmān is Ibn 'Abdullāh Ibn Muslim Al-Jazarī, whose status is unknown; no one has mentioned any criticism or praise of him and he is one of the men in *'Al-Tahẓīb'* (6/196).

ḥadīth are the protectors and preservers of the Religion is considered to be from among the weak and miserable, who do not follow Allāh's Religion. Allāh says to His Prophet (ﷺ):

اللَّهُ نَزَّلَ أَحْسَنَ الْحَدِيثِ كِتَابًا

"Allāh has sent down the best statement, a Book."

[*al-Zumar* (39): 23]

And the Messenger of Allāh (ﷺ) says: "Jibrīl related to me from Allāh, the Almighty, the All-Powerful."[150]

[150] Its chain of narrators is weak,
It contains Al-ʿAlawī, of whom we spoke previously (see report no. 77).

CHAPTER EIGHTEEN

The Fact that the People of Ḥadīth are the Guardians of the Religion due to their Defence of the *Sunan*

80. We were informed by Abū Nuʿaym Al-Ḥāfiẓ that he said that he was told by Aḥmad Ibn Muḥammad Al-Rāzī, in Naysābūr, who said that he was told by ʿAbdu'l-Raḥmān Ibn Abū Ḥātim, who said that he was told by his father, who said that he was told by Qubaysah, who said that he heard Sufyān Al-Thawrī saying:

> "The angels are the guardians of the heaven and the people of ḥadīth are the guardians of the earth."[151]

81. We were told by Muḥammad Ibn Yūsuf Al-Qaṭṭān, who said that he was informed by Muḥammad Ibn ʿAbdullāh Al-Ḍhabbī,

[151] There is no objection to its chain of narrators.
Qubaysah made mistakes in his aḥādīth on the authority of Al-Thawrī and Abū Nuʿaym's Shaikh is Al-Qaṣṣār, of whom Al-Dhahabī said in *'Al-Siyār'* (15/569), "I do not know of any objection to him."

who said that he heard Ḥassān Ibn Muḥammad Al-Faqīh, who said that he heard Al-Ḥasan Ibn Sufyān say that he heard Ṣāliḥ Ibn Ḥātim Ibn Wardan say that he heard Yazīd Ibn Zuray' saying:

> "Every religion has cavalry; and the cavalry of this Religion are the people of the *asānīd* (pl. *isnād*)."[152]

82. We were informed by Muḥammad Ibn 'Abdullāh Ibn Ṣāliḥ Al-Muqrī', in Aṣbāhan, that he said that he was informed by 'Abdullāh Ibn Muḥammad Ibn Ja'far, who said that he heard 'Abdān say that he was told by Al-Qāsim Ibn Naṣr Al-Makhramī, who said that he was told by a man whom he named, but whose name he had forgotten, that he said:

> "I saw the Prophet (ﷺ) in a dream and he (ﷺ) was sleeping. Yaḥyā Ibn Ma'īn was standing at his head guarding him with a fly whisk and when I awoke, I went to Yaḥyā [Ibn Ma'īn] and informed him of what I had seen. He said to me: "We protect the Messenger of Allāh (ﷺ) from lies."[153]

[152] Its chain of narrators is ḥasan.
Sāliḥ Ibn Ḥātim is truthful and a good narrator of ḥadīth.

[153] Its chain of narrators is authentic up to Al-Makhrami.

CHAPTER NINETEEN

The Fact that the People of Ḥadīth are the Heirs of the Messenger (ﷺ)[154] with regard to the Sunnah and the Various Wisdoms that He Bequeathed

83. We were informed by Abū ʿAlī ʿAbdu'l-Raḥmān Ibn Muḥammad Ibn Faḍālah Al-Naysābūrī Al-Ḥāfiẓ, in Al-Rai, who said that he was informed by Abū Aḥmad Al-Ḥāfiẓ—whose name was Muḥammad Ibn Muḥammad Ibn Aḥmad Ibn Isḥāq Al-Karabīsī, who said that he was told by Abū Jaʿfar Muḥammad Ibn Ibrāhīm al-Dailī, in Makkah, who said that he was told by ʿAbdu'l-Ḥamīd Ibn Ṣubayh Al-ʿAnazī, who said that he was told by Ḥammād Ibn Zayd, who reported on the authority of Jarīr Ibn Hāzim, who reported on the authority of Sulaymān Ibn Mahrān [that he said]:

> "One day, while Ibn Masʿūd (*raḍiyAllāhu ʿanhu*) was with a man from among his companions, a Bedouin passed by and he [the Bedouin] asked, "Around what are these

> people gathering?" Ibn Mas'ūd (*raḍiyAllāhu 'anhu*) replied: "[They are gathering] around the inheritance of Muḥammad and sharing it out[155] among themselves."[156]

84. We were informed by Abū Isḥāq Ibrāhīm Ibn Mukhallad Ibn Ja'far Al-Mu'addil and Abū'l-Ḥasan Muḥammad Ibn Aḥmad Ibn Rizq Al-Bazzāz—and the wording is the latter's—who both said that they were told by Muḥammad Ibn 'Alī Al-Haytham Al-Muqrī', who said that he was told by Abū Bakr Ibn Abū Ḥalīmah,[157] a man from Al-Rai, said, "I heard Mūsā Ibn Manṣūr saying:

> "Al-Faḍayl Ibn 'Iyāḍ saw some persons from among the people of ḥadīth and among them were some who were underweight and he said: "O heirs of the Prophets! This is how you are."[158]

85. I recited to Aḥmad Ibn Muḥammad Ibn Ghālib Al-Faqīh, on the authority of Ibrāhīm Ibn Muḥammad Ibn Yaḥyā Al-Muzakkī, who said that he heard Muḥammad Ibn Isḥāq Ibn Khuzaymah, who said that he heard Yūnus—Ibn 'Abdu'l-'Alā'— saying that he heard Al-Shāfi'ī saying:

> "When I see a man from the people of ḥadīth, it is as if I am seeing the living Prophet (ﷺ)."[159]

---

[154] This is from manuscript (B).

[155] In manuscript (B) it says *"dividing it up"*.

[156] Its chain of narrators is *munqaṭi'* (broken) between Al-A'mash and Ibn Mas'ūd (*raḍiyAllāhu 'anhu*) and as for 'Abdu'l-Ḥamīd Ibn Ṣubayh, I have not found any biography for him.

[157] In manuscript (B) it says *"Khaythamah"*.

[158] Its chain of narrators is weak.

A biography was given for Mūsā Ibn Manṣūr by Al-Dhahabī in *'Al-Mīzān'* (4/224) and he said: "Ibn Yūnus said that he is *munkar* in ḥadīth. I say that he is from the same level as the narrator of this report, though he is Egyptian; and it is most likely in my opinion that they are one and the same. And Allāh knows better."

[159] Its chain of narrators is authentic.

The author's Shaikh is Al-Barqānī Al-Ḥāfiẓ (may Allāh have mercy on him).

CHAPTER TWENTY

The Fact that they are those Who Command all that is Good and Forbid all that is Evil

86. We were informed by Muḥammad Ibn Aḥmad Ibn Rizq, who said that he was told by Ja'far Al-Khaldī, who said that he was told by Abū Ya'qūb Isḥāq Ibn Ibrāhīm Al-Baghdādī, in Egypt, who said that he was told by Ma'mūn Abū 'Abdullāh, in Makkah, who reported on the authority of Sa'īd Ibn Al-'Abbās, who said: "Ibrāhīm Ibn Mūsā was asked: 'Who are those who order all that is good and forbid all that is evil?' He said:

> "We are they. We say: 'The Messenger of Allāh (ﷺ) said: 'Do this' and: 'The Messenger of Allāh (ﷺ) said: 'Do not do this'."[160]

[160] I do not know Ma'mūn Abū 'Abdullāh and I have not found any biography for him.

CHAPTER TWENTY-ONE

The Fact that they are the Best of People

87. We were informed by Abū Nu'aym Al-Ḥāfiẓ, who said that he was told by Muḥammad Ibn Ibrāhīm Ibn 'Alī, who said that he was told by Abū 'Urūbah, who said that he was told by Zakariyyah Ibn Al-Ḥakam, who said that he was told by Ḥamzah Ibn Sa'īd Al-Mirwazī, who said:

> "I saw Abū Bakr Ibn 'Ayyāsh striking the forearm of Yaḥyā Ibn Ādam and he said: "There is no people better than the people of ḥadīth; verily, one of them asks me about such-and-such a ḥadīth once and if he wishes, he [then] says, 'Abū Bakr Ibn 'Ayyāsh told me...'."[161]

---

[161] (It is) authentic and the men in the author's chain of narrators are trustworthy, aside from Zakariyyah Ibn Al-Ḥakam; no one declared him trustworthy except Ibn Ḥibbān (8/255).

However, the report has another source given by Al-Ḥākim in *'Ma'rifah 'Ulūm Al-Ḥadīth'* (p. 4): I was told by Abū Bakr Muḥammad Ibn Ja'far Al-Muzakkī, who said that he was told by Abū Bakr Muḥammad Ibn Isḥāq, who said that he heard 'Alī Ibn Khashram

=

88. We were informed by Muḥammad Ibn Al-Ḥusayn Al-Qaṭṭān and Al-Ḥasan[162] Ibn Abū Bakr Ibn Shazān, who both said that they were told by Abū Sahl Aḥmad Ibn Muḥammad Ibn ʻAbdullāh Ibn Ziyād, who said that he was told by Aḥmad Ibn ʻAlī Al-Ubar, who said that he was told by Yūsuf Ibn Mūsā Al-Qaṭṭān, who said:

> "One day, we gathered around Abū Bakr Ibn ʻAyyāsh and he said: "Why do I see heads as if they are the heads of devils?" So we moved back from him and he said: "I know of no people in the world who are better than they. They know my ḥadīth and if they take it and go, who can say anything to them?!"[163]

89. We were informed by ʻAlī Ibn Muḥammad Ibn ʻAbdullāh Ibn Bashrān Al-Mu'addil, who said that he was informed by Ismāʻīl Ibn Muḥammad Al-Saffar, who said that he was told by Muḥammad Ibn Al-Ḥusayn Al-Ḥunaynī, who said that he was told by ʻUmar Ibn Ḥafs, who said that he heard people saying to his father, "O Abū ʻUmar ! What is your opinion of the people of ḥadīth and how have they changed? How have they gone wrong?" He replied:

> "They are following what makes them the best of people."[164]

=

saying that he heard Abū Bakr Ibn ʻAyyāsh: .... And he reported it in a similar manner.

I say: In my opinion, Muḥammad Ibn Jaʻfar is most likely to be Ibn Al-Ḥusayn Ibn Muḥammad Ibn Zakariyyah Al-Warraq and I have not found anyone from his lineage. It was said (that he might be) Al-Muzakka. And Allāh knows better.

[162] In manuscript (A) it says "Al-Ḥusayn".

[163] (It is) authentic.

[164] Its chain of narrators is authentic.

The report was narrated by Al-Ḥākim in *'Maʻrifah ʻUlūm Al-Ḥadīth'* (p. 4) from another source, on the authority of Al-Ḥunaynī.

It was also narrated by Al-Ramāhurmuzī (#28) from a third source, likewise on the authority of Al-Ḥunaynī and it is mentioned in it that the questioner was ʻUmar Ibn Ḥafs himself.

90. I was told on the authority of ʿAbdu'l-ʿAzīz Ibn Jaʿfar Al-Ḥanbalī, who said that he was told by Abū Bakr Aḥmad Ibn Muḥammad Al-Khallāl, who said that he was informed by Abū Bakr Al-Marūzī, who reported that Abū ʿAbdullāh—Aḥmad Ibn Ḥanbal—said:

> "No people in my opinion are better than the people of ḥadīth; they know naught but ḥadīth." Al-Khallāl said: "Muḥammad Ibn Jaʿfar informed us that he was told by Abū'l-Ḥārith that he heard Abū ʿAbdullāh saying, "The people of ḥadīth are the best of those who speak of knowledge.""[166]

91. We were informed by Abū Ḥāzim ʿUmar Ibn Aḥmad Ibn Ibrāhim Al-ʿAbdawī, in Naysābūr, who said that he was informed by ʿAbdullāh Ibn ʿAdiyy in his letter to him, in which he said that he was told by ʿUmar Ibn Sinān Al-Manbajī, who said that he was told by Hashīm[167] Ibn Hammam Al-Ṭabarī, who said that he was told by Hisham Ibn Khālid, who said that he was told by Al-Walīd Ibn Muslim, who said: "Al-Awzāʿī escorted us when we were departing from his house and he remained with us for a long distance—two or three *farsakhs*[168]—and we said to him, "O Shaikh! Is it not difficult for you to walk, due to your advanced age?" He replied:

> "Walk and be silent. If I knew that Allāh had a generation or a people whom He praises, or who were better than you, I would walk with them and escort them, but

[165] In manuscript (B) it says: "We were told by".

[166] Its chain of narrators is authentic.

...were it not that the chain is *munqaṭiʿ* (broken) between Al-Khaṭīb and ʿAbdu'l- ʿAzīz Ibn Jaʿfar.

But in my opinion, it is most likely among the *"ʿIlal"* of Al-Khallāl.

[167] In manuscript (B) it says *"Hamīm"*.

[168] *Farsakh*: An ancient measurement of distance, equivalent to approximately three miles.

you are the best of people."[169]

92. I was told directly by 'Ubaydullāh[170] Ibn Abū'l-Fatḥ, that he said that he was told by Muḥammad Ibn Zayd Ibn Marwān Al-Kūfī, who said that he was told by Abū Bakr Ibn Abū Darim, who said that he was told by Muḥammad Ibn Al-Ḥasan Ibn Muḥammad Ibn Al-Ṣabāḥ, who said that he was told by Abū 'Imran Al-Ṣūfī, Al-Makkī, who said:

> "Aḥmad Ibn Ḥanbal saw some people of ḥadīth when they had departed from the house of a ḥadīth scholar and they had inkwells in their hands and he said: "If these are not the people, then I do not know who are the people."[171]

93. We were informed by 'Alī Ibn Muḥammad Ibn 'Abdullāh Ibn Bashrān, who said that he was informed by 'Uthmān Ibn Aḥmad Al-Daqqāq, who said that he was told by Muḥammad Ibn Aḥmad [Ibn][172] Al-Barra' Al-'Abdī, who said that he heard 'Uthmān Ibn Abū Shaybah saying, when he saw some of the people of ḥadīth in a state of commotion and he said:

> "Verily, the corrupt one (*fāsiq*) among them is better than the devout worshipper who is not one of them."[173]

---

[169] Its narrators are trustworthy, aside from this man, Hashīm, for whom I have not found a biography.

[170] In manuscript (A) it says "'Abdullāh".

[171] Its chain of narrators is extremely weak.

In it is Abū Bakr Ibn Abū Dārim, whose name is Aḥmad Ibn Al-Sara Ibn Yaḥyā, who is a liar. Al-Ḥākim said: "He is a Rafidhite (Shi'ite) and he is not trustworthy." Al-Dhahabī declared him to be a liar, saying, "He is not a trustworthy transmitter."

I say: He is a wicked Rafidhite, who narrates and fabricates slanders. See his biography in *'Al-Mīzān'* (1/139).

[172] It is not in manuscript (A) or (B), but it is necessitated by the text.

[173] Its chain of narrators is authentic.

94. I was informed by Abū'l-Qāsim Al-Azharī, who said that he was informed by 'Umar Ibn Aḥmad Ibn Hārūn Al-Muqrī' that 'Uthmān Ibn 'Abdawayh Al-Bazzāz told them that he heard Ibrāhīm Al-Ḥarbī saying:

> "Abū Yūsuf—Al-Qāḍī—went out one day and found the people of ḥadīth at the door. He said: "There is no one on earth better than you; have you not come (or he said: "arrived early in the morning") to hear the ḥadīth of the Messenger of Allāh (ﷺ)?"[174]

[174] Its chain of narrators is authentic up to Al-Ḥarbī.

CHAPTER TWENTY-TWO

Whoever said: "Verily, the *Abdāl* and the *Awliyā'*[175] are the People of Ḥadīth

95. I was informed by Al-Ḥasan[176] Ibn Abū'l-Ḥasan Al-Warrāq, who said that he was informed by 'Abdullāh Ibn 'Uthmān Al-Ṣaffār, who said that he was told by Abū Bakr Muḥammad Ibn Al-'Abbās Ibn Al-Walīd Ibn Mahdī Al-Ṣā'igh, who said that he was told by Ṣāliḥ Ibn Muḥammad Al-Rāzī that he was asked a question by a man and he replied:

"If the people of ḥadīth are not *al-abdāl*, then I don't

[175] Translator's note: The concept of *awliyā'* and *al-abdāl* as used here is one invented by *Ṣūfīs* and has no basis in the Qur'ān or the authentic aḥadīth of the Prophet (ﷺ). Shaikh Al-Islām Ibn Taymiyyah said: "These names are not found in the words of the Salaf in the manner mentioned there, nor are they narrated in this manner and with these meanings from the Shaikhs who are accepted by the *ummah* in general."

See for a detail discuss on the concept of *awliyā'* and *al-abdāl*, the Friends of Allāh and the Friends of Shayṭān by Shaikh Al-Islām Ibn Taymiyyah, English translation of *'al-Furqān bayna Awliyā' al-Raḥmān wa awliyā' al-Shayṭān'*, published by Dār as-Sunnah Publishers, Birmingham, United Kingdom, 1ed., 2000.

[176] In manuscript (A) and manuscript (B) it says "Al-Ḥusayn", but the correct name is the one we have confirmed. And Allāh knows better.

> know who *al-abdāl* are." He said that these are the words of Yazīd Ibn Hārūn, which he quoted on the authority of Sufyān Al-Thawrī. Then Ṣāliḥ Al-Rāzī said: "The just person is not the one who refrains from unlawful sexual relations, shedding blood or taking the property of others. The just person is the one who testifies to [the words of] the Prophet (ﷺ) and his testimony is accepted."[177]

96. We were informed by Muḥammad Ibn ʿIsā Ibn ʿAbdu'l-ʿAzīz Al-Hamdānī, who said that he was told by Ṣāliḥ Ibn Aḥmad Al-Ḥāfiẓ, who said that he was told by Muḥammad Ibn Muʿādh, who said that he was told by Abū'l-Ḥasan ʿAlī Ibn Ibrāhīm, who said that he heard ʿUmar Ibn Bakkār Al-Qāfilānī, who said that he heard Aḥmad Ibn Ḥanbal saying:

> "If [they],[178] the people of ḥadīth are not *al-abdāl*, then who are they?!"[179]

97. I was informed by Abū'l-Qāsim Al-Azharī, who said that ʿAlī Ibn Al-Ḥasan Al-Qāḍī reported that Muḥammad Ibn Aḥmad Ibn Yaʿqūb informed them, saying that his father told him that he heard Isḥāq Ibn Abū Isrā'īl and Al-Zubayr Ibn Bakār both said that they heard Al-Naḍr Ibn Shumayl saying that he heard Al-Khalīl Ibn Aḥmad say:

---

[177] Its chain of narrators is authentic.

The author's Shaikh is Al-Ḥasan Ibn ʿAlī Al-Jawharī and the *kunyah* (agnomen) of his father, ʿAlī, is also Abū'l-Ḥasan. The remainder of the men in the chain are trustworthy.

[178] This is from manuscript (B).

[179] Its chain of narrators is weak.

The status of ʿUmar Ibn Bakkār is unknown. Ibn Abū Yaʿlā mentioned him in *'Ṭabāqāt Al-Ḥanabilah'* (1/220), saying, "He transmitted things on the authority of our Imām (i.e. Imām Aḥmad)..." and he quoted this report.

> "If the people of the Qur'ān and ḥadīth are not the *awliyā'* of Allāh, then there is no *waliyy* on earth."[180]

98. We were informed by Aḥmad Ibn Muḥammad Ibn Aḥmad Al-Mujahhaz, who said that he was told by Muḥammad Ibn 'Abdullāh Ibn Muḥammad Al-Kūfī, who said that he was told by Ibn Abū Dāwūd, who said that he heard Maḥmūd Ibn Khālid saying that he asked Abū Ḥafs 'Amr Ibn Abū Salāmah:

> "Do you love to narrate ḥadīth?" He replied, "And who would like for his name to be omitted from the record of the righteous?!"[181]

99. We were informed by Al-Ḥasan Ibn Abū Bakr, who said that Muḥammad Ibn Ibrāhīm Al-Khawzī, from Shīrāz, stated that 'Abdān Ibn Aḥmad Al-Hamazānī told them that he heard Abū Ḥātim—Al-Razī—saying that he was told on the authority of Ibn 'Uyaynah that he said:

> "In my whole life, I have not seen anyone who supplicated more than the companions of ḥadīth."[182]

---

[180] Its chain of narrators is weak.
'Alī Ibn Al-Ḥasan Al-Qāḍī is Al-Jarrāḥī; he has a biography in *'Tārīkh Baghdād'* (11/387) and there is (negative) talk about him.

[181] Its chain of narrators is *talif* (broken, bad, worthless).
In it is Muḥammad Ibn 'Abdullāh Al-Kūfī, who is a liar; he was described as having fabricated and stolen *aḥādīth*. He has a biography in *'Tārīkh Baghdād'* (5/466).

[182] Its chain of narrators is *munqaṭi'* (broken, cut off) between Abū Ḥātim Al-Rāzī and Sufyān Ibn 'Uyaynah.

CHAPTER TWENTY-THREE

Whoever said: "Were it not For the [Companions][183] of Ḥadīth, We would Not have Studied Islām."

100. We were informed by Aḥmad Ibn Muḥammad Ibn Ghālib Al-Khawārizmī, who said that he recited to Abū Ḥāmid Aḥmad Ibn 'Umar Ibn Ḥafṣ Al-Mu'allim, a righteous Shaikh in Merv—who said that 'Abdullāh Ibn Maḥmūd told them that he heard Muḥammad Ibn 'Abdullāh say that he heard Ṣadaqah say that he was with Ḥafṣ Ibn Ghiyāth and some people gathered around him. Ḥafṣ said:

> "Were it not that Allāh had placed endeavour in the hearts of these—the seekers of knowledge—this matter—Islām—would have been wiped out."[184]

101. I was informed by Aḥmad Ibn Abū Ja'far Al-Qaṭī'ī, who said

[183] In manuscript (B) it says "people".

[184] Its chain of narrators is ḥasan.

I do not know who this Muḥammad Ibn 'Abdullāh is.

that he was told by 'Abdu'l-Karīm Ibn Aḥmad Ibn Abū Jidār, in Egypt, who said that he was told by Muḥammad Ibn Aḥmad Ibn Yūsuf Al-Khallāl, who said that he was told by Muḥammad Ibn 'Umar Al-Kassī, who said that he was told by 'Abdu'l-Ḥamīd Ibn Ḥamīd, who said that he heard Abū Dāwūd saying:

> "Were it not for this group—the people of ḥadīth —we would not have studied Islām."[185]

102. We were told by Muḥammad Ibn Aḥmad Ibn Ya'qūb, who reported on the authority of Muḥammad Ibn 'Abdullāh Ibn Muḥammad Al-Ḥāfiẓ, who said that he heard Khalaf Ibn Muḥammad Al-Bukhārī, who said that he heard Ibrāhīm Ibn Ma'qal say that he heard Abū 'Abdullāh Muḥammad Ibn Ismā'īl Al-Bukhārī saying:

> "We were three or four [persons] at the door of 'Alī Ibn 'Abdullāh and he said: "I hope that the explanation of this ḥadīth from the Prophet (ﷺ): "A group from among my *ummah* will continue to adhere to the truth and those who forsake them or oppose them will not harm them."—is that it refers to you, because the merchants have busied themselves with trading, the manufacturers have busied themselves with manufacturing and the kings have busied themselves with [the affairs of] their kingdoms, while you keep alive the Sunnah of the Prophet (ﷺ)."[186]

---

[185] In the chain of narrators there is someone whom I do not know.

In addition, 'Abdu'l-Ḥamīd Ibn Ḥamīd is Al-Ḥāfiẓ 'Abd Ibn Ḥamīd, the author of '*Al-Musnad*' and Abū Dāwūd is Al-Ṭayālisī.

[186] Its chain of narrators is extremely weak.

In it is Khalaf Ibn Muḥammad Al-Bukhārī Al-Khayyām, of whom Abū Ya'lā said: "He mixed things up and he is extremely weak; he narrated texts (of ḥadīth) that are unknown and was declared weak by Al-Ḥākim and others."

We were informed by Abū Bakr Aḥmad Ibn Muḥammad Ibn Ja'far Al-Yazdī, in Aṣbāhan, who said that Abū Bakr 'Abdullāh Ibn Muḥammad Ibn Sahrah communicated to him in writing, saying that one of the men of letters communicated to him in a poetic style:

"They strive to carry the lights of Allāh's Religion,
Men who give life to the ḥadīth of Muḥammad,
They transmit the reports from every scholar,
Who is pious, truthful, virtuous and devout,
Their inkwells shine and illuminate, as if,
They are lamps illuminating the centre of a *Masjid*,
Which drive (people) to those who are scholars of *fiqh*,
And to those who write the rulings from every *musnid*."[187]

103. We were told by[188] Aḥmad Ibn Muḥammad Ibn Aḥmad Al-Qaṭī'ī, who said that he was told by Abū Sa'd 'Abdu'l-Raḥmān Ibn Muḥammad Al-Idrīsī, who said that he was told by Muḥammad Ibn 'Ubaydullāh Ibn Muḥammad Ibn Aḥmad Ibn Sahl Al-Madīnī Al-Samarqandī, who said that he was told by 'Umar Ibn Muḥammad Ibn 'Āmir Al-Samarqandī, who said that he was told by Sa'īd Ibn 'Ayyāsh, who said that he was told by Muḥammad Ibn Ṣāliḥ Ibn Yaḥyā Al-'Adawī, who said that he was informed by Shu'ayb Ibn Ḥarb, who said:

> "I was with 'Abdu'l-'Azīz Ibn Abū Rawwād and he noticed a young man who was approaching him (to ask about) a ḥadīth and he said: "Do you not see that in his hand are the lamps of Islām? These are the lamps

[187] *Musnid*: A scholar of ḥadīth who arranges *aḥādīth* according to their *asānīd*.
[188] In manuscript (B) it says: *"haddathanī"* (I was told).

of faith and the signposts of the righteous—bottles of ink."[189]

This is the end of the first section of *Sharaf Aṣḥab al-Ḥadīth*,

All Praise and Thanks be to Allāh, the Lord of the Worlds, and Success is Attained through Allāh.

[189] In the *isnād* there are a number of narrators whom I do not know. And Allāh knows better.

The verifier (may Allāh pardon him) said: "The end of the checking of the first section of *'Sharaf Aṣḥab al-Ḥadīth'*, by Al-Khaṭīb Al-Baghdādī (may Allāh have mercy on him) was achieved through Allāh's Grace and Favour, on Tuesday, the 5th of Rabīʿ Al-Awwal, in the year 1416 AH. All praise and thanks be to Allāh, the Lord of the worlds.

THE SECOND SECTION OF THE BOOK

Sharaf Aṣḥab al-Ḥadīth

The Shaikh, Imām and Ḥāfiẓ Abū Bakr Aḥmad Ibn ʿAlī Ibn Thābit al-Khaṭīb al-Baghdādī (may Allāh have Mercy on him)

The narration of the trustworthy Shaikh: Abū Muḥammad Hibatullāh Ibn Aḥmad In Muḥammad Al-Akfānī, on his authority.

The narration of the trustworthy Shaikh: Abū ʿAbdullāh Muḥammad Ibn Ḥamzah Ibn Muḥammad Ibn Abū'l-Ṣaqr, on his authority.

The narration of: the Shaikh, Imām, scholar and Ḥāfiẓ and eminent member of the Ḥuffāẓ, Jamaluddīn Abī[190] Muḥammad ʿAbdu'l- Qāḍir Ibn ʿAbdullāh Al-Rahāwī, on his authority.

The author of the section, the seeker of Allāh, Most High's mercy, Muḥammad Ibn Aḥmad Ibn Al-Ḥusayn Al-Hakārī, on his authority. All praise and thanks be to Allāh, the Lord of the worlds.

---

[190] In manuscript (A) it says, "Abu".

CHAPTER TWENTY-FOUR

Whoever said: "Verily, the Truth is With the Companions of Ḥadīth"

In the Name of Allāh, the Most Beneficent, the Most Merciful, From Whom We Seek Aid—We were told by the Shaikh, Imām, scholar, Ḥāfiẓ, Mufti of the Sharī'ah and example to the Ḥuffāẓ, Jamaluddīn Abū Muḥammad 'Abdu'l-Qāḍir Ibn 'Abdullāh Al-Rahāwī, then later Al-Ḥarranī, who recited in his own words when I was present, listening in Al-Mawsil, on Monday, the 25th of Dhū'l-Hijjah, in the year 562 AH., when he said that he was informed by the trustworthy Shaikh Abū 'Abdullāh Muḥammad Ibn Ḥamzah Ibn Muḥammad Ibn Abū'l-Ṣaqr, who said that he was informed by the trustworthy Shaikh, Abū Muḥammad Hibatullāh Ibn Aḥmad In Muḥammad Al-Akfānī, who said: "We were informed by the Shaikh, Imām and Ḥāfiẓ, Abū Bakr Aḥmad Ibn 'Alī Ibn Thābit Al-Khaṭīb Al-Baghdādī—may Allāh have mercy on him, who said:

104. I was informed by 'Ubaydullāh Ibn Abū'l-Fatḥ Al-Fārisī, who said that he heard Abū Sa'd Al-Astarabazī, who said that he heard Abū Bakr Muḥammad Ibn 'Abdullāh Ibn Yaḥyā Al-Muzakkir

Al-Naysābūrī, in Astarābaz, who said that he heard 'Abdu'l-'Azīz Al-Khaffāf, in Makkah, who said that he heard Ibrāhīm Ibn Mūsā Al-Baṣrī, who said that he heard Abū 'Abdullāh Muḥammad Ibn Al-'Abbās Al-Miṣrī, who said:

> "I heard Hārūn Al-Rashīd saying: "I sought four [things] and I found them in four [places]: I sought disbelief (*kufr*) and found it among the *Jahmiyyah*.[191] I sought *Kalām*[192] and argument and found them with the *Mu'tazilah*.[193] I sought untruthfulness and found it with the *Rāfiḍah*[194] and I sought truth and found it with the companions of ḥadīth."[195]

105. We were informed by Abū Manṣūr Muḥammad Ibn 'Isā Al-

---

[191] *Jahmiyyah*: Founded by Jahm Ibn Ṣafwān, a theologian who attached himself to Al-Ḥārith Ibn Surayj, a dissident in Khurasān towards the end of the Umayyad period, and who was put to death in 746 AH. by Salm Ibn Aḥwāz. It is said that he taught that only a few Attributes can be ascribed to Allāh, such as Creation, Divine Power and Action, whilst others such as Speech cannot. Therefore, he believed that it was wrong to describe the Qur'ān as the Word of Allāh, since, according to Jahm, Allāh does not speak.

[192] *Kalām*: Speculative theology. As interest in philosophy grew among some Muslims, *Kalām* adopted the dialectic (methodology) of the Greek skeptics and the stoics and attempted to fit Aristotle and Plato into an Islāmic context.

[193] *Mu'tazilah*: The *Mu'tazilah* arose in the beginning of the second century AH. The adherents of the *Mu'tazili* school are best known for rejecting the doctrine of the Qur'ān as uncreated, asserting that if the Qur'ān is the Word of Allāh, He must logically have preceded His own Speech. The philosophical speculation of the *Mu'tazilah* centres on the concepts of Divine Justice (*Al-'Adl*) and divine unity (*tawḥīd*). The school worked to resolve the supposed theological problem of evil: how to reconcile the Justice of an All-Powerful God with the reality of evil in the world, in accordance with the guidance of the Qur'ān. The *Mu'tazilah* reasoned that, since Allāh is Just and Wise, and since He cannot command what is contrary to reason, or act with disregard for the welfare of His creatures, evil must be regarded as something that stems from errors in human acts, arising from man's Divinely bestowed free will.

[194] *Rāfiḍah*: Shi'ites.

[195] In the chain of narrators there is someone whom I do not know.

Hamazānī, who said that Ṣāliḥ Ibn Aḥmad Al-Tamīmī Al-Ḥāfiẓ, who said that he was told by Aḥmad Ibn ʻUbayd Ibn Ibrāhīm, who said that he was told by ʻAbdullāh Ibn Sulaymān Ibn Al-Ashʻath, who said that he heard Aḥmad Ibn Sinān saying:

> "Al-Walīd Al-Karābīsī was my maternal uncle and when death approached him, he said to his sons, 'Do you know anyone more knowledgeable regarding *Kalām* than I?' They replied, 'No.' He said: 'Do you doubt me?' They answered, 'No.' He said: 'Then I advise you; do you accept [my advice]?' They replied, 'Yes.' He said: 'It is incumbent upon you to adhere to what the companions of ḥadīth follow, for I have seen that the truth is with them. I do not mean the leaders, but these tearers, do you not see that when one of them goes to one of their leaders, he accuses him of being in error and censures him'?"[196]

Abū Bakr Ibn Al-Ashʻath said: "He was the most knowledgeable of people regarding *Kalām*, after Ḥafṣ Al-Farḍ Al-Karābīsī. Ḥusayn Al-Karābīsī learnt *Kalām* from him."

106. We were informed by Muḥammad Ibn ʻIsā, who said that he was told by Ṣāliḥ Ibn Aḥmad, who said that he heard Aḥmad Ibn Muḥammad Abā[197] ʻAbdullāh saying that he heard ʻAbdu'l-Raḥmān[198] Ibn ʻAbdu'l-Raḥmān Ibn Muḥammad Ibn Quraysh Al-ʻAnbarī Al-Baṣrī saying:

[196] Its chain of narrators is authentic.
The biography of the author's Shaikh is given in his *'Tārīkh'* (2/406) and he said: "He was truthful." Ṣāliḥ Ibn Aḥmad Al-Tamīmī was trustworthy and he was a Ḥāfiẓ and a protector (of the Religion) and Aḥmad Ibn 'Ubayd has a biography in *'Al-Siyār'* (15/380) and he is trustworthy and may be cited as a proof.

[197] This is how it appears in manuscript (B); it was written as *"abā"* in manuscript (A), as one writes *"anā"*, indicating earwitness.

[198] In manuscript (A) it says "'Abdu'l-Raḥīm".

"Every person who goes along with a saying—a ḥadīth—and flees from it to something other than a ḥadīth, then he is going towards misguidance."[199]

[199] Its chain of narrators is ḥasan.

It contains Aḥmad Ibn Muḥammad Ibn Aws, of whom Ṣāliḥ Ibn Aḥmad said: "I recorded from him... and he is truthful in his narrations."

CHAPTER TWENTY-FIVE

The Fact that the Companions of Ḥadīth are the Most Deserving People to be Saved in the Hereafter and the First of Creation to Enter Paradise

107. We were informed by Aḥmad Ibn Al-Mubārak Al-Barāthī, who said that he was told by 'Alī Ibn Muḥammad Ibn Mūsā Al-Tammār, in Al-Baṣrah, who said that he was told by 'Abdullāh Ibn Muḥammad Ibn Abū Sa'īd, who said that he was told by Ibrāhīm Ibn Muḥammad Ibn Abū'l-Jahīm, who said that he was told by Ḥakkāmah Bint 'Uthmān Ibn Dīnār, who said that she was told by her father, 'Uthmān Ibn Dīnār, who reported on the authority of his brother, Mālik Ibn Dīnār, who reported on the authority of Anas Ibn Mālik (*raḍiyAllāhu 'anhu*), the servant of the Prophet (ﷺ), who reported that the Prophet (ﷺ) said:

> "Verily, the first of you to be saved from the terrors of the Day of Resurrection will be those of you who pray

most in the abode of this world."[200]

108. I read to Muḥammad Ibn Aḥmad Ibn Ya'qūb, who reported on the authority of Muḥammad Ibn Nu'aym Al-Ḍhabbī, who said that he heard Muḥammad Ibn Ṣāliḥ Ibn Hānī, who said that he heard Al-Faḍl Ibn Muḥammad Al-Sha'rānī, who said that he heard Abū Ja'far Al-Nufaylī, who said:

> "If there is anyone on the face of the earth who will be saved, it is these [people] who study ḥadīth."[201]

Abū'l-Qāsim Al-Azhārī recited to me, saying that Abū'l-Faḍl 'Ubaydullāh Ibn 'Abdu'l-Raḥmān Al-Zuhrī recited to him, saying that Abū Muzāḥim Al-Khāqānī recited to him:

> "The people of ḥadīth are the saved ones, if they act,
> On it, if it does not come from anyone accused,
> It has been said that they are the best of slaves due to,
> The virtue that is in them, if they abstain from trials,

[200] (This is) fabricated.

Its weakness lies in Ḥakkāmah Bint 'Uthmān Ibn Dīnār and her father.

As for Ḥakkāmah, Al-'Uqaylī said in *'Al-Dhu'afā'* (3/200), "She narrates false aḥadīth from him (i.e. her father) that are baseless." He added, "The aḥādīth of Hakkamah resemble the sayings of storyteller, that have no basis (in fact)."

As for 'Uthmān Ibn Dīnār, Al-Dhahabī said in *'Al-Mīzān'* (3/33), "(He is) nothing." As for Ibn Ḥibbān, he mentioned him in *'Al-Thiqāt'*, saying, "He narrates on the authority of his brother and his daughter, Ḥakkāmah narrates on his authority—and she is nothing." So it seems as if he considered that the weakness emanates from his daughter.

The ḥadīth was narrated Abū'l-Qāsim Al-Aṣbāhanī in *'Al-Targhīb wa'l-Tarhīb'* (#1667 and #1687) by way of Ḥakkāmah.

Al-Suyūtī attributed it to Al-Daylamī in *'Al-Durr Al-Manthūr'* (5/219).

[201] Muḥammad Ibn Nu'aym is Al-Ḥākim Abū 'Abdullāh, of whom Al-Ḥāfiẓ (Ibn Ḥajr) said in *'Al-Lisān'* (5/461), "This is what Al-Khaṭīb said when he investigated it in his *'Tārīkh'* and in other works."

I say: I have not found any biography for him.

If any of them died in that state, his martyrdom is near,
So the deceased in his grave will be in a pleasant state."

109. We were told directly by Al-Ḥasan Ibn Abū Ṭālib, who said that he was told by 'Alī Ibn 'Amr Ibn Sahl, who said that he was told by Aḥmad Ibn Maḥmūd Al-Qāḍī Al-Aḥwāzī, who said that he was told by 'Alī Ibn Rawḥān, who said that he was told by Aḥmad Ibn Sinān, who said that he heard Shaybān Ibn Yaḥyā—Shaikh Abū Bakr said:[202] "This is how Al-Ḥasan related it to me and the correct statement is that his name is Shāzz Ibn Yaḥyā"—:

> "I do not know of any path to Paradise straighter than that of one who follows the path of ḥadīth."[203]

110. We were informed by Muḥammad Ibn 'Isā Al-Hamazānī, who said he was told by Ṣāliḥ Ibn Aḥmad Al-Ḥāfiẓ, who said that he was informed by Al-Ḥasan Ibn 'Alī by way of reading, who said that he was told by Muḥammad Ibn Ja'far Al-Baghdādī, who said that he was told by Ḥubaysh Ibn Mubshir, who said that he was told by a trustworthy person,[204] who reported on the authority of Ibn Al-Mubārak [that he said]:

> "The steadiest of people on the *Ṣirāṭ* will be the companions of ḥadīth."[205]

---

[202] (This is) from manuscript (A).

[203] Its chain of narrators is weak.

In it is 'Alī Ibn Rawḥān, whose biography was given by Al-Khaṭīb in his *'Tārīkh'* (11/446) and it, does not mention any criticism or praise.

[204] This is how it is written in manuscript (B) and its verifier indicated that the manuscripts upon which he relies are agreed on this, although this copy of ours has the name Baqiyyah.

[205] Its chain of narrators is weak.

This is due to the unknown status of the narrator who reported on the authority of Ibn Al-Mubārak, for the preponderance of opinion is that he is not identified.

111. We were informed by Abū ʿUbayd Muḥammad Ibn Abū Naṣr Al-Naysābūrī, who said that he heard Muḥammad Ibn ʿAlī Al-ʿAlawī Al-Hamazānī, who said that he heard ʿAlī Ibn Ibrāhim Al-Jabbān say that he heard Al-Ḥasan Ibn ʿAlī Al-Tamīmī saying:

> "I was performing circumambulation [of the *Kaʿbah*] and it came to my mind: Who will be in the forefront on the Day of Resurrection? Then a voice said: "[They are] the companions of ḥadīth."[206]

[206] I have not found any biography for ʿAlī Ibn Ibrāhim Al-Jabbān.

CHAPTER TWENTY-SIX

The Virtue of Those Who Travel in Search of Ḥadīth

112. We were informed by[207] Abū Sa'd Al-Malīnī, who said that he was told by 'Abdullāh Ibn 'Adiyy Al-Ḥāfiẓ, who said that he was informed by Aḥmad Ibn Muḥammad Ibn Al-Ḥasan, who said that he heard Muḥammad Ibn Al-Wazīr Al-Wasiṭī, who said that he heard Yazīd Ibn Hārūn, who said that he asked Ḥammād Ibn Zayd, "O Abū Ismā'īl! Has Allāh, the Almighty, the All-Powerful mentioned the companions of ḥadīth in the Qur'ān?" He replied, "Certainly! Have you not heard the Words of Allāh:

وَلِيُنذِرُوا قَوْمَهُمْ إِذَا رَجَعُوٓا إِلَيْهِمْ لَعَلَّهُمْ يَحْذَرُونَ ﴿١٢٢﴾

> "to obtain understanding in the religion and warn [i.e., advise] their people when they return to them that they might be cautious."
>
> [*al-Tawbah* (9):122]?

[207] In manuscript (B) it says *"anbā'nā"* (imparted to us).

This refers to every person who travels for the purpose of seeking knowledge (*'ilm*) and understanding (*fiqh*) and then returns with it to those whom he left behind and teaches it to them."[208]

113. I read to Muḥammad Ibn Aḥmad Ibn Ya'qūb, who reported on the authority of Muḥammad Ibn Nu'aym Al-Ḍhabbī, who said that he heard Abū 'Abdullāh Muḥammad Ibn Muḥammad Ibn 'Ubaydullāh Al-Ḥāfiẓ, who said that he heard Muḥammad Ibn Muslim Ibn Wārah, who said that he heard 'Abdu'l-Razzāq saying regarding the Words of Allāh, Most High:[209]

فَلَوْلَا نَفَرَ مِن كُلِّ فِرْقَةٍ مِّنْهُمْ طَآئِفَةٌ لِّيَتَفَقَّهُوا۟ فِى ٱلدِّينِ
وَلِيُنذِرُوا۟ قَوْمَهُمْ إِذَا رَجَعُوٓا۟ إِلَيْهِمْ لَعَلَّهُمْ يَحْذَرُونَ ﴿١٢٢﴾

> "For there should separate from every division of them a group [remaining] to obtain understanding in the religion and warn [i.e., advise] their people when they return to them that they might be cautious."
>
> [*al-Tawbah* (9):122]

"They are the companions of ḥadīth."[210]

114. We were informed by Riḍwān Ibn Muḥammad Ibn Al-Ḥasan Al-Daynūrī, who said that he was told by Abū 'Abdullāh Muḥammad Ibn 'Alī Ibn Aḥmad Ibn Mahdī, in Wasiṭ, who said

[208] Its chain of narrators is authentic.
Ibn 'Adiyy's Shaikh is most likely Ibn Al-Sharqī Al-Ḥāfiẓ.
However, the author narrated the report in *'Al-Riḥlah Fī Ṭalab Al-Ḥadīth'* (#10) by way of Ibrāhīm Ibn Aḥmad Ibn Al-Ḥasan Al-Qarmansīnī, who said that he was told by Aḥmad Ibn Muḥammad Ibn Al-Ḥasan Ibn Abū Ḥamzah. But I have found no mention of Ibn Al-Sharqī, so his origin would seem to be as the author said. And Allāh knows better.
[209] In manuscript (B) it says *"the Almighty, the All-Powerful"*.
[210] I do not know the author's Shaikh.

that he was told by Muḥammad Ibn Al-Ḥasan Al-Muqrī', who said that he was told by Muḥammad Ibn 'Aṣim, in Merv, who said that he heard 'Abdu'l-Raḥmān Ibn Muḥammad Ibn Ḥātim, who said that Ibrāhīm Ibn Adham said:

> "Verily, Allāh, (Most High) will repel trials and tribulations from this *ummah* due to the travels of the companions of ḥadīth."[211]

115. We were informed on the authority of 'Ubaydullāh Ibn Abū'l-Fatḥ and Al-Ḥasan Ibn Abū Ṭālib, who both said that they were told by Muḥammad Ibn Al-'Abbās Al-Khazzāz, who said that he was told by 'Abdullāh Ibn Abū Dāwūd, who said that he was told by Ja'far Ibn Abū Salāmah, who said that he was told by 'Abdullāh Ibn 'Umar, who said that he was told by Al-Walīd Ibn Bakīr, who reported on the authority of 'Umar Ibn Nafi', who reported on the authority of 'Ikrimah, the freed slave of Ibn 'Abbās (*raḍiyAllāhu 'anhumā*), that he said regarding the Words of Allāh, Most High:

ٱلسَّٰٓئِحُونَ

"The travelers [for His cause]"

[*al-Tawbah* (9):112]

"They are the seekers of ḥadīth."[212]

---

[211] Its chain of narrators is weak.

A biography for the author's Shaikh was given by him in *'Tarīkh Baghdād'* (8/432) and he said: "I know nothing of him except good." As for Muḥammad Ibn Al-Ḥasan Al-Muqrī' is Ibn Ziyād Al-Naqqāsh and he is nothing—and there has been some (negative) talk about him.

The report was narrated by the author in *'Al-Riḥlah Fī Ṭalab Al-Ḥadīth'* (#15) from another source, on the authority of Al-Naqqāsh.

[212] Its chain of narrators is extremely weak.

In it is 'Umar Ibn Nafi' Al-Thaqafī, of whom Ibn Ma'īn said: "He is nothing." Al-Sajī mentioned him, as did Ibn Al-Jarūdī in *'Al-Dhu'afā'*. As for Ibn Ḥibbān, he mentioned him in *'Al-Thiqat'*. Abū Ḥātim said regarding Al-Walīd Ibn Bakīr, "(He is) a Shaikh." Ibn

=

116. I was informed by Abū'l-Qāsim Al-Azhari, who said that he was informed by Abū Ḥāmid Aḥmad Ibn Ibrāhim Al-Naysābūri, who said that he heard Abū 'Abdullāh Muḥammad Ibn Aḥmad Ibn Ḥāmid Al-Faqīh, in Al-Damighan, who said that he was told by Abū Ja'far Al-Tahawī, who said that he heard Naṣr Ibn Marzūq saying, "When 'Alī Ibn Ma'bad saw the companions of ḥadīth, he said:

> "Their hair is unkempt, their garments are soiled and their faces are dusty. If there is no reward for this, then by Allāh, that is a punishment."[213]

[Shaikh Abū Bakr Al-Khaṭīb [Al-Baghdādī] said:][214] "We believe strongly, without a shred of doubt, that the seeker of ḥadīth is rewarded for his seeking; and the least benefit in it is in what follows:

117. I was informed by 'Ubaydullāh Ibn Aḥmad Al-Sayrāfi, who said that he was told by 'Umar Ibn Aḥmad Al-Marūrūzī, who said that he was told by Ja'far Ibn Muḥammad Al-Naqid, who said that he heard Abū Hishām Al-Rifā'ī, who said that he heard Wakī' Ibn Al-Jarrah, who said:

> "Were it that a man did not receive any reward for a ḥadīth except that it keeps him from heresy, he would

=

Ḥbbān also mentioned him in his 'Thiqat', while Al-Daraquṭnī said: "(He is) abandoned in matters of ḥadīth."

The report was narrated by the author in *'Al-Riḥlah Fī Ṭalab Al-Ḥadīth'* (#11).

[213] In it (chain of narrators) is Abū Ḥāmid Ibn Ibrāhīm Al-Naysābūrī, whose biography was given by Al-Khaṭīb in *'Tārīkh Baghdād'* (4/20) and by Al-Dhahabī in *'Al-Siyār'* (16/496), both of whom mentioned his abstemiousness and his devoutness, but they did not mention anything that would prove him to be precise and exacting, but he is recorded as being of the best status.

[214] In manuscript (B) it says *"I said"*.

have acquired [benefit] from it."[215]

118. I was told on the authority of 'Abdu'l-'Azīz Ibn Ja'far Al-Faqīh, who said that he was told by Abū Bakr Al-Khallāl, who said that he was told by Muḥammad Ibn Ja'far, who said that he was told by Isḥāq Ibn Ibrāhīm, who said that he asked Abū 'Abdullāh—Aḥmad Ibn Ḥanbal—:

> "[What if] a people write ḥadīth and one does not see the signs of it upon them and they have no dignity?" Abū 'Abdullāh said: "They will be led by ḥadīth to goodness."[216]

119. We were informed by Muḥammad Ibn Aḥmad Ibn Rizq, who said that he was told by 'Uthmān Ibn Aḥmad Al-Daqqāq, who said that he was told by Muḥammad Ibn Aḥmad Ibn Al-Barā', who said that he was told by Aḥmad Ibn Ibrāhīm, who said that he was told by Yaḥyā Ibn Suwayd Al-Ḥanafī, who said that he heard Ḥammād Ibn Zayd saying:

> "Ayyūb would be informed of the death of a young man from among the companions of ḥadīth and [the effect of] that would be seen in him and he would be informed of the death of a man who was said to have been devout and [the effect of] that would not be seen in him."[217]

---

[215] Its chain of narrators is extremely weak.

Abū Hishām Al-Rifā'ī is Muḥammad Ibn Yazīd Ibn Muḥammad Al-Rifā'ī; most of the scholars are in agreement that he is weak and some of them accused him of stealing aḥadīth.

[216] Its chain of narrators is munqati', but the report is authentic.

[217] The men in the chain of narrators are trustworthy and biographies are given for them in *'Tārīkh Baghdād'*—aside from Yaḥyā Ibn Suwayd Al-Ḥanafī, for whom I have not found any biography. Aḥmad Ibn Ibrāhīm is Al-Dawraqī and he is among the narrators mentioned in *'Al-Tahẓīb'*.

CHAPTER TWENTY-SEVEN

Combining the Goodness of the Life of this World and the Hereafter by Hearing Ḥadīth and Recording Them

120. I was told byAbū Ṣāliḥ Aḥmad Ibn ʿAbdu'l-Mālik Al-Naysābūrī and Abū Saʿīd Masʿūd Ibn Nāṣir Al-Sajzī—and the wording is that of the latter—that they said that they were told by ʿAbdu'l-Raḥmān Ibn Ḥamdān Al-Naḍrawiyyī,[218] who said that he was informed by Abū Muḥammad Al-Ḥasan Ibn Aḥmad Ibn Muḥammad, in Tostar, who said that he heard ʿAlī Ibn Abū'l-Ḥusayn[219] Ibn Isḥāq [and in the ḥadīth of Abū Ṣāliḥ, it says: "Ibn Al-Ḥasan"][220] Ibn Isḥāq, who said that he heard Sahl Ibn ʿAbdullāh Al-Zāhid saying:

> "Whoever desired the life of this world and that of the Hereafter, let him record ḥadīth, for in that there

[218] In manuscript (A) and manuscript (B) it says, *"Al-Naḍrawī"*, but the correct version is what we have confirmed from *'Al-Siyār'* (17/553).
[219] In manuscript (B) it says *"Al-Ḥasan"*.
[220] This is from manuscript (B), but the correct version is *"Ibn Al-Ḥusayn"*.

is benefit in this world and in the Hereafter."[221]

121. I was informed by Muḥammad Ibn Al-Muẓaffar Ibn 'Alī Al-Muqrī', who said that he was told by Ibrāhīm Ibn Muḥammad Ibn Yaḥyā Al-Naysābūrī, who said that he was told by Muḥammad Ibn Al-Musayyib, who said that he was told by Zayd Ibn Akhzam Al-Ṭā'ī, who said that he heard 'Abdullāh Ibn Dāwūd saying:

> "The ḥadīth is strength; whoever desired to attain thereby the life of this world [will have] it and whoever desired to attain thereby the life of the Hereafter [will have] it."[222]

122. We were informed by Al-Ḥasan Ibn 'Alī Ibn Muḥammad Al-Jawharī, who said that he was informed by Muḥammad Ibn Zayd Ibn Marwān Al-Anṣarī, who said that he was told by 'Abdullāh Ibn Al-Ṣaqr, who said that he was told by Zayd Ibn Akhzam, who said that he heard 'Abdullāh Ibn Dāwūd say regarding ḥadīth:

> "Whoever desired to attain thereby the life of this world[will have] it and whoever desired to attain thereby the Hereafter [will have] it."[223]

---

[221] Al-Naḍrawiyyī is a Shaikh whose biography is given in *'Al-Siyār'* (17/553). His Shaikh was most likely Abū Muḥammad Al-Mukhalladī, who is truthful and whose earwitness testimony is correct. A biography is given for him in *'Al-Siyār'* (16/539).

The report was narrated by Al-Dhahabī in *'Al-Siyār'* (13/331) by way of Al-Ḥasan Ibn Aḥmad Al-Adīb, in Tostar, who said that he was told by 'Alī Ibn Al-Ḥusayn Al-Daqīqī, who said: "I heard Sahl Ibn 'Abdullāh saying..." and he quoted the report.

If Al-Adīb is not Al-Mukhalladī, then I do not know him and I have not found any biography for Al-Daqīqī.

[222] Its chain of narrators is authentic.

Muḥammad Ibn Al-Musayyib is Al-Urghiyani Al-Ḥāfiẓ; is biography is given in *'Al-Siyār'* (14/422).

[223] Its chain of narrators is authentic.

Muḥammad Ibn Zayd Ibn Marwān Al-Anṣarī is Muḥammad Ibn Zayd Ibn 'Alī Ibn Ja'far Ibn Marwān Ibn Rashīd and he is trustworthy and reliable; a biography is given for him in *'Tārīkh Baghdād'* (5/289).

123. We were informed by Riḍwān Ibn Muḥammad Al-Daynūrī, who said that he was informed by 'Abdu'l-Raḥmān Ibn Al-Khalīl Al-Qāḍī, who said that he was told by Zayd Ibn Akhzam, who said that he heard 'Abdullāh Ibn Dāwūd say that he heard Sufyān Al-Thawrī saying:

> "Hearing ḥadīth is a strength for the one who desired to attain thereby the life of this world and it is integrity for the one who desired to attain thereby the Hereafter."[224]

Abū'l-Muẓaffar Hannād Ibn Ibrāhīm Al-Nasfī recited to me, saying that Abū Bakr Muḥammad Ibn Najīd Al-Baghawī had recited to him and Aḥmad Ibn Manṣūr Al-Shīrāzī recited to one of them:

"It is upon you to learn ḥadīth, for there is nothing,
Equivalent to it on any side,
I have advised you, for the Religion is advising,
And I do not hide obligatory advices,
We have found in the narrations all *fiqh*,
And rulings, and from all dialects,
Citing the chains of narrators,
And preserving knowledge is the best of benefits,

[224] Its chain of narrators is *shāzz*.

What has been recorded is that it is *mawqūf* to 'Abdullāh Ibn Dāwūd. As for 'Abdullāh Ibn Muḥammad Ibn 'Abdu'l-Raḥmān, his biography has been given by the author in his *'Tārīkh'* (10/117-118) and he transmitted on the authority of Ṣāliḥ Ibn Aḥmad Al-Ḥāfiẓ the words: "I met him, but I was unable to hear (ḥadīth) from him. However, his speech proves that he is truthful." Al-Dhahabī gave a biography for him in *'Al-Siyār'* (14/303) and he described him as, "the Shaikh and truthful scholar."

I say: He contradicted both Muḥammad Ibn Al-Musayyib Al-Ḥāfiẓ and 'Abdullāh Ibn Al-Ṣaqr Al-Sukkarī—and their narration is the more correct one from the saying of 'Abdullāh Ibn Dāwūd. And Allāh knows better.

Whoever learns ḥadīth benefits from a treasure store,
And a bounty, then a sure Religion,
It is upon you to study the narrations that,
Were reported by Mālik, the purest of narrators,
And Shu'bah and Ibn 'Amr and Ibn Zayd,
And Sufyān: the trustworthy from the trustworthy,
And Yaḥyā and Ibn Ḥanbal, the purified,
And Isḥāq Al-Riḍā and Ibn Al-Furāt,
And our stellar Imāms, and did Rashīd,
Speak of the dazzling stars?"

CHAPTER TWENTY-EIGHT

Those of the Caliphs Who Set Aside a Provision from the Treasury for the Companions of Ḥadīth

124. Abū Muḥammad ʿAbdu'l-Raḥmān Ibn ʿUthmān Ibn Al-Qāsim Al-Dimashqī wrote to me and Muḥammad Ibn Yūsuf Al-Naysābūrī [also] told me that from him, saying that he was informed by Abū'l-Maymūn ʿAbdu'l-Raḥmān Ibn ʿAbdullāh Al-Bajlī, who said that he was informed by Abū Zurʿah ʿAbdu'l-Raḥmān Ibn ʿAmr Al-Naṣrī, who said that he was told by Muḥammad Ibn Al-Mubārak, who said that he was told by Ibn ʿAyyāsh, who reported on the authority of Abū Bakr Ibn Abū Maryam that he said that ʿUmar Ibn ʿAbdu'l-ʿAzīz wrote to the Governor of Ḥimṣ, saying:

> "Order for the righteous people from the Treasury something—a stipend—that will suffice them, so that nothing preoccupies them from reading the Qur'ān and

from reciting what they know of ḥadīth."[225]

[225] Its chain of narrators is weak.
In it is Abū Bakr Ibn Abū Maryam and he is weak in ḥadīth.

CHAPTER TWENTY-NINE

Attracting the Young to Hear the Ḥadīth

125. I was informed by Muḥammad Ibn Al-Ḥusayn[226] Ibn Al-Faḍl Al-Qaṭṭān, who said that he was informed by Daʿlaj Ibn Aḥmad, who said that he was informed by Aḥmad Ibn ʿAlī Al-Ubār, who said that he was told by Abū Umayyah Al-Ḥarrānī, who said that he was told by Miskīn Ibn Bukayr, who said:

> "A man passed by Al-Aʿmash and he was relating ḥadīth and he said to him, 'Do you relate ḥadīth to these young ones?' Al-Aʿmash then said:[227] 'These young ones preserve your Religion for you.'"[228]

[226] In manuscript (A) it says "Al-Ḥasan" but the correct version is the one that we have confirmed.

[227] In manuscript (A) it says "Al-Aʿmash said".

[228] Its chain of narrators is weak, but the report is authentic.

Miskīn Ibn Bukayr is weak in memorising and further, Al-Aʿmash has not been mentioned as being one of his Shaikhs. However, his narrations are accepted.

Al-Ramāhurmuzī narrated it in *'Al-Muḥaddith Al-Fāsil'* (#65) by way of Yazīd Ibn Mahrān Abū Khālid, who said that he was told by Abū Bakr Ibn ʿAyyāsh, who said: "We

=

126. I was informed by Al-Ḥasan Ibn Abū Ṭālib, who said that he heard Muḥammad Ibn ʿAbdullāh Ibn Hamām Al-Kūfi saying that he heard ʿAbdullāh Ibn Sulaymān say that he heard Al-Musayyib Ibn Wāḍiḥ, at Tall Mannas[229] saying that when Ibn Al-Mubārak (may Allāh have mercy on him) saw the sons of the companions of ḥadīth with inkwells in their hands, he went up to them and said: "These are the seedlings of the Religion. We were informed that the Messenger of Allāh (ﷺ) said:

> "Allāh will continue to plant seeds in this Religion through which He will strengthen the Religion; they are today your young ones and soon they will be adults after you'."[230]

127. We were informed by Muḥammad Ibn Aḥmad Ibn Rizq, who said that he was told by Jaʿfar Ibn Muḥammad Ibn Naṣīr, who said that he was told by Aḥmad Ibn Muḥammad Ibn Maṣrūq, who said that he was told by Muḥammad Ibn Ḥamīd, who said that he was told by Ibn Al-Mubārak ʿAbdullāh, who said that he was told by Jarīr Ibn Hāzim, who reported on the authority of ʿAbdullāh

=

were with Al-Aʿmash and we were (sitting) around him, writing ḥadīth, then a man passed by him and said: '...' and he quoted the narration. Its chain of narrators is authentic.

[229] Tall Mannas: A village in the Idlīb Governorate of Syria.

[230] Its chain of narrators is weak.

In it is Al-Musayyib Ibn Wāḍiḥ, who is weak and narrates things that are *munkar*.

The last part of it is *marfūʿ* (reported from the Prophet [ﷺ]) and is authentic, due to it having been narrated from the words of ʿUrwah Ibn Al-Zubayr, for it was narrated by Al-Ramāhurmuzī (#68) by way of Ḥammād Ibn Zayd, who said that he heard Hishām Ibn ʿUrwah saying that his Father used to say, "O my son! We were the young of a people and we became their elders. You today are the young of a people and soon you will be their elders and there will be no good in an adult and he will have no knowledge, so it is incumbent upon you to adhere to the Sunnah." And its chain of narrators is authentic.

It was also reported on the authority of a number of narrators mentioned by Al-Sakhāwī in *'Al-Maqaṣid Al-Ḥasanah'* (p. 421/no. 621) and see the following report.

Ibn 'Ubayd Ibn 'Umayr, who said that 'Amr Ibn Al-'Āṣ (*raḍiyAllāhu 'anhu*) stopped by a circle of people from Quraysh and he said:

> "Why have you excluded these young boys? Do not do so. Widen the gathering for them, let them hear the ḥadīth and instruct them in it, for they are the young of a people and soon they will be the elders of a people. You were previously the young of a people and today you are that people's elders."[231]

[231] Its chain of narrators is extremely weak, but the report is authentic up to 'Abdullāh Ibn 'Ubayd Ibn 'Umayr.

In it is Muḥammad Ibn Ḥamīd Al-Rāzī Al-Ḥāfiẓ and he is extremely weak; in fact, Abū Zur'ah declared him to be a liar, though his narrations have been accepted.

It was narrated by Al-Bayhaqī in *'Al-Madkhal'* (#621):

'Affan Ibn Muslim was told it by Jarīr and at the beginning there is an addition.

I say: Its chain of narrators is authentic up to 'Abdullāh Ibn 'Ubayd Ibn 'Umayr and I do not know if it is true that he heard from 'Amr or not. But in my opinion, most likely it is *munqaṭi'*. And Allāh knows better.

CHAPTER THIRTY

Whoever said that it is Incumbent Upon a Man to Force His Son to Hear Ḥadīth

128. I was informed by Muḥammad Ibn Al-Faraj Ibn ʿAlī Al-Bazzār, who said that he was informed by Muḥammad Ibn Zayd Ibn Marwān Al-Kūfī, who said that he was told by ʿAbdullāh Ibn Najiyah.

And we were informed by Ridhwan Ibn Muḥammad Al-Daynūrī, who said that he was informed by ʿUmar Ibn Ibrāhīm Al-Muqrī', in Baghdād, who said that he was told by Al-Baghawī, who both said that they were told by Zayd Ibn Akhzam, who said that he heard ʿAbdullāh Ibn Dāwūd saying:

> "It is incumbent upon a man to force his son to listen to ḥadīth." And he used to say, "The Religion is not [preserved] by *Kalām*, but by traditions."[232]

[232] Its chain of narrators is authentic.

=

129. We were informed by Al-Ḥasan Ibn ʿAlī Al-Jawharī, who said that he was informed by Muḥammad Ibn Zayd Ibn Marwān Al-Anṣarī, who said that he was told by ʿAbdullāh Ibn Al-Ṣaqr, who said that he was told by Zayd Ibn Akhzam, who said that he heard ʿAbdullāh Ibn Dāwūd saying:

> "It is incumbent upon a man to force his son to learn ḥadīth..." and he quoted something similar [to the above].[233]

130. We were informed by ʿAbdu'l-Mālik Ibn Muḥammad Ibn ʿAbdullāh Ibn Bashrān [Al-Muʿaddil][234] Al-Wāʿiẓ, who said that he was informed by Daʿlaj Ibn Aḥmad, who said that he was told by Muḥammad Ibn Nuʿaym, who said that he told heard Abū Ṭālib Zayd Ibn Akhzam say that he heard ʿAbdullāh Ibn Dāwūd saying:

> "Let a man force his son to learn ḥadīth." And he said: "The Religion is not [preserved] by *Kalām*, only by traditions."

And he said regarding ḥadīth, "As for one who desires the life of this world [he will have] the life of this world, while as for one who desires the Hereafter [he will have] the Hereafter."[235]

= ʿAbdullāh Ibn Najiyah is the son of Muḥammad Ibn Najiyah and he is trustworthy and reliable. A biography is given for him in *'Tārīkh Baghdād'* (10/104).

233 Its chain of narrators is authentic.

There was disagreement regarding ʿAbdullāh Ibn Dāwūd.

It was narrated by Abū Nuʿaym in *'Al-Ḥilyah'* (6/365) on the authority of Al-Jaʿābī, who said that he was told by ʿAbdullāh Ibn Bishr Ibn Ṣāliḥ, who said that he was told by Zayd Ibn Akhzam, who said that he heard ʿAbdullāh Ibn Dāwūd say that he heard Al-Thawrī report it.

I say: This is *munkar*, it contains ʿAlī Al-Jaʿābī Al-Ḥāfiẓ, regarding whom there has been talk.

234 This is from manuscript (B).

235 It is not clear to me who Muḥammad Ibn Nuʿaym is. He is not Al-Naṣībī, who is ac- =

CHAPTER THIRTY-ONE

Whoever Trained His Son to Listen to Ḥadīth

131. We were informed by Muḥammad Ibn Aḥmad Ibn Rizq, who said that he was informed by Muḥammad Ibn Al-Ḥasan Ibn Ziyād Al-Naqqāsh, who said that he was told by Muḥammad Ibn Maḥmūd Abū ʻAmr, in Nasā, who said that he was told by Ḥumayd Ibn Zanjawayh, who said that he was told by Ibrāhīm Ibn Muḥammad Al-Firyābī, who said that he was told by Al-Naḍr Ibn Al-Ḥārith, who said that he heard Ibn Ibrāhīm Ibn Adham say that his father said to him:

> "O my son! Learn ḥadīth, for every time you listen to a ḥadīth and memorise it, you will have a *dirham*." He said: "So I learnt ḥadīth due to this."[236]

=

cused (of dishonesty), for he came earlier. Nor is he Al-Ḥākim, who came later. But the tradition is authentic from two previously mentioned sources. And Allāh knows better.

[236] Its chain of narrators is extremely weak.

In it is Muḥammad Ibn Al-Ḥasan Ibn Ziyād Al-Naqqāsh and he is accused of lying. A biography is given for him in Al-Khaṭīb's *'Tārīkh'* (2/201).

CHAPTER THIRTY-TWO

Whoever Censured the Shaikhs Who Did Not Hear Ḥadīth

132. I was informed by Al-Ḥusayn Ibn ʿAlī Al-Ṭanājīrī, who said that he was told by ʿAlī Ibn Ḥibbān[237] Ibn Qays Al-Asadī, in Al-Kūfah, who said that he was told by Ḥāmid Ibn ʿAbdullāh Ibn Al-Ḥasan Al-Ḥalwānī, who said that he was told by Muḥammad Ibn Yūnus, who said that he was told by ʿAbbād Ibn Mūsā Al-Khatlī, who said that he heard Sufyān Al-Thawrī saying, when he saw a Shaikh who did not write ḥadīth:

"May Allāh not reward you with goodness for Islām."[238]

133. We were informed by Abū Muḥammad ʿAbdullāh Ibn Yaḥyā Ibn ʿAbdu'l-Jabbār Al-Sukkarī, who said that he was informed by Sahl Ibn Ismāʿīl, Abū Ṣāliḥ Al-Ṭarsūsī, who said that he was told by Abū Jaʿfar Muḥammad Ibn Muḥammad Ibn ʿUqbah Al-Shaybānī,

[237] In manuscript (B) it says *"Ḥayyān"*.

[238] In it(s chain of narrators) is Muḥammad Ibn Yūnus and it is likely that he is Al-Kadīmī, the liar accused of fabricating ḥadīth. If it is not he, then I do not know who he is.

who said that he was told by Hārūn Ibn Ḥātim Al-Bazzāz Al-Muqrī', who said that he heard 'Uthām Ibn 'Alī, who said that he heard Al-A'mash saying:

> "If you see a Shaikh[239] who does not recite the Qur'ān and does not write ḥadīth, then slap him, for he is one of the Shaikhs of the Moon."

Abū Ṣāliḥ said: "I asked Abū Ja'far, 'What are the Shaikhs of the Moon?' He replied, 'They are Dahris,[240] who gather on the nights of the [full] moon to remind one another of the times of the people and none of them performs ablution well for prayer'."[241]

---

[239] In manuscript (B) it says *"the Shaikh"*.

[240] Dahris: Atheists who believe that only time destroys, hence the term Dahrī (from Arabic word *'dahr'*, meaning 'time').

[241] Its chain of narrators is weak.

In it is Hārūn Ibn Ḥātim; Abū Zur'ah Al-Rāzī and Abū Ḥātim Al-Rāzī heard from him and they rejected narrations from him. Nasā'ī said: "He is not trustworthy," while Al-Daraquṭnī said: "He is weak," and Abū Ḥātim maligned him.

CHAPTER THIRTY-THREE

Whoever said: "It is Incumbent for Ḥadīth to Be Written Until the Time of Death

134. I was informed by 'Ubaydullāh Ibn Abū'l-Fatḥ, who said that he was told by Muḥammad Ibn Al-'Abbās Al-Khazzāz, who said that he was told by 'Abdullāh Ibn Abū Dāwūd, who said that he was told by 'Abdullāh Ibn Khubayq, who reported on the authority of one of his Shaikhs that he said that it was said to Ibn Al-Mubārak,

> "Until when should ḥadīth be written?" He replied, "It may be that I have not yet heard the word from which I will benefit."[242]

135. [The Shaikh said][243] that he was told on the authority of

[242] Its chain of narrators is weak.

This is due to the unknown status of the person who narrated on the authority of Ibn Al-Mubārak. Also, a biography has been given for 'Abdullāh Ibn Khubayq in *'Al-Jarḥ wa'l-Ta'dīl'* (2/2/46) and there is nothing in that to indicate his status.

[243] This is from manuscript (B).

ʿAbdu'l-ʿAzīz Ibn Jaʿfar, who said that he was informed by Aḥmad Ibn Muḥammad Ibn Hārūn Al-Khallāl, who said that he was told by Abū Muḥammad Al-Ṣā'igh, our companion, whose name is Al-Qāsim Ibn Aḥmad, who said that he was told by Yaʿqūb Ibn Al-ʿAbbās Al-Hāshimī, who said that he heard Al-Ḥasan Ibn Manṣūr Al-Jaṣṣāṣ say that he said [to Aḥmad Ibn Ḥanbal]:[244]

> "Until when should a man write ḥadīth?" He replied, "Until he dies."[245]

136. We were informed by Abū'l-Ḥasan Muḥammad Ibn Aḥmad Ibn ʿUmar [Ibn ʿAlī][246] Al-Ṣābūnī, who reported from memory that he heard Abū Bakr Ibn Khazzam saying that he heard ʿAbdullāh Ibn Muḥammad Al-Baghawī saying that he heard Abū ʿAbdullāh Aḥmad Ibn Ḥanbal saying:

> "I will seek knowledge until I enter the grave."[247]

137. I was informed by ʿUbaydullāh Ibn Abū'l-Fatḥ, who said that he was told by Muḥammad Ibn Al-Muẓaffar Al-Ḥāfiẓ, who said that he was told by Aḥmad Ibn Al-Ḥasan Al-Muqrī', who said that he was told by Muḥammad Ibn Yaḥyā Al-Kasaʿī Al-Muqrī', who said that he was told by Abū'l-Ḥārith Al-Layth Ibn Khālid

---

[244] This is from manuscript (B).

[245] Its chain of narrators is weak.

Al-Ḥasan Ibn Manṣūr Al-Jaṣṣāṣ was mentioned by Ibn Abū Yaʿlā in *'Ṭabāqāt Al-Ḥanabilah'* (1/140) and he reported this tradition from him, though he did not report anything that indicated his status.

[246] This is from manuscript (B).

[247] The author's Shaikh is truthful; a biography is given for him in *'Tārīkh Baghdād'*. ʿAbdullāh Ibn Muḥammad Al-Baghawī is the son of Bint Manīʿ, Abū'l-Qāsim, while I do not know who Abū Bakr Ibn Khazzām is; it might be that he is Abū Bakr Al-Shāfiʿī, who is mentioned among Al-Ṣābūnī's Shaikhs and is among those who narrated on Al-Baghawī's authority. But I have not found anyone who states that his name was Ibn Khazzām. And Allāh knows better.

Al-Mirwazī, who said that he was told by Abū Muḥammad Yaḥyā Ibn Al-Mubārak Al-Yazīdī, who reported on the authority of Abū 'Amr Ibn Al-'Alā', who said that Al-Ḥasan Ibn 'Alī was asked about a man who was aged eighty years and was still writing ḥadīth. He replied:

> "If he is [doing that well], then it is good that he lives."[248]

[248] Its chain of narrators is weak.

The author has given biographies for Muḥammad Ibn Yaḥyā Al-Kasa'ī and Al-Layth Ibn Khālid in *'Tārīkh Baghdād'* (3/421 and 13/16) but he mentioned neither praise nor criticism for either of them.

CHAPTER THIRTY-FOUR

[Confirmation][249] That the Companion of Ḥadīth is a Proof

138. We were informed by Abū Bakr Aḥmad Ibn Muḥammad Ibn Ghālib Al-Khawarizmī, who said that it was recited to Al-Qāḍī Abū'l-Ḥasan Muḥammad Ibn Ṣāliḥ Al-Hāshimī while he was listening, that Muḥammad Ibn Muḥammad Ibn ʿUqbah told them that he was told by Muḥammad Ibn Yazīd, who told him that he was told by Wakīʿ, who said that Al-Aʿmash said:

> "Between me and the Companions of Muḥammad (ﷺ) there is a screen which I raise and then I look at them."[250]

139. I was told by ʿUbaydullāh Ibn Abū'l-Fatḥ Al-Fārisī, who said that he was told by Abū'l-Qāsim Al-Ḥasan Ibn Aḥmad Ibn Jaʿfar Al-Ṣūfī, from his memory, who said that he was told by Abū

[249] This is from manuscript (B).

[250] Its chain of narrators is extremely weak.

In it is Muḥammad Ibn Yazīd Abū Hishām Al-Rifāʿī, of whom we have spoken previously.

Bakr Al-Naysābūrī, who said that he heard Al-Mizanī say that he heard Al-Shāfi'ī saying:

> "Whoever learnt the Qur'ān, his rank will be enhanced, whoever studied Islāmic Jurisprudence (*fiqh*), his standing will be ennobled and whoever wrote ḥadīth, his status as a proof will be strengthened."[251]

140. We were informed by Abū'l-Faḍl Aḥmad Ibn Muḥammad [Ibn Ja'far][252] Al-Jawwāz, in Aṣbāhanī, who said that he heard Abū Bakr Ibn Al-Muqrī' saying that he heard Abū 'Urwah Al-Ḥarrānī saying:

> "If the jurist (*faqīh*) is not a companion of ḥadīth, he will be crippled."[253]

[251] This is authentic.

In it is Al-Ḥasan Ibn Aḥmad Ibn Ja'far Al-Ṣūfī; he was mentioned by the author in his *'Tārīkh'* (7/376) and he narrated from him this tradition, but he did not mention criticism or praise of him.

However, he is accepted (by scholars).

I was narrated by Al-Bayhaqī in *'Al-Madkhal'* (#511) by way of Ja'far Ibn Aḥmad Al-Shāmātī, who reported on the authority of Al-Mizanī, in a version that is longer than this wording.

Al-Shāmātī is a Shaikh who has a biography written for him in *'Al-Siyār'* (14/15).

It was also narrated by Abū Nu'aym in *'Al-Ḥilyah'* (9/133) by way of Al-Rabī'.

Its chain of narrators is authentic, aside from Abū Nu'aym's Shaikh, whose name is 'Uthmān Ibn Muḥammad Al-'Uthmānī, who was mentioned Al-Sam'ānī in *'Al-Ansāb'* (4/159) and neither criticism not praise have been reported regarding him.

Then I found that Al-Bayhaqī narrated it from numerous sources on the authority of Al-Mizanī in *'Manaqib Al-Shāfi'ī'* (1/281-282). So the tradition is authentic, Allāh Willing.

[252] This is from manuscript (B).

[253] I have not found any biography for the author's Shaikh.

CHAPTER THIRTY-FIVE

The Description of One Who Seeks to Learn Ḥadīth and the One Who is Self-Denying

141. We were informed by Abū ʿAlī Al-Ḥasan Ibn Al-Ḥusayn Ibn Al-ʿAbbās Al-Naʿālī, who said that he was informed by Aḥmad Ibn ʿAbdullāh Ibn Naṣr Al-Dhāriʿ, who said that he was told by Ṣadaqah Ibn Mūsā, who said that he was told by Al-ʿAbbās Ibn Bakkar, who said that he was told by Abū Bakr Al-Hazlī.

And I was informed by Aḥmad Ibn ʿUmar Ibn ʿAlī Al-Qāḍī, who said that he was informed by Aḥmad Ibn ʿAlī Ibn Muḥammad Ibn Al-Jahm Al-Kāṭib, who said that he was told by Muḥammad Ibn Jarīr Al-Ṭabarī, who said that he was told by ʿAbdu'l- Quddūs Ibn Muḥammad Ibn ʿAbdu'l-Karīm Al-ʿAṭṭār, who said that he was told by ʿAmr Ibn ʿAṣim, who said that he was told by Bakr Ibn Salām Abū'l-Haytham, who said that he was told by Abū Bakr Al-Hazlī, who said that Al-Zuhrī said to him:

> "O Hazli! Do you like ḥadīth?" I replied, "Yes. Is it not the case that the males among men like it, while the females among them dislike it?"[254]

142. We were informed by Al-Ḥasan Ibn Abū Bakr, who said that he was informed by Ja'far Ibn Muḥammad Ibn Aḥmad Ibn Al-Ḥakam Al-Mu'addib, who said that he was told by Muḥammad Ibn Yūnus, who said that he was told by Muḥammad Ibn 'Ubaydillāh Al-'Atbī, who said that he was told by Sa'īd Al-Khassaf, who reported on the authority of Al-Zuhrī, who said:

> "No one among men studies ḥadīth except the males and none of them neglects it except the females among them."

Al-Ḥasan Ibn 'Alī Ibn Muḥammad Al-Balkhī, in Aṣbāhanī, recited to me, saying that Abū'l-Faḍl Al-'Abbās Ibn Muḥammad Al-Khurasanī recited the following verses to him:

"I travelled in earnest pursuit of the foundation of knowledge,
And a man's beauty in this life is seen in ḥadīth,
None seeks knowledge except a mature male,
And none dislikes it except the effeminate,
Do not be enamoured by wealth, for you will leave it,
This world is only inheritances."[255]

---

[254] Its chain of narrators is extremely weak.

In it is Abū Bakr Al-Hazlī and he is *matrūk*. As for Al-'Abbās Ibn Bakkār, Al-Daraquṭnī said of him, "He is a liar," and he was accused by others of fabricating ḥadīth, as is made clear in his biography in *'Al-Lisān'* (3/299).

The tradition was also narrated by Ibn 'Abdu'l-Barr, in *'Jami' Bayān Al-'Ilm wa Faḍlihi'* (2/35) and by Al-Ramāhurmuzi (#33).

[255] Its chain of narrators is talif (bad, broken) and the tradition is weak.

In it is Muḥammad Ibn Yūnus Al-Kadīmī and he is a liar, accused of fabricating ḥadīth.

=

CHAPTER THIRTY-SIX

Evidence of the People of the Sunnah Based on Their Love for the Companions of Ḥadīth

143. We were informed by Abū Manṣūr Muḥammad Ibn ʿAlī Ibn Isḥāq Al-Kātib, who said that he was informed by Muḥammad Ibn Aḥmad Ibn Al-Ḥasan Al-Ṣawwāf, who said that he was told by Jaʿfar Ibn Muḥammad Ibn Al-Ḥasan Al-Qāḍī, who said that he heard Qutaybah Ibn Saʿīd saying:

> "If you see a man who loves the people of ḥadīth, such as Yaḥyā Ibn Saʿīd Al-Qaṭṭān, ʿAbdu'l-Raḥmān Ibn Mahdī, Aḥmad Ibn Ḥanbal and Isḥāq Ibn Rāhawayh," and he mentioned some other people, "then [know that]

=

It was also narrated Al-Ramāhurmuzī (#31) by way of Bishr Ibn Ādam, who said that it was told to him by Muḥammad Ibn ʿUbaydillāh Al-ʿUtbī.

Al-ʿUtbī is Muḥammad Ibn ʿUbaydillah Ibn ʿAmr Ibn Muʿāwiyah, whose biography was given by Al-Khaṭīb in his *'Tārīkh'* (2/324) and he said: "He used to report traditions and narrations regarding good manners and he was among the most literate and erudite of people." He did not report either criticism or praise of him.

he is upon the Sunnah; and whoever opposes this, then [know that] he is an innovator."[256]

'Abdu'l-Ghaffār Ibn Muḥammad Ibn Ja'far Al-Muktib recited to me and he said that 'Umar Ibn Aḥmad Al-Wā'iẓ recited to him, who said that Aḥmad Ibn Kāmil recited to Abū Ja'far Al-Khawwāṣ:

"I went to the land of the innovators,
And it was their rope, but then it broke,
Do they have, O my people, in their innovations,
Any jurist or any Imām that is followed?
Such as Sufyān, the brother of Thawr, who,
Taught the people the ways of piety,
Or Sulaymān, the brother of Al-Taym, who,
Abandoned sleep for the sunrise,
Or the hero of Islām, I mean Aḥmad,
If the reciters fought with him, he would strike,
And he would not fear their scourge if they sought to frighten,
Nay, nor their sword when it gleams."

[256] Its chain of narrators is authentic.
The tradition was reported by Qutaybah Ibn Sa'īd in his book, *'Al-Īmān'*.
The tradition was also narrated by Al-Ṣabūnī in *'I'tiqād Ahl Al-Sunnah'* (#172) and by Al-Lalāka'ī in *'Sharḥ Usūl Al-I'tiqād'* (#59) by way of Qutaybah Ibn Sa'īd.

CHAPTER THIRTY-SEVEN

Evidence Against the Innovators Based on Their Hatred of Ḥadīth and its People

144. I was told by Al-Ḥasan Ibn Abū Ṭālib, who said that he was told by ʿUmar Ibn Aḥmad Al-Wāʿiẓ, who said that he was told by Muḥammad Ibn Hārūn Ibn Ḥumayd, who said that he was told by Hammām, who said that he was told by Baqiyyah, who said that Al-Awzāʿī said to him, "O Abū Aḥmad! What do you say about a people who hate the ḥadīth of their Prophet?" I said: "An evil people." He said:

> "Every innovator whose innovation is contradicted by the ḥadīth of the Messenger of Allāh (ﷺ) hates ḥadīth."[257]

145. We were informed by Abū Nuʿaym Al-Aṣbāhanī, who said that he was informed by Abū ʿAlī Al-Ḥusayn Ibn ʿAlī Al-Ḥāfiẓ [who

[257] Its chain of narrators is ḥasan.

Abū Hammām is Al-Sakūnī, whose name is Al-Walīd Ibn Shujāʿ, who is truthful, but whose memorisation is weak; however, his ḥadīth do not fall below the level of ḥasan except when he contradicts (something proven).

wrote] in his book that he heard Ja'far Ibn Aḥmad Ibn Sinān saying:

> "There is no innovator in the world who does not hate the people of ḥadīth and when a man innovates, the sweetness of ḥadīth is taken from his heart."[258]

146. We were informed by Abū Bakr Aḥmad Ibn Muḥammad Ibn 'Abdu'l-Wāḥid Al-Marūrūzī, who said that he was told by Muḥammad Ibn 'Abdullāh Ibn Muḥammad Al-Ḍhabbī Al-Ḥāfiẓ, in Naysābūr, who said that he heard Abū Naṣr Ibn Salām Al-Faqīh, in Bukhāra, saying:

> "There is nothing more burdensome to the apostates, nor more hateful to them than hearing ḥadīth and reciting it with its *isnād*."[259]

147. And we were also informed by Abū Bakr, who said that he was told by Muḥammad Ibn 'Abdullāh Al-Ḥāfiẓ, who said that he heard Abū'l-Ḥusayn Ibn Aḥmad Al-Hanzalī, who said that he heard Abū Ismā'īl Muḥammad Ibn Ismā'īl Tirmidhī, who said:

> "Aḥmad Ibn Al-Ḥasan Tirmidhī and I were with Abū

---

[258] Its narrators are trustworthy and the tradition is authentic.

—Except that it is *mudallas*; the *mudallis* is Abū Nu'aym Al-Ḥāfiẓ, for he did not hear from Abū 'Alī Al-Ḥāfiẓ, which is why he mentioned him in his book; and the scholars consider that this does not permit an assumption of him having heard directly from him. See also the comments made by Al-Dhahabī in *'Al-Mūqiẓah'* (p. 57). However, it was narrated by Al-Ḥākim in *'Ma'rifah 'Ulūm Al-Ḥadīth'* (p. 5), on the authority of Aḥmad Ibn Sahl.

It was also narrated by way of Al-Ṣābūnī (#165).

[259] The author gave a biography for his Shaikh in his *'Tārīkh'* (5/59) and he said: "He was virtuous, literate and a poet." I say: This pertains to his honesty and not to his accuracy and it is most likely that he is unknown.

However, the tradition was narrated by Al-Ḥākim in *'Ma'rifah 'Ulūm Al-Ḥadīth'* (p. 5), on the authority of Aḥmad Ibn Sahl. Al-Ṣābūnī also narrated it from his source (#165).

'Abdullāh Aḥmad Ibn Ḥanbal and Aḥmad Ibn Al-Ḥasan said to him: 'O Abū 'Abdullāh! Some people in Makkah mentioned the companions of ḥadīth to Abū Qatīah and he said: 'The companions of ḥadīth are bad people.' On hearing this, Abū 'Abdullāh stood up, dusting off his garments and said: '[He is] a *zindīq*, a *zindīq*!' And then he entered his house."[260]

[260] Its chain of narrators is weak.

In it is the author's Shaikh and we have spoken of him previously, however, he was accepted by Al-Ḥākim in *'Al-Ma'rifah'* (p. 5), on the authority of Al-Hanzalī, whose name is Muḥammad Ibn Aḥmad Ibn Tamīm—as it has been written in some manuscripts—and Al-Khaṭīb gave a biography for Abū'l-Ḥusayn Al-Qantarī in his *'Tārīkh'* (1/283) and he mentioned that he is not strict.

The tradition from Al-Ḥākim's source was narrated by Al-Ṣābūnī (#164) and Ibn Abū Ya'lā in *'Al-Ṭabāqāt'* (1/38 and 280).

CHAPTER THIRTY-EIGHT

Whoever Combined Praise of the Companions[261] of Ḥadīth with Censure of the People of Opinion and Wicked *Kalām*

148. We were informed by Abū'l-Ḥusayn 'Alī Ibn Muḥammad Ibn 'Abdullāh Ibn Basharān Al-Mu'addal, who said that he was informed by Ismā'īl Ibn Muḥammad Al-Ṣaffār, who said that he was told byAḥmad Ibn Manṣūr Al-Ramādī, who said that he was told by 'Abdu'l-Razzāq, who said that he was informed by Al-Thawrī, who reported on the authority of Ibn Abjar, who said that Al-Sha'bī said to him:

> "Whatever they transmit to you from the Companions of Muḥammad (ﷺ), accept it and whatever they say to you from their opinion, reject it."[262]

[261] This is from manuscript (B).

[262] Its chain of narrators is authentic.

The tradition was narrated by 'Abdu'l-Razzāq in *'Al-Jam'i'* (11/256) and his version has some additional words. =

149. We were informed by Al-Ḥasan Ibn Abū Bakr, who said that he was told by Ḥāmid Ibn Muḥammad Al-Harawī, who said that he was told by Muḥammad Ibn ʿAbdu'l-Raḥmān Al-Sāmī, who said that he heard ʿAbdullāh Ibn Aḥmad Ibn Shabawayh, who said that he heard his father saying:

> "Whoever desired knowledge of the grave, he should study the traditions and whoever desired knowledge of bread, let him study opinion."[263]

150. We were informed by Muḥammad Ibn Aḥmad Ibn Rizq Al-Bazzār, who said that he was told by Jaʿfar Ibn Muḥammad Ibn Nuṣayr Al-Khaldī, who said that he was told by Muḥammad Ibn ʿAbdullāh Ibn Sulaymān Al-Ḥaḍramī, who said that he was told by ʿAbdullāh Ibn Aḥmad Ibn Shabawayh, who said that he heard Abū Rajā' saying that he heard Yūnus Ibn Sulaymān Al-Saqṭī—who was trustworthy—saying:

> "I studied the matter and found that there was ḥadīth and opinion. In the ḥadīth, I found mention of the Lord, Most High and His Lordship, His Majesty and His Might. I also found mention of His Throne, descriptions of Paradise and Hell, mention of the Prophets and the Messengers, the lawful and the unlawful, encouragement to maintain the ties of kinship and good communities therein. Then I looked at opinion and I

=

And by way of ʿAbdu'l-Razzāq, it was narrated by Abū Nuʿaym in *'Al-Ḥilyah'* (4/319), by Ibn ʿAbdu'l-Barr in *'Jamiʿ Bayān Al-ʿIlm'* (2/32) and by Al-Bayhaqī in *'Al-Madkhal'* (#814).

[263] Its chain of narrators is ḥasan.

A biography was given for ʿAbdullāh Ibn Aḥmad Ibn Shabawayh by Ibn Abū Ḥātim in *'Al-Jarḥ wa'l-Taʿdīl'* (2/2/6) and neither criticism nor praise of him was mentioned. However, Ibn Ḥibbān mentioned him in *'Al-Thiqāt'* (8/366) and he said: "He is straight in matters of ḥadīth." So his narration remains at the level of ḥasan. And Allāh knows better.

found in it deception, perfidy, subterfuge, cutting of the ties of kinship and evil communities therein."[264]

151. We were informed by Al-Ḥusayn Ibn Muḥammad Ibn Al-Ḥasan Al-Mu'addib, who said that he was told by 'Abdu'l-Raḥmān Ibn Muḥammad Al-Idrīsī, who said that he heard Abū Bakr Aḥmad Ibn 'Abdu'l-Raḥmān Al-Nasafī Al-Muqrī', in Samarqand, who said:

> "Our Shaikhs named Abū Bakr Ibn Ismā'īl as Abū Thamūd, because he had been one of the companions of ḥadīth and he became one of the companions of opinion and Allāh, Most High says:
>
> وَأَمَّا ثَمُودُ فَهَدَيْنَٰهُمْ فَٱسْتَحَبُّوا۟ ٱلْعَمَىٰ عَلَى ٱلْهُدَىٰ
>
> "And as for Thamūd, We guided them, but they preferred blindness over guidance."
>
> [*Fuṣṣilat* (41):17]

I was informed by Muḥammad Ibn Abū 'Alī Al-Aṣbāhanī, who said that he was told by Al-Ḥusayn Ibn Muḥammad Ibn Al-Walīd Al-Tustarī, who said that he heard 'Abdullāh Ibn Muḥammad Ibn Sallām saying:

"'Abdah Ibn Ziyād Al-Aṣbāhanī recited to me from his words:

"The Religion of the Prophet is traditions,
The best expedient for a young man is reports,
Do not be misled away from the ḥadīth and its people,
For opinion is night and ḥadīth is day,
And it is possible that a young man might stray
from the path of guidance,

[264] Its chain of narrators is authentic up to Ibn Shabawayh. And it is not clear to me who Abū Raja' is.

And the breaking sun is radiant."[265]

152. We were informed by 'Abdu'l-Mālik Ibn Muḥammad Ibn 'Abdullāh Ibn Bashrān, who said that he was informed by 'Umar Ibn Muḥammad Al-Jumhī, in Makkah, who said that he was told by 'Alī Ibn 'Abdu'l-'Azīz, who said that he was told by Abū'l-Walīd Al-Qurashī, who said that he was told by Muḥammad Ibn 'Abdullāh Ibn Bakkār Al-Qurashī, who said that he was told by Sulaymān Ibn Ja'far, who said that he was told by Muḥammad Ibn Yaḥyā Al-Rab'ī, who said that Ibn Shabramah said that he and Abū Ḥanīfah visited Ja'far Ibn Muḥammad Ibn 'Alī and Ja'far said to him:

> "Fear Allāh and do not compare the Religion with your opinion, for on the morrow, we—and you—will stand before Allāh, Most High and we will say: 'Allāh said...' and 'The Messenger of Allāh (ﷺ) said...' while you and your companions will say: 'We heard...' and 'We considered...' Then Allāh will do as He wills with us and with you."[266]

153. We were informed by Abū Bakr Al-Barqānī, who said that he was told by Ya'qūb Ibn Mūsā Al-Ardabīlī, in Baghdād, who said that he was told by Aḥmad Ibn Ṭāhir Ibn Al-Najm, who said that he was told by Sa'īd Ibn 'Amr Al-Barza'ī, who said that he was told by Abū Zur'ah Al-Rāzī, who reported on the authority of 'Abdullāh Ibn Al-Ḥasan Al-Hasinjānī, who said:

> "I was in Egypt and I saw one of their judges in Al-Masjid Al-Jami' while I was in poor health. I heard the

---

[265] Its chain of narrators is ḥasan up to Al-Nasafī.

A biography was given for the author's Shaikh by Al-Khaṭīb in his *'Tārīkh'* (8/108) and he said: "We wrote about him and there is no objection to him."

[266] Abū'l-Walīd Al-Qurashī is Aḥmad Ibn 'Abdu'l-Raḥmān Ibn Bakkār and 'Alī Ibn 'Abdu'l-'Azīz is Al-Baghawī, Al-Ḥāfiẓ. In the chain there are a number of people whom I do not know.

judge saying, "The people of ḥadīth are *masākīn*[267] and they are not proficient in Islāmic Jurisprudence." So I went towards him and said to him, 'The Companions of the Prophet (ﷺ) differed regarding injuries to men and injuries to women. So what did 'Alī Ibn Abū Ṭālib say? And what did Zayd Ibn Thābit say? And what did 'Abdullāh Ibn Mas'ūd say?' He remained silent, so I said to him, 'You have claimed that the companions of ḥadīth are not proficient in Islāmic Jurisprudence and I am one of the most minor of the companions of ḥadīth and I asked you about this, and you were unable to answer. So how can you disparage a people and claim that they are not proficient in something, when you are not proficient in it yourself?'."[268]

Abū 'Abdullāh Muḥammad Ibn 'Alī Al-Sūrī personally recited to me:

"Say to one who opposes ḥadīth and attacks it,
Censuring its people and those who lay claim to it,
'Is it with knowledge that you say this?
Or is it with ignorance?
For ignorance is the characteristic of the foolish,
Shall those who preserve the Religion be accused,
Of concerning themselves with trifles and of falsification,
When to their words and what they have narrated,
Every scholar and jurist refers?"

154. We were informed by Al-Qāḍi Abū Muḥammad Al-Ḥasan Ibn Al-Ḥusayn Ibn Rāmīn Al-Astarābazī, who said that he was told by Abū Muḥammad 'Abdu'l-Raḥmān Ibn Muḥammad Ibn Ja'far

[267] *Masākīn* (sing. = *miskīn*): poor, miserable, wretched.
[268] Its chain of narrators is authentic.

Al-Jurjānī, who said that he heard Abū Muḥammad ʿAbdullāh Ibn Muḥammad Ibn Ḥamzah Al-Muqrī' saying that one of his Shaikhs related to him on the authority of Hārūn Al-Rashīd that he said:

> "Manliness is found among the companions of ḥadīth, *kalām* among the Mu'tazilites and lies among the Rafidhites."[269]

155. We were informed by Muḥammad Ibn Yūsuf Abū ʿAbdu'l-Raḥmān Al-Naysābūri, who said that he was informed by Al-Ḥusayn Ibn Muḥammad Al-Thaqafī, in Al-Dāmighān, who said that he was told by Al-Faḍl Ibn Al-Faḍl Al-Kindī, who said that he was told by Zakariyya Ibn Yaḥyā Al-Baṣrī, who said that he was told by Muḥammad Ibn Ismāʿīl, who said that he heard Abū Thawr and Al-Ḥusayn[270] Ibn ʿAlī saying that they heard Al-Shāfiʿī saying:

> "My ruling on the companions of *kalām* is that they should be beaten with palm leaves, that they should be borne on camels and carried among the clans and the tribes and it should be called out upon them: 'This is the reward of those who abandon the Book (of Allāh) and the Sunnah and adopted *kalām*'."[271]

Aḥmad Ibn Abū Jaʿfar Al-Qaṭīʿī recited to us, saying that Muḥammad Ibn Al-ʿAbbās Al-Khazzāz recited to him, saying that Abū Muzahim Al-Khāqānī personally recited to him:

"The people of *kalām* and the people of opinion have no,

[269] Its chain of narrators is weak.

This is due to the unknown status of the its narrator on the authority of Hārūn Al-Rashīd from one source and from another source, 'Abdu'l-Raḥmān Ibn Muḥammad has a biography in *'Tārīkh Jurjān'* (p. 258-259), but there is nothing to indicate his status.

[270] In manuscript (A) it says *'Al-Ḥasan'*.

[271] (This is) authentic. =

Knowledge of ḥadīth by which a man may be saved,
If they knew the traditions, they would not turn away,
From them towards anything else, but they are ignorant."

Abū 'Alī Al-Ḥasan Ibn Shihāb Al-'Akbarī recited to us, saying that Abū 'Āmir Al-Ḥasan Ibn Muḥammad Al-Nasawī recited to him, that Abū Zayd, the jurist to some scholars in Shāsh recited to him:

"All *kalām* aside from the Qur'ān is atheism,
Except for ḥadīth, understanding of the Religion,
And knowledge preceded by *"haddathana"*
(we were told) should be followed,
Anything aside from that is the whispering of Satan."

=

Muḥammad Ibn Ismā'īl is Abū Ismā'īl Tirmidhī Al-Ḥāfiẓ, Abū Thawr is Ibrāhīm Ibn Khālid and Ḥusayn is Ibn 'Alī Al-Karabīsī.

The tradition was narrated by Al-Bayhaqī in *'Manāqib Al-Shāfi'ī'* (1/462), by Ibn Ḥajr in *'Tāwalī Al-Tā'sīs'* (p. 111) from another source on the authority Al-Sajī.

CHAPTER THIRTY-NINE

What Has Been Narrated Regarding the Reward for Memorising Ḥadīth and Conveying It

156. We were informed by Muḥammad Ibn Aḥmad Ibn Rizq Al-Bazzāz, who said that he was informed by Al-Qāḍi Abū Naṣr Ibn Muḥammad Al-Zaʿfarānī Al-Bukhārī, who said that he was told by Al-Ḥusayn Ibn Muḥammad Ibn Mūsā Al-Qummī, who said that he was told by ʿAbdu'l-Raḥīm Ibn Ḥabīb, who said that he was told by Ismāʿīl Ibn Yaḥyā Ibn ʿUbaydillāh Al-Tamīmī,[272] who said that he was told by Sufyān, who reported on the authority of Layth, who reported on the authority of Ṭāwūs, who reported on the authority Ibn ʿAbbās (*raḍiyAllāhu ʿanhumā*) that he said that the Messenger of Allāh (ﷺ) said:

> "Whoever conveyed a ḥadīth to my *ummah* in order to establish a Sunnah thereby or to discredit an innovation thereby, he will have Paradise."[273]

[272] This is what it says in manuscript (A); in manuscript (B) it says *'Al-Taymī'*.
[273] (This is) fabricated. =

157. We were informed by Muḥammad Ibn Al-Ḥusayn Ibn Al-Faḍl Al-Qaṭṭān and Ghaylān Ibn Muḥammad Ibn Ibrāhīm Al-Samsār, who both said that they were told by Muḥammad Ibn ʿAbdullāh Ibn Ibrāhim Al-Shāfiʿi, who said that he was told by Muḥammad Ibn Khālid Ibn Yazīd Al-Barzāʿī, in Makkah, who said that he was told by ʿAṭiyyah Ibn Baqiyyah, who said that he was told by his father, who said that he was told by Ḥamzah Ibn Ḥassān, who said that he was told by a Shaikh whose agnomen was Abū'l-Ḥasan, who reported on the authority of Nafīʿ Ibn Al-Ḥārith, who reported on the authority of Al-Barā' Ibn ʿĀzib (*raḍiyAllāhu ʿanhu*), who reported that the Messenger of Allāh (ﷺ) said:

> "Whoever learnt two ḥadīths by which he benefits himself, or teaches them to someone else and that person benefits from them, it will be better for him than worshipping for sixty years."[274]

=

Its weakness is Ismāʿīl Ibn Yaḥyā Ibn ʿUbaydillah Al-Taymī, who is described as talif (bad, broken, damaged). Ṣāliḥ Jazarah said: "He used to fabricate ḥadīth." He was described as weak by Ibn ʿAdiyy, while Al-Azdī said: "He is one of the pillars of untruthfulness."

Layth is Ibn Abū Sulaym, who is weak in ḥadīth.

The ḥadīth was also narrated by Abū Nuʿaym in *'Al-Ḥilyah'* (10/44) by way of ʿAbdu'l-Raḥīm Ibn Ḥabīb and he is similar to his Shaikh with regard to his weakness. Ibn Maʿīn said: "He is nothing," while Ibn Ḥibbān said: "It is likely that he fabricated more than five hundred aḥadīth that he (falsely) attributed to the Messenger of Allāh (ﷺ)."

He was reported from by someone similar to him and he is Al-ʿAlā' Ibn Maslamah, who reported on the authority of Ismāʿīl Al-Taymī.

It was narrated by Ibn ʿĀsakir in *'Al-Arbaʿīn'* (#7).

As for Al-ʿAlaʿ Ibn Maslamah, Ibn Ṭāhir said: "He used to fabricate ḥadīth." Ibn Ḥibbān said: "He narrates fabrications on the authority of trustworthy narrators."

[274] (This is) fabricated.

The person accused (of untruthfulness) is Nafīʿ Ibn Al-Ḥārith, Abū Dāwūd Al-Nakhāʿī Al-A'mā (the blind man); it is not correct that he heard from Al-Barā' and he was declared a liar by Qatādah. Ibn Maʿīn said: "He is nothing," while Abū Zurʿah said: "He was nothing." And Al-Daraquṭnī said: "(He is) abandoned." As for Abū'l-Ḥasan, he is unknown, while ʿAṭiyyah Ibn Baqiyyah was careless, though truthful.

The ḥadīth was also narrated by Abū Nuʿaym in *'Akhbār Aṣbāhanī'* (2/126).

158. We were informed by Abū Nuʿaym Aḥmad Ibn ʿAbdullāh Al-Ḥāfiẓ, who said that he was told by Abū Muḥammad Ibn Ḥayyān, who said that he was told by Isḥāq Ibn Ibrāhim Ibn Jamīl, who said that he was told by Abū Hishām Al-Rifāʿī, who said that he was told by Ibn Yaman, who said that he was told by a Shaikh, who reported on the authority of Abū Jaʿfar Muḥammad Ibn ʿAlī, who said that the Messenger of Allāh (ﷺ) said:

> "Hasten to seek knowledge, for a ḥadīth on the authority of a truthful person is better than the earth and all of the gold and silver that it contains."[275]

[275] (This is) *munkar.*

There are weaknesses in its chain of narrators.

The first is *iʿḍāl* (having two or more narrators missing from its chain). Abū Jaʿfar is Al-Bāqir, Muḥammad Ibn ʿAlī Ibn Al-Ḥusayn Ibn ʿAlī Ibn Abū Ṭālib and his narration from the Prophet (ﷺ) is most likely *muʿḍahl.*

The second is the unknown status of Ibn Yaman's Shaikh.

The third is the weakness of Abū Hishām Al-Rifāʿī, of whom we spoke previously.

The fourth is the leniency of Isḥāq Ibn Ibrāhīm Ibn Jamīl, whose biography was given by Abū Al-Shaikh in *'Ṭabāqāt Aṣbāhanī'* (4/262) and he said: "He was truthful, but reported many *gharīb* narrations.

It is likely that the ḥadīth is fabricated.

It was narrated in a longer form than this with a different chain of narrators, which was mentioned by Al-Albānī (may Allāh have mercy on him) in *'Al-Ḍaʿīfah'* (2/337).

CHAPTER FORTY

Whoever said that Seeking Ḥadīth is Better than[276] Acts of Worship

159. I was informed by Al-Qāḍī Abū Naṣr Aḥmad Ibn Al-Ḥusayn Al-Daynūrī, who said that he was informed by Abū Bakr Aḥmad Ibn Muḥammad Ibn Isḥāq Al-Sunnī, who said that he was told by Aḥmad Ibn Muḥammad Ibn Sallām[277] Al-Kātib, who said that he was told by Ja'far Ibn 'Amir, who said that he heard Isḥāq Ibn Al-Bahlūl, who said that he heard Wakī' saying that he heard Sufyān saying:

> "I do not know of any action on the face of the earth that it better than seeking ḥadīth for one who desires Allāh's Countenance."[278]

[276] In manuscript (B) it says: "...is one of the best acts of worship".

[277] In manuscript (B) it says *"Salāmah"*.

[278] Its chain of narrators is extremely weak, but the report is authentic.

In it is Ja'far Ibn 'Amir, of whom Al-Dhahabī said in *'Al-Mīzān'*, "It was reported on the authority of Aḥmad Ibn 'Ammar, the brother of Hisham with an untruthful report; he was accused (of lying) by Ibn Al-Jawzī." Isḥāq Ibn Al-Bahlūl is truthful; he has a biography in *'Al-Jarḥ wa'l-Ta'dīl'* (1/1/214).

It was narrated by Al-Bayhaqī in *'Al-Madkhal'* (#470) by way of Abū Mu'āwiyah Al- =

160. We were informed by Al-Ḥasan Ibn ʿAlī Ibn Al-Tamīmī, who said that he was informed by Aḥmad Ibn Jaʿfar Ibn Ḥamdān, who said that he was told by ʿAbdullāh Ibn Aḥmad Ibn Ḥanbal, who said that he heard ʿAlī Ibn Ḥakīm saying that he heard Wakīʿ saying that Sufyān said:

> "There is nothing more frightening to me than ḥadīth and there is nothing better than it for one who desires what is with Allāh, the Almighty, the All-Powerful."[279]

161. We were informed by Abū Bakr Muḥammad Ibn ʿAbdullāh Ibn Abān Al-Hītī Al-Taghlibī, who said that he was told by Aḥmad Ibn Salmān Al-Najjād, who said that he was told by Abū Jaʿfar Al-Fasawī, who said that he was told by Abū Bakr Al-Azraq, who said that he was told by Huyay Ibn Ḥātim, who said that he was told by Wakīʿ, who said that he heard Sufyān Al-Thawrī saying:

> "I know of nothing better than it—ḥadīth—for one who desires Allāh thereby." And he said: "Verily, the people are in need of it with regard to their food and their drink."[280]

=

Ghulabī, who said that he was told by Wakīʿ Ibn Al-Jarrāḥ, who said he heard Sufyān Al-Thawrī saying.. and he quoted something similar. Its chain of narrators is authentic.

He also narrated it from another source (#471) on the authority of Nuʿaym Ibn Ḥammād, who reported on the authority of Ibn Al-Mubārak from his own words. This was narrated by Al-Bayhaqī (#472) and it is the more authentic.

It was also narrated by Abū Nuʿaym in *ʿAl-Ḥilyah'* (6/366) by way of Muḥammad Ibn Yūsuf Al-Firyābī, who reported something similar on the authority of Al-Thawrī, and its chain of narrators is authentic. See what follows it.

[279] Its chain of narrators is authentic.

ʿAlī Ibn Ḥakīm is Al-Awaddī, who is trustworthy and is one of the men in *ʿAl-Tahẓīb'*.

The tradition was narrated by Al-Ramāhurmuzī (p. 177) who said that he was told by ʿAbdullāh Ibn Ghannām Al-Kūfī, who said that he was told by ʿAlī Ibn Ḥakīm Al-Awaddī...

[280] Its chain of narrators is weak, but the tradition is authentic.

162. I was told by 'Abdu'l-'Azīz Ibn Abū'l-Ḥasan Al-Qirmīsīnī, in his own words, that he was told by Aḥmad Ibn 'Abdullāh Ibn Al-Khiḍr Al-Muqrī', who said that he was told by 'Alī Ibn Muḥammad Ibn Sa'īd, who said that he was told by Abū Ya'lā Al-Mawsilī, who said that he heard Ibrāhīm Ibn Sa'īd Al-Jawharī, who said that he heard Wakī' Ibn Al-Jarrāḥ saying:

> "Allāh is not worshipped by anything better than ḥadīth."[281]

163. I was informed by Al-Ḥasan Ibn 'Alī Ibn Muḥammad Al-Jawharī, who said that he was told by Muḥammad Ibn Al-'Abbās Al-Khazzāz, who said that he was told by Abū'l-Faḍl Al-Sandalī, who said that he was informed by Ya'qūb Ibn Bakhtan Al-Qazzāz, who said that he heard Bishr Ibn Al-Ḥārith saying:

> "I do not know of any deed on the face of the earth better than seeking knowledge and ḥadīth for one who fears Allāh and whose intention is good. As for me, I ask Allāh's Forgiveness for every step I have taken therein."[282]

In it is the author's Shaikh, whose biography was given in his *'Tārīkh'* (5/475); he said: "The principles of Abū Bakr Al-Hītī are weak and he made many mistakes." However, he has a blameless record and was righteous, poor and without property, well known for his goodness. He was known to be forgetful, in spite of his absorption with ḥadīth knowledge. He reported to us on the authority of his Shaikh's Shaikh and he is unknown." See the previous narration.

[281] Its chain of narrators is authentic.

The author's Shaikh is 'Abdu'l-'Azīz Ibn 'Alī Ibn Aḥmad Al-Azjī, who was named thus in the biography of Aḥmad Ibn 'Abdullāh Ibn Al-Khiḍr in *'Al-Tārīkh'*. Al-Khaṭīb said (10/468), "We wrote of him and he was truthful and authored many books."

[282] Its chain of narrators is authentic.

Abū'l-Faḍl Al-Sandalī is Ja'far Ibn Muḥammad, who is a native of Baghdād and is trustworthy, as is Ya'qūb Ibn Bakhtān.

CHAPTER FORTY-ONE

Whoever said that Narrating Ḥadīth is Better than *Tasbīḥ*[283]

164. We were informed by Al-Ḥusayn Ibn Al-Ḥasan Ibn Muḥammad Al-Makhzūmī, Muḥammad Ibn Aḥmad Ibn Rizq and Al-Ḥasan Ibn Abū Bakr [Al-Ḥasan said: *'Akhbarana'*—we were informed], while the other two said: *'Ḥaddathana'*—we were told] by 'Uthmān Ibn Aḥmad Al-Daqqāq, who said that he was told by Aḥmad Ibn Bishr Al-Marthadī, who said that he was told by Hārūn Ibn Sufyān Al-Mustamilī, who said that he was told by Zakariyyā Ibn 'Adiyy, who said that he heard Wakī' saying:

> "Were it not that ḥadīth is better than in my view than *tasbīh*, I would not have related ḥadīth."[284]

[283] *Tasbīḥ*: Glorifying Allāh by saying: *'Subḥān Allāh'*.

[284] In it is Hārūn Ibn Sufyān Al-Mustamili, known as Makhalah. His biography is given by Al-Khaṭīb in his *'Tārīkh'* (14/25), but he did not report anything that would prove his status, aside from the words of Abū Nu'aym to him: "O Hārūn! Find for yourself some work other than ḥadīth, for it seems as if you report ḥadīth that are rubbish." It would appear that this is *tajrīḥ* (criticism)—and Allāh knows better.

Similar narrations have been authentically reported; see no. #167.

CHAPTER FORTY-TWO

Whoever said that Relating Ḥadīth is of the Same Status as Studying the Qur'ān

165. We were informed by ʿAlī Ibn Muḥammad Ibn ʿAbdullāh Ibn Bashrān, who said that he was informed by Ismāʿīl Ibn Muḥammad Al-Ṣaffār, who said that he was told by Saʿdān Ibn Naṣr, who said that he was told by Muʿādh Ibn Muʿādh, who said that he was told by Sulaymān Al-Taymī, who said that he was with Abū Mujliz, who was relating aḥadīth to them, when a man said: "Perhaps if you were to recite a *Sūrah*..." Abū Muljiz replied:

> "That in which we are engaged is of no less importance[285] to me than reciting a *Sūrah* from the Qur'ān."[286]

---

[285] In manuscript (A) it says *"no less disliked..."*

[286] Its chain of narrators is authentic.

The tradition was narrated by Al-Ramāhurmuzī (#29) by way of Al-Muʿtamir Ibn Sulaymān, who reported something similar on the authority of his father, though there is something added at the start.

CHAPTER FORTY-THREE

Whoever said that relating Ḥadīth has the Same Reward as Prayer

166. We were told by Abū Ṭālib Yaḥyā Ibn 'Alī Ibn Al-Ṭayyib Al-Daskari, in his words at Ḥalwān, that he said that he was informed by Abū Bakr Ibn Al-Muqrī', in Aṣbāhanī, who said that he was told by Ibrāhim Ibn Muḥammad Ibn Al-Ḥasan, the Imām of the Congregational Masjid at Aṣbāhanī, who said that he was told by Ibrāhīm Ibn Sa'īd, who said that he was told by Rūḥ Ibn 'Ubādah, who said that he was told by Dāwūd Ibn Qays, who reported on the authority of Muḥammad Ibn 'Amr Ibn 'Aṭā' that he said that Mūsā Ibn Yasar was with him, relating ḥadīth and Ibn 'Amr said to him:

> "When you have finished with your ḥadīth, make *taslīm*, for you are in prayer."[287]

[287] The men in the chain of narrators are trustworthy except for the author's Shaikh, for whom I have not found any biography.

As for Ibrāhīm Ibn Muḥammad Ibn Al-Ḥasan, he is Ibn Mutawayh; a biography is given for him in *'Al-Siyār'* (14/142) and he is truthful and a Ḥāfiẓ.

CHAPTER FORTY-FOUR

Whoever said that relating Ḥadīth is Better than Voluntary Prayer

167. We were informed by Abū'l-Fatḥ Hilāl Ibn Muḥammad Ibn Ja'far Al-Ḥaffār, who said that he was told by 'Alī Ibn Muḥammad Ibn Aḥmad Al-Miṣrī, who said that he heard Abū Bakr Ibn 'Alī saying that he heard Yūsuf Al-Qaṭṭān saying that he heard Wakī' saying:

> "If I knew that (voluntary) prayer was better than ḥadīth, I would not relate ḥadīth."[288]

168. Our Shaikh, Abū'l-Ḥasan 'Alī Ibn Yaḥyā Ibn Ja'far Al-Aṣbāhanī stated that 'Abdullāh Ibn Al-Ḥasan Ibn Bandar told them that he heard 'Abdullāh Ibn Muḥammad Ibn Muḥammad Ibn Al-Nu'mān saying that he heard his father saying Al-Qa'nabī saying:

---

[288] Its chain of narrators is authentic.

It is most likely in my view, that Abū Bakr Ibn 'Alīs Aḥmad Ibn 'Alī Ibn Sa'īd Al-Mirwazī, who is the trustworthy Ḥāfiẓ, for he narrated from the people of Yūsuf Ibn Qaṭṭān's generation. And Allāh knows better.

> "If I knew that (voluntary) prayer was better than it, I would not relate ḥadīth."[289]

169. Aḥmad Ibn Muḥammad Ibn Al-Ṣalt Al-Ahwāzī imparted to us that he was told by 'Abdu'l-Ghāfir Ibn Salāmah Al-Ḥimṣī, who said that he was told by Abū Thawbān Yazdād[290] Ibn Jamīl Al-Bahrānī, who said that he asked 'Umar Ibn Suhayl—man from among the companions of ḥadīth—Al-Mu'āfā Ibn 'Imrān:

> "O Abū 'Imrān! What is most beloved to you? That I pray, or that I write ḥadīth?" He said: "Writing a single ḥadīth is more beloved to me than standing at night in prayer."[291]

Someone else said of 'Abdu'l-Ghafir that he reported from 'Amr Ibn Ismā'īl, rather than 'Umar Ibn Suhayl. [This is what Shaikh Abū Bakr—may Allāh have Mercy on him—said to us].[292]

170. We were informed by Abū 'Uthmān Sa'īd Ibn Al-'Abbās Ibn Muḥammad Al-Qurashī Al-Harawī, who said that he heard Abū'l-'Abbās 'Abdullāh Ibn Muḥammad Ibn Ja'far, in Būshanj [Pushang], saying that he heard Abū Muḥammad 'Abdu'l-Raḥmān Ibn Muḥammad Ibn Idrīs saying:

---

[289] Its chain of narrators is extremely weak.

In it is Muḥammad Ibn Muḥammad Ibn Al-Nu'mān, who is Shibl Al-Bahilī; Al-Daraquṭnī maligned him and accused him (of untruthfulness). See his biography in *'Al-Lisān'* (1/24).

[290] This is how it is written in manuscript (A) and manuscript (B). See the comment on the sanad.

[291] Its chain of narrators is weak.

In it is Yazdad (or it was said: Izdad). And he is Ibn Jamīl Ibn Mūsā (or it was said: Ibn Mūsā Ibn Jamīl). A biography is given for him by Al-Khaṭīb with both names in two places (7/49 and 14/335), but neither criticism nor praise was mentioned for him.

The tradition was also narrated by Ibn 'Abdu'l-Barr in *'Al-Jami'* (1/24).

[292] This is from manuscript (B).

"I went out to Ailah, to Muḥammad Ibn 'Azīz Al-Ailī and my father and Abū Zur'ah had written a letter to him for me—as recommendations—and Muḥammad Ibn 'Azīz began to recite to me on a Friday and he did not pray that day except two rak'ahs for the Friday prayer and four rak'ahs for the 'Aṣr prayer. And he recited ḥadīth to me, based on the belief that reciting ḥadīth is better than voluntary prayer."[293]

[293] The author cited a biography for his Shaikh, in his *'Tārīkh'* (9/113) and he declared him to be trustworthy. Al-Dhahabī mentioned in *'Al-Siyār'* (17/553) that he was alone in narrating on the authority of a group, while as for 'Abdullāh Ibn Muḥammad Ibn Ja'far, I have not found a biography for him and it is likely that he was alone in narrating from them.

CHAPTER FORTY-FIVE

Whoever said that relating Ḥadīth is Better than Voluntary Fasting

171. We were informed by 'Abdu'l-Ghaffār Ibn Abū Al-Ṭayyib Al-Mu'addib, who said that he was told by 'Umar Ibn Aḥmad Ibn 'Uthmān, who said that he was told by Muḥammad Ibn Aḥmad Ibn Abū Al-Thalj, who said that he was told by his grandfather, who said that he asked Aḥmad Ibn Ḥanbal, "O Abū 'Abdullāh! Which of the two is better, that a man writes ḥadīth or that he fasts and prays?" He replied:

> '[It is better that] he writes ḥadīth.' I said: 'How can you prefer writing ḥadīth to fasting and prayer?' He replied, 'So that none may say, 'I saw a people doing something and so I followed them'."[294]

---

[294] Its chain of narrators is weak.

'Abdu'l-Ghaffār Ibn Abū Al-Ṭayyib Al-Mu'addib is Ibn Muḥammad Ibn Ja'far Ibn Zayd. Al-Khaṭīb said (11/116), "I wrote on his authority and I heard Abū 'Abdullāh Al-Sūrī maligning him and saying things about him that necessitate him being declared weak."

As for Ibn Abū Al-Thalj and his grandfather, they are both trustworthy. A biography is given for the former in *'Tārīkh Baghdād'* (1/338), while the latter is one of the men of *'Al-Tahẓīb'*.

Shaikh Abū Bakr Al-Ḥāfiẓ said[295]:

> "Studying ḥadīth in this time is better than all kinds of acts of obedience, due to the prevailing ignorance of the Sunan and the need to learn them, and the appearance of innovations and the rise of its people."

172. We were informed by Abū Ṭāhir Al-'Alawī Muḥammad Ibn Al-Ḥasan Ibn Zayd Ibn Al-Ḥasan Ibn Aḥmad Ibn 'Isā Ibn Yaḥyā Ibn Al-Ḥusayn Ibn Zayd Ibn 'Alī [Ibn Al-Ḥusayn][296] Ibn 'Alī Ibn Abū Ṭālib, in Al-Rai, who said that he was told by Abū'l-Ḥasan Aḥmad Ibn Muḥammad Ibn Sahl Al-Bazzār, who said that he was told by Muḥammad Ibn Ayyūb, who said that he was informed by 'Abdullāh Ibn 'Umar, who said that he heard Yaḥyā Ibn Yamān saying that he heard Yaḥyā Ibn Yamān saying:

> "There is nothing better than studying ḥadīth today." We said: "O Abū 'Abdullāh! They study it without intention." He replied, "Their studying of it is [their] intention."[297]

[295] In manuscript (B) it says: *"Al-Khaṭīb said..."*

[296] This is confirmed in manuscript (B).

[297] Its chain of narrators is weak.

If Muḥammad Ibn Ayyūb is Ibn Hishām Al-Rāzī—and that is most likely, in my opinion—then he was declared to be a liar by Abū Ḥātim, while Abū'l-Ḥusayn Ibn Babawayh in *'Tārīkh Al-Rai'* and the author of *'Al-Lisān'* (5/99) said that he is weak. There was talk about him and it was said that he was a Shi'ite.

Yaḥyā Ibn Yamān is weak, especially when he narrates on the authority of Al-Thawri.

It has another source on the authority of Ibn Yamān.

It was narrated by the author in *'Al-Jami''* (#772) by way of Surayj Ibn Yūnus, who said that he was told by Yaḥyā...

And Ibn Yamān was accepted.

The author narrated it in *'Al-Jami''* (#771) by way of Ibn Mahdi and by Al-Ramāhurmuzī (#40), by way of 'Abdu'l-Ṣamad Ibn Ḥassān, both of whom narrated on the authority of Al-Thawrī.

CHAPTER FORTY-SIX

Whoever Sought a Cure by Reciting Ḥadīth

173. We were informed by Aḥmad Ibn Muḥammad Ibn Ghālib Al-Faqīh, who said that Abū'l-Ḥasan Al-Dāraquṭnī said to him that Muḥammad Ibn Mukhallad said to him:

> "Whenever Al-Ramādī complained of anything, he would say, 'Bring the companions of ḥadīth,' and when they came to him, he would say: 'Recite ḥadīth to me'."[298]

[298] Its chain of narrators is authentic.
The author's Shaikh is Al-Barqānī Al-Ḥāfiẓ—may Allāh have mercy on him.

CHAPTER FORTY-SEVEN

A Report of 'Umar Ibn Al-Khaṭṭāb's (*raḍiyAllāhu 'anhu*) Prohibition of Reciting Ḥadīth and the Explanation of the Sense and Meaning of That

174. We were told by[299] Abū Sa'd Aḥmad Ibn Muḥammad Ibn Aḥmad Al-Malīnī, who said that he was informed by 'Abdullāh Ibn 'Adiyy Al-Ḥāfiẓ, who said that he was informed by Aḥmad Ibn Shu'ayb Nasā'ī, who said that he was told by Isḥāq Ibn Mūsā Al-Anṣārī.

And we were told by Abū Sa'd also that he said that he was informed by 'Abdullāh Ibn 'Adiyy, who said that he was told by Aḥmad Ibn Al-Ḥusayn Ibn Naṣr Al-Ḥadhā', Muḥammad Ibn Ṣāliḥ Ibn Zurayḥ, Al-Ḥusayn Ibn 'Abdullāh Ibn Yazīd and Ismā'īl Ibn Ḥammād Abū Al-Naḍr, who said that they were told by Isḥāq Ibn Mūsā...

[299] In manuscript (B) it says: *"informed by"*.

And we were informed by 'Alī Ibn Aḥmad Al-Razzāz, who said that he was informed by 'Alī Ibn Ibrāhīm Ibn Ḥammād Ibn Isḥāq Al-Qāḍī, who said that he was told by Ibn Najiyah, who said that he was told by Abū Mūsā Al-Anṣārī—whose name is Isḥāq Ibn Mūsā—who said that he was told by Ma'an Ibn 'Isā, who said that he was told by Mālik Ibn Anas, who reported on the authority of 'Abdullāh Ibn Idrīs, who reported on the authority of Shu'bah, who reported on the authority of Sa'd Ibn Ibrāhīm, who reported on the authority of his father that he said:

> "'Umar Ibn Al-Khaṭṭāb (*raḍiyAllāhu 'anhu*) sent messages to 'Abdullāh Ibn Mas'ūd, Abū'l-Dardā' and Abū Mas'ūd Al-Anṣārī (*raḍiyAllāhu 'anhu*), saying: "What is this ḥadīth that you narrate so much from the Messenger of Allāh (ﷺ)?" Then he confined them to Al-Madīnah until he was martyred."[300]

[Their wording is the same].[301]

Shaikh Abū Bakr said: "Mālik did not narrate any ḥadīth on the authority of 'Abdullāh Ibn Idrīs except this one and he did not report on the authority of the people of Al-Kūfah except from him,[302] because he followed his opinion that *nabīth* is unlawful and he is not in Ma'an's *'Muwaṭṭa'*."

---

[300] This is authentic.

Sa'd Ibn Ibrāhīm is Ibn 'Abdu'l-Raḥmān Ibn 'Awf.

Ibn Kathīr reported another source for it in *'Musnad Al-Fārūq'* (2/624) from the narration of Muḥammad Ibn Isḥāq, who reported on the authority of Ṣāliḥ Ibn Ibrāhīm Ibn 'Abdu'l-Raḥmān Ibn 'Awf, who reported it on the authority of his father.

The saying of the narrator: "He confined them in Al-Madīnah" means that he ordered them to live with him in Al-Madīnah.

[301] This is from manuscript (A).

[302] This is from manuscript (B), while in manuscript (A) it says: *"nor from him"*.

175. We were informed by 'Abdu'l-Mālik Ibn Muḥammad Ibn 'Abdullāh Ibn Bashrān Al-Wā'iẓ, who said that he was informed by 'Umar Ibn Muḥammad Al-Jamhī, in Makkah, who said that he was told by 'Alī Ibn 'Abdu'l-'Azīz, who said that he was told by Sa'īd Ibn Manṣūr, who said that he was told by Khālid Ibn 'Abdullāh, who reported on the authority of Bayān, who reported on the authority of 'Amir Al-Sha'bī, who reported on the authority of Qarzah Ibn Ka'b that he said:

> "We went out and we accompanied 'Umar to Ṣirār, then he called for water and performed ablution, after which he said to us, 'Do you know why I came out with you?' We said: 'You wanted to accompany us and honour us.' He replied, 'In addition to that, I came out to fulfil a need; you are going to a town where the sound of the Qur'ān resonates like the sound of bees. Do not repel those people with aḥādīth from the Messenger of Allāh (ﷺ) and I will be your supporter." Qarzah said: "After that, I did not narrate any ḥadīth from the Messenger of Allāh (ﷺ) again."[303]

[The Shaikh said][304]: "If someone asked, 'What was the reason for 'Umar's disapproval of the Companions' narrating from the Messenger of Allāh (ﷺ) and his sternness towards them for doing that?' It would be said to him, "Umar (*raḍiyAllāhu 'anhu*) only did that because of his concern for the Religion and his desire to protect the Muslims, because he feared that they would refrain

[303] The men of the *isnād* are trustworthy, aside from Al-Jamhī, for whom I have not found any biography.

The report was narrated by Ibn Mājah (#28) by way of Mujālid, who reported it on the authority of Al-Sha'bī.

Ibn Kathīr said in *'Musnad Al-Fārūq'* (2/624), "Its chain of narrators is good."

I say: Rather, it is weak, for Mujālid is Ibn Sa'īd and he is weak in ḥadīth.

[304] This is from manuscript (B).

from performing [good] deeds and rely on the apparent meaning of traditions, when the apparent meaningsof aḥadīth are not always the correct ones and not everyone who hears a ḥadīth understands it. It is possible that a ḥadīth might be reported by someone and the meaning and explanation might be derived from it by someone else, so he feared that the ḥadīth might be conveyed with some other meaning, or be taken literally when the apparent meaning was not the intended one. An example of this would be the following ḥadīth:

176. We were informed by Aḥmad Ibn Muḥammad Ibn Ghālib Al-Khawārizmī, who said that he recited to Abū'l-'Abbās Ibn Ḥamdān, saying that Al-Ḥusayn Ibn Muḥammad Ibn Ziyād Al-Qabbānī told them that Abū Bakr Ibn Abū Shaybah told him that Al-Khawārizmī said that he recited to Abū Bakr Al-Ismā'īlī, who informed him that Abū Ya'lā—Al-Mawsilī—informed him that Khalaf Ibn Hishām was told by Abū'l-Ahwāṣ, who reported on the authority of Abū Isḥāq, who reported on the authority of 'Amr Ibn Maymūn Al-Awaddī, who reported on the authority of Mu'ādh (*raḍiyAllāhu 'anhu*) that he said:

> "I was mounted behind the Messenger of Allāh (ﷺ) on a donkey belonging to him that was called 'Ufayr and he said: 'O Mu'ādh! Do you know what is the right of Allāh upon the slaves and what is the right of His slaves on Him?' I replied, 'Allāh and His Messenger know better.' He said: 'Allāh's right on His slaves is that they should worship Him (Alone) and that they should not worship any other besides Him, while the slave's right on Allāh is that He should not punish one who worships none besides Him.' I said: 'O Messenger of Allāh! Should I not inform the people of this good

news?' He said: 'Do not inform them of it, lest they should depend on it (absolutely)'."[305]

177. We were informed by Abū Bakr Aḥmad Ibn 'Alī Ibn Muḥammad Al-Aṣbāhanī Al-Ḥāfiẓ, in Naysābūr, who said that he was informed by Abū 'Amr Ibn Ḥamdān, who said that he was informed by 'Imrān Ibn Mūsā Ibn Mujashi', who said that he was told by Muḥammad Ibn Khallād, who said that he was told by Mu'tamir, who reported on the authority of his father that he said that he was told by Anas (*raḍiyAllāhu 'anhu*) that he said: "It was mentioned to me that the Prophet (ﷺ) said to Mu'ādh (*raḍiyAllāhu 'anhu*):

> "Whoever met Allāh (the Almighty, the All-Powerful)[306] without associating anything with Him will enter Paradise." He said: "O Prophet of Allāh! Shall I not give the people the glad tidings?" He (ﷺ) replied, "No. I fear that they may depend on it."[307]

178. We were informed by Al-Ḥasan Ibn Abū Bakr, who said that Abū 'Alī Al-Tūmarī said:

> "We were with Abū'l-'Abbās Aḥmad Ibn Yaḥyā Tha'lab and a man said to him, 'What is the meaning of the saying of the Prophet (ﷺ) to 'Alī when Abū Bakr and 'Umar (*raḍiyAllāhu 'anhu*) approached and he said: 'These two are the masters of the elder people among

[305] This is authentic.

It was narrated by Al-Bukhārī (2/146), by Muslim (1/58), by Abū Dāwūd (#2559) in an abbreviated form, by Tirmidhī (#2643) and by Nasā'ī in *'Al-Kubrā'* (*tuḥfah*: 8/411) by way of Abū Isḥāq.

[306] This is from manuscript (B).

[307] This is authentic.

It was narrated by Al-Bukhārī (1/37) by way of Mu'tamir Ibn Sulaymān and it has another source on the authority of Anas (*raḍiyAllāhu 'anhu*).

> the inhabitants of Paradise. But do not inform them, 'Alī. I fear that they will reduce their [good] deeds [because of it]'."[308]

[Shaikh][309] Abū Bakr [Al-Ḥāfiẓ][310] said: "[I said][311]: Likewise, 'Umar (*raḍiyAllāhu 'anhu*) forbade the Companions (*raḍiyAllāhu 'anhum*) from narrating a lot of aḥādīth, due to fear that the people would refrain from [good] deeds, due their dependence on the ḥadīth."

'Umar's sternness towards the Companions' narration and memorisation of the aḥādīth of the Messenger of Allāh (ﷺ) was the fear that people who were not from among the Companions (*raḍiyAllāhu 'anhu*) might add things to the Sunan that were not from them. He also feared that Satan might influence a person to see untruth in a favourable light.

179. We were informed by Abū'l-Faraj 'Abdu'l-Salām Ibn 'Abdu'l-Wahhāb Al-Qurashī, in Aṣbāhanī, who said that he was informed by Sulaymān Ibn Aḥmad Ibn Ayyūb Al-Ṭabāranī, who said that he was told by Abū Yazīd Al-Qaratīsī, who said that he was told by Asad Ibn Mūsā, who said that he was told by Mu'āwiyah Ibn Ṣāliḥ, who said that he was told by Rabī'ah Ibn Yazīd, who reported on the authority of 'Abdullāh Ibn 'Amir Al-Yahsabī, who said that he heard Mu'āwiyah (*raḍiyAllāhu 'anhu*) on the pulpit in Damascus, saying:

---

[308] Its chain of narrators is weak.

In it is Abū 'Alī Al-Tūmarī, whose name is 'Isā Ibn Muḥammad , of whom there has been talk, due to the fact that he narrated things without any basis. Ibn Makūla said: "They did not approve of him." Abū'l-Ḥasan Ibn Al-Furāt said: "It would appear that he had no basis (for his narrations) ... and he used to confuse things towards the end of his life."

[309] This is from manuscript (A).

[310] This is from manuscript (A).

[311] This is from manuscript (B).

> "O people! I warn you against [narrating] the aḥadīth of the Messenger of Allāh (ﷺ), aside from a ḥadīth that was reported during the era of 'Umar (*raḍiyAllāhu 'anhu*), for 'Umar (*raḍiyAllāhu 'anhu*) used to make the people fear Allāh, the Almighty, the All-Powerful."[312]

And 'Umar (*raḍiyAllāhu 'anhu*)[313] supported the meaning that we mentioned when he requested that Abū Mūsā Al-Ash'arī (*raḍiyAllāhu 'anhu*) bring a man with him who would bear witness that he had heard from the Messenger of Allāh (ﷺ) the ḥadīth of Al-Salām.

180.We were informed by Abū'l-Ḥusayn 'Alī Ibn Muḥammad Ibn 'Abdullāh Ibn Bashrān Al-Mu'addil, who said that he was informed by Ismā'īl Ibn Muḥammad Al-Ṣaffār, who said that he was told by Aḥmad Ibn Manṣūr Al-Ramādī, who said that he was told by 'Abdu'l-Razzāq, who said that he was informed by Ma'mar, who reported on the authority of Sa'īd Al-Jarīrī, who reported on the authority of Abū Naḍrah, who reported on the authority of Abū Sa'īd Al-Khudrī (*raḍiyAllāhu 'anhu*), who said that he heard the Messenger of Allāh (ﷺ) saying:

> "If one of you delivers salutations of peace three times and he is not answered, then he should return." 'Umar (*raḍiyAllāhu 'anhu*) said: "By Allāh! We will ask Abū Mūsā to bring witnesses for it." [Abū Mūsā went to a gathering of the Anṣar and said:] "Did anyone of you hear this from the Prophet (ﷺ) ?" Ubayy Ibn Ka'b (*raḍiyAllāhu 'anhu*) said: "By Allāh, none will go with you but the youngest of the people [as a witness]." Abū Sa'īd

[312] This is authentic.
It was narrated by Muslim (2/718) by way of Zayd Ibn Al-Ḥabbāb, who said that he was informed of it by Mu'āwiyah Ibn Ṣāliḥ.
[313] This is from manuscript (B).

> (*raḍiyAllāhu ʿanhu*) was the youngest of them, so I went with Abū Mūsā (*raḍiyAllāhu ʿanhu*) and informed ʿUmar (*raḍiyAllāhu ʿanhu*) that the Prophet (ﷺ) had said so."[314]

[Shaikh Abū Bakr Al-Ḥāfiẓ said][315]: "ʿUmar (*raḍiyAllāhu ʿanhu*) did not ask Abū Mūsā (*raḍiyAllāhu ʿanhu*) to produce one man who would bear witness to this ḥadīth with him, because he did not consider that a report from one fair witness was acceptable. And how could this be, when he accepted the narration of ʿAbdu'l-Raḥmān Ibn ʿAwf from the Prophet (ﷺ) regarding the acceptance of the *jizyah* from the *Majūs*[316] and acted upon it, and no one narrated it aside from ʿAbdu'l-Raḥmān [Ibn ʿAwf]?[317] Likewise, the ḥadīth of Al-Daḥḥāk Ibn Sufyān Al-Kilābī, regarding the inheritance of the wife of Ushaym Al-Dhababī from the blood money of her husband. ʿUmar (*raḍiyAllāhu ʿanhu*) also did not do this, because he suspected the reliability of Abū Mūsā's narration; however, he did it based on the premise which we have mentioned, which was prudential in order to preserve the Sunan and to warn against narration. And Allāh knows better.

And an encouragement to spread aḥādīth, memorise them and remind people of them has been narrated on the authority of a number of the Companions (*raḍiyAllāhu ʿanhum*) and the *Tabiʿūn* —and we shall convey as many of those narrations as possible, if Allāh (Most High)[318] wills it.

---

[314] This is authentic.

It was narrated by Muslim (3/1695) and by Tirmidhi (#690) by way of Al-Jarīrī.

Al-Jarīrī used to mix things up, however Shuʿbah heard from him from early on and he narrated this report from him in Muslim's narration. In addition, others accepted his narrations.

[315] This is from manuscript (B).

[316] *Majūs*: Magians.

[317] This is from manuscript (A).

[318] This is from manuscript (B).

CHAPTER FORTY-EIGHT

Mention of Some of the Narrations from the Companions and the *Tabiʿūn* Regarding the Encouragement to Memorise Aḥādīth and to Disseminate Them and Remind People of Them

181. We were informed by Abū'l-Ḥusayn ʿAlī Ibn Aḥmad Ibn Ibrāhim Al-Bazzār, in Al-Baṣrah, who said that he was told by Abū ʿAlī Al-Ḥasan Ibn Muḥammad Ibn ʿUthmān Al-Fasawī, who said that he was told by Yaʿqūb Ibn Sufyān, who said that he was told by ʿAbdu'l-Raḥmān Ibn Ḥammād Al-Shuʿaythī, who said that he was told by Kahmas, who reported on the authority of ʿAbdullāh Ibn Buraydah, who said that ʿAlī Ibn Abū Ṭālib (*ʿalayhis-salām*)[319] said:

[319] This is from manuscript (B). Translator's note: Ibn Kathīr said in his *'Tafsīr'*: "It has become normalfor many writers to single out ʿAlī (*raḍiyAllāhu ʿanhu*) by specifically saying "*'ʿalayhis-salām'* or *'Karram Allāhu wajhahu'*—may Allāh honour his countenance —when mentioning his name and not when mentioning the names of other Companions =

"Visit one another and remind each other of ḥadīth, for if you do not do so, it will be extinguished."[320]

182. We were informed by Abū 'Alī Al-Ḥusayn Ibn Yūsuf Al-'Atbī,[321] who said that he was told by Muḥammad Ibn 'Abdullāh [Ibn Ibrāhim][322] Al-Shāfi'ī, who said that he was told Muḥammad Ibn Ismā'īl Tirmidhī, who said that he was told by Muḥammad Ibn 'Abdullāh Al-Anṣārī, who said that he was told by Kahmas Ibn Al-Ḥasan.

And we were informed by Al-Qāḍī Abū Bakr Aḥmad Ibn Al-Ḥasan Ibn Aḥmad Al-Harashī, who said that he was told by Abū'l-'Abbās Muḥammad Ibn Ya'qūb Al-Aṣamm, who said that he was told by Al-Ḥasan Ibn 'Alī Ibn 'Affan, who said that he was told by Yaḥyā Ibn Ādam, who reported on the authority of Isra'īl, who reported on the authority of Kahmas Ibn Al-Ḥasan, who reported on the authority of 'Abdullāh Ibn Buraydah, who reported on the authority of 'Alī Ibn Abū Ṭālib (*raḍiyAllāhu 'anhu*) that he said:

=

(*raḍiyAllāhu 'anhum*). Though the meaning is correct, one should place all the Companions (*raḍiyAllāhu 'anhum*) on the same footing in this regard, because if this is said about him as a way or honouring him and glorifying him, then Abū Bakr, 'Umar and 'Uthmān should have priority over him."

[320] Its chain of narrators is *mursal.*

The person who gave a biography for Ibn Buraydah did not mention any narration for him on the authority of 'Alī (*raḍiyAllāhu 'anhu*) and it is unlikely that he heard from him. As for 'Abdu'l-Raḥmān Ibn Ḥammād, he has a biography in *'Al-Lisān'* (3/503); Abū Ḥātim said: "He is *munkar* in ḥadīth." Ibn Ḥibbān and others said: "He cannot be cited as a proof." However, he was accepted by the one who made *takhrīj* of the tradition.

The tradition was narrated by Al-Dārimī (#626), by Al-Ḥākim (1/95), by Al-Bayhaqī in *'Al-Madkhal'* (#420), by Ibn 'Abdu'l-Barqī in *'Jami' Bayān Al-'Ilm wa Faḍlihi'* (1/101) from a number of sources on the authority of Kahmas.

[321] In manuscript (A) it says: *'Al-'Anabī'.*

[322] This is from manuscript (B).

[323] Its chain of narrators is mursal.

See what has preceded.

> "Visit one another and remind each other of ḥadīth, for if you do not, it will be extinguished."[323]

183. We were informed by Abū Sa'īd Muḥammad Ibn Ya'qūb Al-Aṣamm, who said that he was told by 'Abdullāh Ibn Aḥmad Ibn Ḥanbal, who said that he was told by his father, who said that he was told by Yaḥyā Ibn Ādam, who said that he was told by Abū Isrā'īl Al-Mallā'ī, who reported on the authority of 'Aṭā' Ibn Al-Sā'ib, who reported on the authority of Abū'l-Ahwaṣ, who reported on the authority of 'Abdullāh that he said:

> "Remind one another of ḥadīth, for its life is [dependent on] reminding."[324]

184. We were informed by 'Alī Ibn Muḥammad Ibn 'Abdullāh Ibn Bashrān, who said that he was informed by Da'laj Ibn Aḥmad [Ibn Da'laj],[325] who said that he was told by Ibn Shayrawayh, who said that he was told by Isḥāq, who said that he was informed by Jarīr, who reported on the authority of Ya'qūb Al-Qummī.

And I was told by 'Abdu'l-'Azīz Ibn Abū'l-Ḥasan, who said that he was informed by Abū Zur'ah Muḥammad Ibn Yūsuf Al-Jurjānī, in Makkah, who said that he was informed by Aḥmad Ibn Khālid Al-Rāzī, who said that he was told by Muḥammad Ibn Ḥumayd, who said that he was told by Ya'qūb Ibn 'Abdullāh Ibn Sa'd, who said that he was told by Ja'far Ibn Abū'l-Mughīrah, who reported

---

[324] Its chain of narrators is weak.

In it is Abū Isrā'īl Al-Mallā'ī, whose name is Ismā'īl Ibn Khalīfah and he is weak, due to his poor memory. In addition, 'Aṭā' Ibn Al-Sā'ib used to mix things up. And if it were correct that he heard from Abū Ismā'īl before he began to mix things up, we would not accept it, due to the weakness of Al-Mallā'ī.

The tradition was also narrated by Al-Dārimī (#619), by Al-Ḥākim in *'Ma'rifah 'Ulūm Al-Ḥadīth'* (p. 175) and by Al-Bayhaqī in *'Al-Madkhal'* (#421) by way of Al-Malla'ī.

[325] This is from manuscript (B).

on the authority of Sa'īd Ibn Jubayr, who reported on the authority of Ibn 'Abbās (*raḍiyAllāhu 'anhu*) that he said:

> "Remind one another of these aḥadīth so that they do not slip away from you—be forgotten—for it [ḥadīth] does not have the same status as the Qur'ān, in that the whole of the Qur'ān is memorised. Whereas, if you do not remind one another of these aḥadīth, they will slip away from you. So let none of you say: 'I related ḥadīth yesterday,' nor let him say: 'I am relating ḥadīth today.' Rather say: 'I related ḥadīth yesterday, I am relating ḥadīth today and I will relate ḥadīth tomorrow'."

And the wording is that of the ḥadīth of Ibn Ḥumayd.[326]

185. We were informed by Abū Ṭālib Muḥammad Ibn Al-Ḥusayn Ibn Aḥmad Ibn 'Abdullāh Ibn Bakīr, who said that he was informed by 'Abdullāh Ibn Ibrāhīm Ibn Māsī, who said that he was informed by Abū Aḥmad Ibn 'Abdūs, who said that he was told by Abū Ma'mar, who said that he was told by 'Abdu'l-Salām Ibn Ḥarb, who reported on the authority of Ḥajjāj, who reported on the authority of 'Aṭā' that Ibn 'Abbās (*raḍiyAllāhu 'anhumā*) said:

> "If you hear anything from us, then remind one another of it."[327]

---

[326] It is ḥasan.

There has been (some slightly negative) discussion about Ya'qūb Ibn 'Abdullāh Al-Qummī and Ja'far Ibn Abū'l-Mughīrah, which does not cause their narration to descend below the level of ḥasan.

The tradition was also narrated by Al-Dārimī in *'Al-Sunan'* (#600): We were informed by Ismā'īl Ibn Uban, who said that he was told by Ya'qūb Ibn 'Abdullāh Al-Qummī...

[327] Its chain of narrators is weak.

In it is Ḥajjāj Ibn Arta'ah, who has been described as a *mudallis* and he used to commit

=

186. We were informed by ʿAbdu'l-Raḥmān Ibn ʿUbaydillāh Al-Ḥarbī,[328] who said that he was told by Aḥmad Ibn Salmān Al-Faqīh, who said that he was told by Al-Ḥasan Ibn Makram, who said that he was told by Abū Al-Naḍr, who said that he was told by Shuʿbah, who reported on the authority Saʿīd Al-Jarīrī, who reported on the authority of Abū Naḍrah, who reported on the authority of Abū Saʿīd Al-Khudrī (*raḍiyAllāhu ʿanhu*) that he said:

"Remind one another of ḥadīth."[329]

187. We were informed by Al-Ḥasan Ibn Abū Bakr, who said that he was informed by Abū Sahl Aḥmad Ibn Muḥammad Ibn ʿAbdullāh Ibn Ziyād Al-Qaṭṭān, who said that he was told by Muḥammad Ibn ʿAbdullāh Ibn Sufyān Al-Ziyyāt, who said that he was told by ʿAbdullāh Ibn Ṣāliḥ, who said that he was told by Isrāʾīl Ibn Kahmas, who reported on the authority of Abū Naḍrah, who reported on the authority of Abū Saʿīd Al-Khudrī (*raḍiyAllāhu ʿanhu*) that he said:

"Remind one another of ḥadīth."[330]

=

ʿaʾanah (i.e. to report a ḥadīth using the word *ʿan* (on the authority of) consecutively, to connect two or more narrators in the chain, from which it is inferred that these narrators did not actually meet and hear from each other). In addition to this, there was discussion regarding his memory.

The tradition was also narrated by Al-Dārimī (#607) by way of ʿAbdu'l-Salām Ibn Ḥarb.

[328] In manuscript (B) it says *'Al-Ḥarfī'*.

[329] This is authentic.

The author cited a biography for his Shaikh in his *'Tārīkh'* (10/303) and he said: "We recorded from him and he was truthful, though some of the narrations that he heard and reported on the authority of Al-Najjād were confused."

Shuʿbah's hearing from Al-Jarīrī was from before he began to mix things up.

The ḥadīth was narrated by Al-Dārimī (1/155) and by Al-Bayhaqī in *'Al-Madkhal'* from a number of sources on the authority of Abū Naḍrah.

[330] This is authentic. See previous narration.

We were informed by Al-Ḥasan Ibn Abū Bakr, who said that he was informed by Abū Sahl Aḥmad Ibn Muḥammad Ibn Ziyād Al-Qaṭṭān, who said that he was told by Muḥammad Ibn 'Abdullāh Ibn Sufyān Al-Ziyyāt, who said that he was told by 'Abdullāh Ibn Ṣāliḥ, who said that he was told by Isrā'īl, who reported on the authority of Kahmas, who reported on the authority of Abū Naḍrah, who reported on the authority of Abū Sa'īd Al-Khudrī (*raḍiyAllāhu 'anhu*) that he said:

> "Transmit ḥadīth, for ḥadīth cause you to remind one another."

188. We were informed by Muḥammad Ibn Al-Ḥusayn Ibn Abū Sulaymān Al-Mu'addil, who said that he was informed by Aḥmad Ibn Ja'far Ibn Ḥamdān, who said that he was told by Ja'far Ibn Muḥammad Al-Qāḍī, who said that he was told by Al-Walīd Ibn 'Utbah, who said that he was told by Al-Walīd Ibn Muslim, who said that he was told by 'Uthmān Ibn Abū'l-'Atikah, who said that Sulaymān Ibn Ḥabīb told him that Abū Umāmah Al-Bahīlī (*raḍiyAllāhu 'anhu*) said to them:

> "Verily, this gathering is from what Allāh has conveyed to you and verily, the Messenger of Allāh (ﷺ) has conveyed what was sent to him. So you should convey from us the best of what you hear."[331]

189. We were informed by 'Abdu'l-Salām Ibn 'Abdu'l- Wahhab Al-Qurashi, who said that he was informed by Sulaymān Ibn Aḥmad [Ayyūb][332] Al-Ṭabāranī, who said that he was told by Aḥmad Ibn 'Abdu'l-Wahhab Ibn Najdah, who said that he

[331] Its chain of narrators is weak.
In it is 'Uthmān Ibn Abū'l-'Atikah, who is weak in ḥadīth, in particular, his narrations on the authority of 'Alī Ibn Yazīd Al-Alhānī.

[332] This is from manuscript (B).

was told by Abū'l-Yaman Al-Ḥakam Ibn Nafi', who said that he was told by Safwān Ibn 'Amr,who reported on the authority of Sulaym Ibn 'Amir that he said that they were sitting around Abū Umāmah Al-Bahīlī (*raḍiyAllāhu 'anhu*), who was relating numerous aḥādīth to them from the Messenger of Allāh (ﷺ), and when he had finished, he said:

> "Understand, and convey from us as I have conveyed to you."[333]

190. I recited to Abū Bakr Al-Barqānī, on the authority of 'Alī Ibn 'Umar Al-Ḥāfiẓ, who said that he was told by Isḥāq Ibn Muḥammad Ibn Al-Faḍl Al-Ziyyāt, who said that he was told by Yaḥyā Ibn 'Ayyāsh Al-Qaṭṭān, who said that he was told by Ḥafṣ Ibn 'Umar Al-Ailī, who said that he was told by 'Abdullāh Ibn Al-Muthannā, who said that he was told by his two uncles, Al-Naḍr and Mūsā, sons of Anas, who reported on the authority of their father, Anas Ibn Mālik (*raḍiyAllāhu 'anhu*), that he ordered them to write down aḥādīth and traditions from the Messenger of Allāh and to learn them and he [Anas] said:

> "We did not consider the knowledge of anyone to be [true] knowledge if they did not write it down."[334]

[333] This is authentic.

It was narrated by Al-Ṭabāranī in *'Al-Mu'jam Al-Kabīr'* (8/187) and its chain of narrators is authentic.

[334] Its chain of narrators is weak.

'Abdullāh Ibn Al-Muthannā is weak in ḥadīth and Yaḥyā Ibn 'Ayyāsh Al-Qaṭṭān's biography was given by Al-Khaṭīb in his *'Tārīkh'* (14/219), but he did not mention any criticism or praise of him.

The tradition was also narrated by the author in *'Taqyīd Al-'Ilm'* (p. 96).

And it was narrated by Abū Khaythamah in *'Al-'Ilm'* (120), by Ibn Sa'd in *'Al-Ṭabāqāt'* (7/14), by Al-Khaṭīb in *'Taqyīd Al-'Ilm'* (p. 96) by way of Muḥammad Ibn 'Abdullāh Ibn Al-Muthannā, who reported on the authority of his father, who reported on the authority of Thumāmah Ibn 'Abdullāh, who said: "Anas (*raḍiyAllāhu 'anhu*) told his sons: "O my sons! Confine knowledge to writing."

191. Al-Qāḍī Abū Bakr Aḥmad Ibn Al-Ḥasan Al-Ḥarshī and Abū Sa'īd Muḥammad Ibn Mūsā Al-Ṣayrafī said that they were told by Abū'l-'Abbās Muḥammad Ibn Ya'qūb Al-Aṣamm, who said that he was told by Al-'Abbās Ibn Muḥammad Al-Dawrī, who said that he was told by Al-Ḥamānī, who said that he was told by Al-A'mash, who reported on the authority of Ibrāhīm, on the authority of 'Alqamah (*raḍiyAllāhu 'anhu*), who said:

> "Remind one another of ḥadīth, because it is kept alive by mentioning it."[335]

192. We were informed by 'Alī Ibn Aḥmad Ibn 'Umar Al-Muqrī', who said that he was told by 'Abdullāh Al-Sahfi'ī, who said that he was told by Mu'ādh Ibn Al-Muthannā, who said that he was told by Musaddad, who said that he was told by Abū 'Awanah, who reported on the authority of Al-Mughīrah, who reported on the authority of Ibrāhīm, who reported on the authority of 'Alqamah (*raḍiyAllāhu 'anhu*) that he said:

> "Prolong the recollection of ḥadīth, so that it is not erased."[336]

193. We were informed by Muḥammad Ibn 'Alī Al-Ḥarbī, who said that he was informed by 'Umar Ibn Ibrāhīm Al-Muqrī', who said that he was informed by 'Abdullāh Ibn Muḥammad Ibn 'Abdu'l-'Azīz, who said that he was told by Abū Khaythamah, who said that he was told by Muḥammad Ibn Fuḍayl, who said that he

[335] This is authentic.

It was narrated by Abū Khaythamah in *'Al-'Ilm'* (#71), by Al-Ḥākim in *''Ulūm Al-Ḥadīth'* (p. 175), by Al-Bayhaqī in *'Al-Madkhal'* (#423) by way of Al-Hamani.

Al-Ḥamānī is weak, but he was accepted by Al-Thawrī, according to Al-Darimi (#603).

[336] Its chain of narrators is weak.

This is because Al-Mughīrah is described as being a *mudallis*, especially when he narrates on the authority of Al-Nakha'ī; he also perpetrated *'an'anah* in this chain.

was told by Yazīd Ibn Abū Ziyād, who reported on the authority of ʿAbdu'l-Raḥmān Ibn Abū Laylā, who said:

> "Preserving ḥadīth is achieved by reminding each other of it, so remind one another of it."[337]

194. We were informed by Al-Ḥasan Ibn Abū Bakr, who said that he was informed by ʿUthmān Ibn Aḥmad Al-Daqqāq, who said that he was told by Al-Ḥasan Ibn Salām, who said that he was told by ʿĀṣim—Ibn ʿAlī—who said that he was told by Al-Masʿūdī, who reported on the authority of Ḥabīb Ibn Abū Thābit, who reported on the authority of Ṭalq Ibn Ḥabīb, who said:

> "Remind one another of ḥadīth, for ḥadīth awakens ḥadīth."[338]

195. We were informed by ʿAlī Ibn Abū ʿAlī Al-Baṣrī, who said that he was told by ʿAlī Ibn ʿAmr[339] Al-Ḥarīrī, who said that he was told by ʿAbdullāh Ibn Sulaymān Ibn Al-Ashʿath, who said that he was told by Al-ʿAbbās Ibn Al-Faraj Al-Riyashī, who said that he was told by Abū Dāwūd Al-Ṭayālisī, who said that he was told by Shuʿbah, who reported on the authority of a man, who reported on the authority of Abū'l-ʿĀliyah that he said:

> "If you are informed of a ḥadīth from the Messenger of Allāh (ﷺ), then memorise it."[340]

[337] Its chain of narrators is weak.

In it is Yazīd Ibn Abū Ziyād, who is weak in ḥadīth.

The report was narrated in a longer version by Abū Khaythamah (#72) and by Al-Dārimī (#610), by way of Ibn Fuḍayl.

[338] Its chain of narrators is weak. This is because ʿĀṣim Ibn ʿAlī only heard from Al-Masʿūdī after he began to mix things up.

[339] In manuscript (A) it says ʿUmar , but the correct version is what we have confirmed.

[340] Its chain of narrators is weak, due to the unknown status of the man who reported on the authority of Abū'l-ʿĀliyah.

CHAPTER FORTY-NINE

Whoever Desired the Narration of Ḥadīth from the Caliphs and Considered that the Scholars of Ḥadīth are the Best of the Scholars

196. We were informed by Abū'l-Ḥasan 'Alī Ibn Al-Qāsim Ibn Al-Ḥasan Al-Shahīd, in Al-Baṣrah, who said that he was told by Abū 'Alī Al-Ḥasan Ibn Muḥammad Ibn 'Uthmān Al-Fasāwī, who said that he was told by Al-Ḥusayn Ibn 'Ubaydillāh Al-Abzārī, who said that he was told by Ibrāhīm Ibn Sa'īd Al-Jawharī, who said that when Al-Ma'mūn conquered Egypt, Faraj Al-Aswad stood up and said:

> "O Commander of the Faithful! All praise and thanks be to Allāh. He has granted you success against your enemy and caused the two Iraqs, *Al-Shamāt*[341] and Egypt to submit to you; and you are the paternal uncle of the

[341] *Al-Shamāt*: The lands of *Al-Shām* (i.e. Syria, Jordan, Palestine and Lebanon).

> Messenger of Allāh (ﷺ)." He replied to him, "O Faraj! Woe to you! I have a natural characteristic, which is that when I sit in a gathering and the *mustamillī*[342] comes and says, 'Whom have you quoted, may Allāh be pleased with you?'I reply, 'The two Ḥammāds, Ḥammād Ibn Salāmah Ibn Dīnār and Ḥammād Ibn Zayd Ibn Dirhām, who both said that they were told by Thābit Al-Bunānī, who reported on the authority of Anas Ibn Mālik (*raḍiyAllāhu ʿanhu*) that the Prophet (ﷺ) said: "Whoever financially supported two or three daughters or two or three sisters until they die or until he dies, will be with me like these two in Paradise," and he indicated by crossing his forefinger and his middle finger."[343, 344]

Shaikh Abū Bakr Al-Ḥāfiẓ said: "In this report there is an ugly mistake and it would seem likely that Al-Maʿmūn narrated it on the authority of a man, who reported on the authority of the two Ḥammāds. The mistake is that Al-Maʿmūn was born in the year

[342] *Mustamillī*: A person who repeats the words of the scholar in large gatherings, so that those sitting further away can hear.

[343] After this tradition, the following addition was mentioned: The Shaikh and Imām said: "We heard this ḥadīth with the license of the Shaikh."

[344] This is a fabrication.

In it is Al-Ḥusayn Ibn 'Ubaydillāh Al-Abzārī; his biography was given by Al-Khaṭīb in *'Tārīkh Baghdād'* (8/56-57) and he said: "I read in the book of Abū'l-Fatḥ 'Ubaydillāh Ibn Aḥmad Al-Nahwī, who heard it from Aḥmad Ibn Kāmil Al-Qāḍī, who said that Al-Ḥusayn Ibn 'Ubaydillāh Al-Abzārī was a strange joker, who lied regarding these aḥādīth which he related with chains of narrators from the Caliphs and he added that he did not record them from him for this reason.

I say: And it is this which incurred Al-Khaṭīb's disapproval from the words of Al-Maʿmūn: We were told by Al-Ḥammādan, for if Ḥammād Ibn Salāmah did not meet the other two, then it is unlikely that he narrated on the authority of Ḥammād Ibn Zayd.

It was also narrated by Al-Ramāhurmuzī (#35), by way of Al-Samʿānī in *'Adab Al-Imlā'* (p. 19), by way of Ibrāhīm Ibn Yūnus Al-Baṣrī, who said that he was told by Abū Ghassān Naṣr Ibn Manṣūr Al-Tafawi, who said that he was told by Abū 'Aṣim Al-Daḥḥāk Ibn Mukhallad, who said that he visited Al-Maʿmūn... and he quoted the narration.

But I have not found any biography for Ibrāhīm Ibn Yūnus, or Al-Tafāwī.

170 AH. and Ḥammād Ibn Salāmah was born in the year 167 AH., three years before Al-Ma'mūn's birth. As for Ḥammād Ibn Zayd, he died in the year 179 AH.

197. I was told by Muḥammad Ibn Yūsuf Al-Naysābūrī, who said that he was informed by Abū 'Abdullāh Al-Ḥusayn Ibn Muḥammad Ibn Aḥmad Al-Raqqī, who said that he was told by Aḥmad Ibn 'Ubayd Ibn Aḥmad [Ibn 'Ubayd][345] Al-Ṣaffār, who said that he was told by Aḥmad Ibn 'Alī Al-Qāḍī, who said that he was told by Muḥammad Ibn Ibrāhīm, who said that he was told by Muḥammad Ibn 'Abdullāh Al-Muqrī', who said that he was told by Yaḥyā Ibn Aktham, who said: "Al-Rashīd said [to me],[346] 'What are the noblest ranks?' I replied, 'O Commander of the Faithful! It is that in which you are.' He asked, 'Do you know someone more exalted than I?' I said: 'No.' He said: 'But I do: [It is] a man in a circle who says, 'So-and-so told us, on the authority of So-and-so, who said:

> 'The Messenger of Allāh (ﷺ) said...' I said: 'O Commander of the Faithful! This [person] is better than you, and you are the nephew of the Messenger of Allāh (ﷺ) and the heir to the [rule of] the Muslims?' He replied, 'Yes. Woe to you! This [person] is better than I, because his name is linked with the name of the Messenger of Allāh (ﷺ) and he will never die. We will die and vanish away, while the scholars will remain for all time."[347]

---

[345] This is from manuscript (B).

[346] This is from manuscript (B).

[347] Its chain of narrators is talif (bad, broken, damaged).

Yaḥyā Ibn Aktham was declared a liar by Ibn Ma'īn, while Ibn Al-Junayd said: "They (the scholars) were in no doubt that he used to steal ḥadīth." I say: He was the Qāḍī of Al-Ma'mūn and his age was twenty years, but I do not know what is the status of his narration on the authority of Al-Rashīd. The tradition was narrated by Al-Sam'ānī (p. 220) by way of Al-Raqqī.

198. We were informed by Abū Bakr Aḥmad Ibn Muḥammad Ibn Ghālib Al-Faqīh, who said that he was told by Abū Bakr Muḥammad Ibn 'Amr Ibn 'Alī Ibn 'Amrawayh Al-Isfarayīnī, who said that he heard Khaythamah Ibn Sulaymān Al-Qurashī, in Atrablus, who said that he heard Abū'l-Khanajir saying:

> "We were in the gathering of Yazīd Ibn Hārūn [in Baghdād][348] and the people had gathered to him. Al-Mutawakkil and his soldiers passed by and he looked towards the gathering of Yazīd Ibn Hārūn and as he looked at him, he said: 'This is the king'."[349]

Shaikh [Abū Bakr Al-Ḥāfiẓ][350] said: "[I said][351] This is how Khaythamah narrated this tradition and in it there is a huge and clear error, which is that Yazīd Ibn Hārūn died in the year 86 AH,[352] while Al-Mutawakkil was born in 87 AH.[353] It is possible that the person who passed by Yazīd with his army was Al-Ma'mūn. And Allāh knows better.

199. I was informed by Muḥammad Ibn Aḥmad Ibn Mūsā Al-Shīrazī Al-Wā'iẓ, who said that he was informed by Aḥmad Ibn Muḥammad Ibn 'Imrān, who said that he was told by Al-Ḥusayn Ibn Al-Qāsim Al-Kawkabī, who said that he was told by Abū'l-'Abbās Al-Kudaymī, who said that he was told by 'Amr Ibn Ḥabīb

[348] This is from manuscript (B).

[349] The men in the chain of narrators are trustworthy, aside from Al-Barqānī's Shaikh, for whom I have not found any biography—and it is likely that the error come from him. The tradition was narrated by Al-Sam'ānī (p. 22), by way of the author's chain.

[350] This is from manuscript (A).

[351] This is from manuscript (A).

[352] This is how it appears in manuscript (A), while in manuscript (B) it says 186 AH and that is the correct version.

[353] This is how it appears in manuscript (A), while in manuscript (B) it says 187 AH and that is the correct version.

Al-ʿAdawī Al-Qāḍī, who said that the Commander of the Faithful, Al-Maʾmūn said to him:

> "My soul has not requested from me anything except that I have achieved it, aside from this ḥadīth, for I would love to sit on a chair and for it to be said to me, 'Who related ḥadīth to you?' and for me to say, 'I was told by So-and-so, who reported on the authority of So-and-so.' I said: 'O Commander of the Faithful! Do so [and why should you not relate ḥadīth?'].[354] He said: 'It is not fitting for a king or a Caliph to relate ḥadīth to the people'."[355]

Al-Maʾmūn was the greatest of the Caliphs from Banul ʿAbbās with regard to his interest in ḥadīth and his learning and memorisation of it. He also had a great yearning for knowledge of narration and he had narrated many aḥādīth to his close companions and he loved to transmit ḥadīth in open gatherings, which were attended by many listeners. And he used to compel himself to do that.

200. I was told by Muḥammad Ibn Yūsuf Al-Qaṭṭān, who said that he was informed by Muḥammad Ibn ʿAbdullāh Ibn Nuʿaym Al-Ḍhabbī, who said that he was informed by Muḥammad Ibn Aḥmad Ibn Tamīm Al-Qantarī, in Baghdād, who said that he was told by Al-Ḥusayn Ibn Fahm, who said that he was told by Yaḥyā Ibn Aktham Al-Qāḍī, who said that Al-Maʾmūn said to him one

[354] This is from manuscript (B).

[355] Its chain of narrators is extremely weak.

In it is the author's Shaikh, for whom he has given a biography in his *'Tārīkh'* (1/359-360) and he said: "I was told something of him by one of our companions that proves his weakness in ḥadīth." And he mentioned something regarding his status that showed his apparent abstemiousness and devoutness.

Al-Kudaymī is Muḥammad Ibn Yūnus, who is a liar and was accused of fabricating ḥadīth.

The tradition was also narrated by Al-Samʿānī (p. 20) by way of the author.

day:

> "O Yaḥyā! I wish to relate ḥadīth."He said: "And who is worthier to relate ḥadīth than the Commander of the Faithful?" He said: "Place for me a pulpit on the concourse." Then he ascended it and related aḥādīth, the first of which was: "Imru'ul Qays[356] is the standard bearer of the poets on their way to the Fire." Then he related thirty other similar aḥādīth, after which he descended and said: "O Yaḥyā! What did you think of our lecture?" H replied, "O Commander of the Faithful! It was the most sublime lecture: the elite and the common folk gained understanding." He replied, "Nay! By your life, I find no sweetness in your company. The real lectures belong only to those dressed in rags and bearing inkwells—the scholars of ḥadīth—."[357]

201. I was informed by Abū'l-Qāsim Al-Azharī, who said that he was informed by 'Ubaydullāh Ibn 'Uthmān Ibn Yaḥyā Al-Daqqāq, who said that he was informed by 'Alī Ibn Al-Ḥusayn Al-Aṣbāhanī, who said that he was told by his paternal uncle, who said that he was told by Ibn Abū Sa'd, who said that he was told by Ḥusayn Ibn Qaddas, who said that he heard Mūsā Ibn Dāwūd saying:

> "Muḥammad Ibn Sulaymān Ibn 'Alī entered the Sacred Masjid and he saw the companions of ḥadīth walking

---

[356] Imru'ul Qays: A renowned Arab poet of the pre-Islāmic era.

[357] Its chain of narrators is *talif* (bad, broken, damaged).

Yaḥyā Ibn Aktham is accused (of untruthfulness) and we have spoken of him earlier. Al-Ḥusayn Ibn Fahm is Ibn Muḥammad Ibn 'Abdu'l-Raḥmān Ibn Fahm and Al-Daraquṭnī and Al-Ḥākim said that he is not strong. A biography was given for Muḥammad Ibn Aḥmad Ibn Tamīm by Al-Khaṭīb in his *'Tārīkh'* (1/283) and he stated that Ibn Abū'l-Fawaris declared him to be layyin (not strict).

The tradition was also narrated by Al-Sam'ānī in *'Adab Al-Imlā' wa'l-Istimlā'* (p. 22) by way of the author.

behind a man from among the ḥadīth scholars and they were keeping close to him. Then he turned to look at those with him and said: 'That these people should walk behind me is more beloved to me than the Caliphate'."[358]

[358] Its chain of narrators is extremely weak.

'Alī Ibn Al-Ḥusayn is Abū'l-Faraj, the author of *'Al-Aghanī'*, who was accused by some of stealing (narrations). And I have not found any biography for Ḥusayn Ibn Qaddas and those between him and Al-Aṣbāhanī.

The tradition was also narrated by Al-Sam'ānī in *'Adab Al-Imlā' wa'l-Istimlā"* (p. 22) by way of the author.

CHAPTER FIFTY

Whoever Delighted in Relating Ḥadīth and Sitting with the Companions of Ḥadīth

202. We were informed by Al-Ḥasan Ibn Abū Bakr, who said that he was informed by Ismāʿīl Ibn ʿAlī Al-Khuṭabī, who said that he was told by Muḥammad Ibn ʿIsā Al-Wāsiṭī, who said that he was told by Muḥammad Ibn Al-Ṣabāh Al-Jarjarāʿī, who reported on the authority of Sufyān Ibn ʿUyaynah, who said that Muṭarrif said:

> "Sitting with you is more beloved to me than sitting with my family."[359]

203. We were informed by Muḥammad Ibn Al-Ḥasan Ibn Aḥmad Al-Ahwāzī, who said that he heard Muḥammad Ibn Aḥmad Ibn Isḥāq Al-Daqqāq, in Al-Ahwāz, who said that he heard Yūsuf Ibn Yaʿqūb saying that he heard his Father say that he heard Yazīd Ibn

[359] Its chain of narrators is authentic.

Hārūn saying:

> "The companions of ḥadīth have troubled me, but if they were absent from me, they would fill me with sadness."[360]

204. We were informed by Abū Ḥāzim Al-A'raj, in Naysābūr, who said that he was informed by Abū Aḥmad Ibn Aḥmad Al-'Abdī, in Jarjān, who said that Abū Khalīfah said that he heard Muḥammad Ibn Ḥafṣ Abū 'Abdu'l-Raḥmān saying:

> "The companions of ḥadīth came in large numbers to Yaḥyā Ibn Sa'īd Al-Qaṭṭān and he became annoyed with them, so I said: 'Would you like them to be kept away from you?' He replied, 'If it be due to dislike, then no'."[361]

205. I was informed by Muḥammad Ibn Al-Ḥusayn Al-Qaṭṭān, who said that he was informed by Da'laj Ibn Aḥmad, who said that he was informed by Aḥmad Ibn 'Alī Al-Abbar, who said that he was told by 'Ubaydullāh Ibn 'Umar, who said that he heard Ḥammād Ibn Zayd saying that Abū Jablah said to him:

> "O Abū Ismā'īl! Do you not see what the people of ḥadīth have done to me this day?" I said: "And what have they done to you?" He replied, "They said: 'We shall go to him.' Shall I wait for them until the Hour comes? They have not come'."[362]

---

[360] I have not found any biography for Yūsuf Ibn Ya'qūb; his father is Ya'qūb Ibn Ibrāhīm Al-Dawrāqī.

[361] Its chain of narrators is extremely weak.

In it is Muḥammad Ibn Ḥafṣ Al-Qaṭṭān, of whom Al-Dhahabī said in *'Al-Mīzān'*, "He is from Baghdād and he was accused of lying." Ibn Mindah said: "He related *munkar* reports on the authority of Sufyān and Yaḥyā Al-Qaṭṭān."

[362] Its chain of narrators is authentic.

206. We were informed by Abū Bakr Al-Barqānī, who said that he recited to Muḥammad Ibn 'Alī Ibn Al-Naḍr,[363] saying that Aḥmad Ibn 'Amr told them Ibn 'Uthmān, who said that 'Abdullāh Ibn Abū Sa'd told him that Muḥammad Ibn 'Abdullāh Ibn 'Ulwān said to Bishr Ibn Al-Ḥārith:

> "Why do you not relate ḥadīth?" He replied, "I desire to relate ḥadīth and if I desire something, I leave it."[365]

207. We were informed by Muḥammad Ibn Aḥmad Ibn Rizq, who said that he was told by Ismā'īl Ibn 'Alī Al-Khiṭbī, who said that he was told by Al-Ḥārith Ibn Muḥammad Ibn Abū Usāmah, who said that one of his companions said to him that he heard Yaḥyā Ibn Aktham Al-Qāḍī saying:

> "I was appointed as a judge, as chief justice, as Wāzir and as such-and-such, but I have not been happy with anything as much as I have been pleased with hearing the *mustamilli* say, 'Whom have you quoted, may Allāh be pleased with you?'[366]

208. We were informed by Abū Isḥāq [Ibrāhīm][367] Ibn Mukhallad

[363] In manuscript (B) it says 'Ibn Abū Al-Naḍr'.

[364] This is how it is written in manuscripts (A) and (B), in *'Tārīkh Baghdād'* (3/92) it says "Umar '.

[365] It was narrated by the author in his *'Tārīkh'* (7/70), on the authority of Al-Azharī, who reported on the authority of Muḥammad Ibn 'Alī Ibn Al-Naḍrah.

Muḥammad Ibn 'Abdullāh Ibn 'Ulwān, who attributed it to Al-Mizzī in *'Al-Tahẓīb'* (4/101) and he said: *"Al-Ḥanafī"*. And he mentioned him among those who narrated on the authority of Bishr Al-Ḥāfī, but I have not found any biography for him.

[366] Its chain of narrators is weak.

This is due to the unknown status of the person who narrated on the authority of Yaḥyā Ibn Aktham—and Yaḥyā Ibn Aktham is weak, as we said earlier.

The tradition was narrated by Al-Sam'ānī (p. 104) by way of Al-Ḥusayn Ibn Fahm: "I heard Yaḥyā Ibn Aktham..." and he reported something similar. But Al-Ḥusayn Ibn Fahm is also weak, as we said earlier.

[367] This is from manuscript (B).

Al-Qāḍī, who said that he was told by Muḥammad Ibn Aḥmad Ibn Ibrāhīm Al-Ḥakīmī, who said that he was told by Ḥamdān Ibn ʿAlī, who said that he heard ʿAbdu'l-Ṣamad Ibn Al-Nuʿmān saying that they were with Qays—Ibn Al-Rabīʿ—one day and when he saw the people who had come to him, he struck his chin with his hand and said:

> "All praise and thanks be to Allāh, after a long period of stagnation!"[368]

209. We were informed by Ismāʿīl Ibn Aḥmad Al-Ḍarīr Al-Ḥayrī,[369] who said that he was informed by Zāhir Ibn Aḥmad Al-Sarkhasī, who said that he was told by Abū Lubayd Al-Sāmī, who said that he was told by Maḥmūd—Ibn Ghaylān—who said that he was told by ʿAbdu'l-Razzāq that he said that he heard Muʿammar saying:

> "There is no commodity more difficult for its owner if it is unprofitable than this ḥadīth."[370]

210. We were informed by Al-Ḥasan Ibn Abū Bakr, who said that he was informed by his father that ʿAbdu'l-ʿAzīz Aḥmad Al-

[368] Its chain of narrators is ḥasan.

Ḥamdān Ibn ʿAlī is Muḥammad Ibn ʿAlī Ibn ʿAbdullāh Al-Warrāq is trustworthy and reliable and he is one of the companions of Imām Aḥmad. There is a difference of opinion regarding ʿAbdu'l-Ṣamad Ibn Al-Nuʿmān. Ibn Maʿīn said that he is trustworthy and Abū Ḥātim said that he is truthful. However, Al-Dāraquṭnī and Nasā'ī said that he is *layyin* (not strict).

I say: His report does not descend below the level of ḥasan, especially when he is not alone in reporting, or the traditions have short chains of narrators.

[369] In manuscript (A) it says Al-Khabrī and the copier ascribed him to Khabr, a village in Shīraz. But what we have written is the correct version and what the copier has stated is simply fancy.

[370] Its chain of narrators is ḥasan.

Biographies are given for Zāhir Al-Sarkhasī and Abū Lubayd Muḥammad Ibn Idrīs Al-Sāmī in *'Al-Siyār'*.

Ghafiqi said that he was told by Ya'qūb Ibn Ka'b, who said that he was told by Yaḥyā Ibn Al-Yaman, who said that he heard Sufyān Al-Thawrī saying:

> "If they did not come to me, I would go to them in their houses—the companions of ḥadīth—."[371]

211. We were informed by Abū Naṣr Aḥmad Ibn Al-Ḥusayn Al-Qāḍī, in Al-Daynūr,who said that he was informed by Abū Bakr Aḥmad Ibn Muḥammad Ibn Isḥāq Al-Sunnī Al-Ḥāfiẓ, who said that he was told by Muḥammad Ibn Ḥamdan Ibn Sufyān, who said that he was told by Muḥammad Ibn 'Abdu'l-Nūr Al-Khazzāz, who said that he was told by Al-Ḥasan Ibn Al-Rabī' Al-Būranī, who said that Sufyān Al-Thawrī said:

> "I warn you and myself against the hidden desire, which is implicit in my words to you: Do not come to me, and if you do not come to me, I will come to you. And if I do not relate ḥadīth to you, I will relate it to the walls."[372]

212. We were told by Abū Ṭālib Yaḥyā Ibn 'Alī Ibn Al-Ṭayyib Al-'Ajalī, in Ḥalwān, who said that he was informed by Abū Bakr Muḥammad Ibn Ibrāhīm Al-Muqrī', who said that he was told by 'Umar Ibn 'Uthmān Al-Ra'aynī, in Antakiyah [Antioch], who said

[371] Its chain of narrators is weak, but it is authentic.

Yaḥyā Ibn Yaman is weak, especially when he narrates on the authority of Al-Thawrī. However, Zayd Ibn Al-Ḥabbāb also reported it on the authority of Al-Thawrī with this wording: "If I knew that someone was seeking it (i.e. ḥadīth) with (a good) intention, I would follow him even into his house to relate it to him."

It was narrated by the author in *'Al-Jami'* (#770) but there is weakness in Zayd Ibn Al-Habbab. However, Al-Ramāhurmuzi also narrated it (#41) via Muḥammad Ibn 'Abdu'l- Wahhāb Al-Qannād, so the tradition is authentic, if Allāh wills.

[372] Its chain of narrators is weak.

A biography is given for Muḥammad Ibn 'Abdu'l-Nūr Al-Khazzāz by Al-Khaṭīb in his *'Tārīkh'* (2/392-393), but he did not mention anything that would prove his status.

that he heard Ibrāhīm Ibn Saʿīd Al-Jawhārī saying that in the ḥadīth of the Messenger of Allāh (ﷺ) there is the hidden desire. He said:

> "From the hidden desire is that I say to you, 'Do not come to me,' when I desire you to come to me."[373]

This is the end of the second section of *'Sharaf Aṣḥāb al-Ḥadīth'*

And may the choicest blessings and peace of Allāh be upon Muḥammad, the best of His creation. Mention will follow in the third section, if Allāh, Most High wills, of what has been narrated by the righteous of dreams of the companions of ḥadīth, regarding the honour and reward they receive. All praise and thanks be to Allāh, the Lord of the worlds.

---

[373] I have not found any biography for Al-Raʿainī.

The verifier said: "The completion of the verification of the second section of the book *'Sharaf Aṣḥāb al-Ḥadīth'*, by Al-Khaṭīb Al-Baghdādī (may Allāh have Mercy on him) was achieved on the night of Wednesday, the 8th of Jumad Al-Awwal 1416 AH.

All praise and thanks be to Allāh, for His Sublime Grace and His Abundant Kindness and may the Blessings and Peace of Allāh be upon our Prophet, Muḥammad (ﷺ).

THE THIRD SECTION OF THE BOOK

Sharaf Aṣḥāb al-Ḥadīth

The Shaikh, Imām and Ḥāfiẓ Abū Bakr Aḥmad Ibn ʿAlī Ibn Thābit al-Khaṭīb al-Baghdādī (may Allāh have Mercy on him)

The narration of the trustworthy Shaikh: Abū Muḥammad Hibatullāh Ibn Aḥmad In Muḥammad Al-Akfānī, on his authority.

The narration of the trustworthy Shaikh: Abū ʿAbdullāh Muḥammad Ibn Ḥamzah Ibn Muḥammad Ibn Abū'l-Ṣaqr, on his authority.

The narration of: the Shaikh, Imām, scholar and Ḥāfiẓ and eminent member of the Ḥuffāẓ, Jamaluddīn Abī[190] Muḥammad ʿAbdu'l- Qāḍir Ibn ʿAbdullāh Al-Rahāwī, on his authority.

The author of the section, the seeker of Allāh, Most High's mercy, Muḥammad Ibn Aḥmad Ibn Al-Ḥusayn Al-Hakārī, on his authority. All praise and thanks be to Allāh, the Lord of the worlds.

CHAPTER FIFTY-ONE

Mention of the Dreams Seen by the Righteous of the People of Ḥadīth and the Honour and Reward They Received

In the Name of Allāh, the Most Beneficent, the Most Merciful—We were told by the Shaikh, Imām, scholar, Ḥāfiẓ and example to the Ḥuffāẓ, Jamaluddīn Abū Muḥammad 'Abdu'l-Qāḍir Ibn 'Abdullāh Al-Rahāwī—may Allāh grant him the best of success—in Al-Mawsil, on Tuesday, the 26th of Dhū'l-Hijjah, in the year 592 AH., who said that he was informed by the steadfast Shaikh, Abū 'Abdullāh Muḥammad Ibn Ḥamzah Ibn Muḥammad Ibn Abū Jamīl Al-Qurashī, who said that he was informed by the steadfast and righteous Shaikh, Abū Muḥammad Hibatullah Ibn Aḥmad Al-Akfānī, who said that he was informed by the Shaikh, Imām and Ḥāfiẓ, Abū Bakr Aḥmad Ibn 'Alī Ibn Thābit Al-Khaṭīb Al-Baghdādī—may Allāh have mercy on him—who said:

213. We were informed by Al-Ḥasan Ibn Abū Bakr, who said

that he was told by Aḥmad Ibn Kamil Al-Qāḍī, who said that he was told by Aḥmad Ibn Ḥarb Ibn Musmiʿ, who said that he was told by Al-ʿAishī, who said that he was told by Mahdī Ibn Maymūn, who said that he was told by ʿUthmān Ibn ʿUbayd Al-Rāsibī, who said that he heard Abū Al-Ṭufayl relating ḥadīth on the authority of Hudayfah (*raḍiyAllāhu ʿanhu*), who reported from the Prophet (ﷺ) that he said:

> "Prophethood has gone; there is no prophethood after me. But *al-mubashshirāt* remain: a good dream experienced by a Muslim or a dream experienced by another that concerns him." [374]

214. We were informed by Abū Nuʿaym Aḥmad Ibn ʿAbdullāh Al-Ḥāfiẓ, who said that was told by ʿAbdullāh Ibn Jaʿfar Ibn Aḥmad Ibn Fāris, who said that he was told by Yūnus Ibn Ḥabīb, who said that he was told by Abū Dāwūd, who said that he was told by Ḥarb Ibn Shidād, who said that he was told by Yaḥyā Ibn Abū Kathīr, who said that he was told by Abū Salāmah Ibn ʿAbdu'l-Raḥmān, who said that he was advised that ʿUbādah Ibn Al-Ṣāmit asked the Prophet (ﷺ) about the Words of Allāh, Most High:

ٱلَّذِينَ ءَامَنُوا۟ وَكَانُوا۟ يَتَّقُونَ ﴿٦٣﴾ لَهُمُ ٱلْبُشْرَىٰ
فِى ٱلْحَيَوٰةِ ٱلدُّنْيَا وَفِى ٱلْءَاخِرَةِ

"Those who believed and were fearing Allāh. For them

[374] This is ḥasan.

It was narrated by Al-Ṭabāranī in *'Al-Muʿjam Al-Kabīr'* (3/200) and by Al-Bazzār in *'Al-Musnad'* (*Kashf Al-Astar*) (#2121), by way of Abū ʿĀsim Al-Nabīl Al-Daḥḥāk Ibn Mukhallad, who reported on the authority of Mahdī Ibn Maymūn.

I say: This chain of narrators is ḥasan. Abū Al-Ṭufaylis a minor Companion (*raḍiyAllāhu ʿanhu*), whose name is ʿĀmir Ibn Wāthilah. ʿUthmān Ibn ʿUbayd Al-Rāsibī was mentioned by Ibn Ḥibbān in *'Al-Thiqāt'* (5/159) and by Ibn Abū Ḥātim in *'Al-Jarḥ wa'l-Taʿdīl'* (1/3/158) and he said: "I asked my father about ʿUthmān Ibn ʿUbayd and he said: "He is a man of honourable status."

> are good tidings in the worldly life and in the Hereafter. No change is there in the words [i.e., decrees] of Allāh. Thatis what is the great attainment."
>
> [*Yūnus* (10): 63-64].

> He (ﷺ) said: "It is a righteous dream that a Muslim man has, or another person has about him."[375]

215. We were informed by Abū'l-Ḥusayn ʿAlī Ibn Muḥammad Ibn ʿAbdullāh Al-Mu'addil, who said that he was informed by Al-Ḥusayn Ibn Ṣafwān Al-Barzaʿī, who said that he was told by ʿAbdullāh Ibn Muḥammad Ibn Abū Al-Dunyā, who said he was told by [Isḥāq],[376] Al-Nursī, who said that he was told by Abū ʿAbdullāh Al-Mirwazī that a man saw Yazīd Ibn Hārūn in a dream after his death and he said to him,

> "How did Allāh treat you?" He replied, "He has allowed Paradise for me." He asked, "Was it due to the Qur'ān?" He answered, "No." The man asked, "Then due to what?" He replied, "Due to the ḥadīth."[377]

216. I was informed by Muḥammad Ibn Al-Muẓaffar Ibn ʿAlī Al-Muqrī' Al-Daynūrī, who said that he was told by Ibrāhīm Ibn Muḥammad Al-Muzakkī, in Baghdād, who said that he heard Aḥmad Ibn Muḥammad Al-Hayrī Al-Muzakkī, who said that he was told by ʿAbdullāh Ibn Al-Ḥārith Al-Sanʿānī, who said that

[375] Its chain of narrators is *munqaṭiʿ*.

The break in the chain is between Abū Salāmah and ʿUbādah Ibn Al-Ṣāmit (*raḍiyAllāhu ʿanhu*), because Abū Salāmah did not hear from ʿUbādah and that is clear from this narration.

The ḥadīth was also narrated by Tirmidhī (#2275), by Ibn Mājah (#3898) and by Al-Dārimī (#2136), by way of Yaḥyā Ibn Abū Kathīr, but in the versions of Ibn Mājah and Al-Dārimī, it does not say *"advised"*.

[376] This is from manuscript (B).

[377] I do not know who Isḥāq Al-Nursī and Abū ʿAbdullāh Al-Mirwazī are; it is possible that the former is Ibn Abū Isrā'īl.

he heard Ḥawtharah Ibn Muḥammad Al-Manqarī Al-Baṣrī, who said:

> "I saw Yazīd Ibn Hārūn Al-Wāsiṭi in a dream after he died on four nights and I said: "How did Allāh treat you?" He replied, "Allāh has accepted my good deeds and pardoned me for my transgressions and He has granted me forgiveness for any acts of injustice I may have committed." I said: "And what was there after that?" He answered, "Is there anything but generosity from the Most Generous? He has forgiven me my sons and admitted me to Paradise." I asked, "Due to what did you attain what you have attained?" He replied, "Due to the gatherings for the purpose of *dhikr*, my having spoken the truth, my honesty in narrating ḥadīth, my standing for long periods in prayer and my patience when faced with poverty."I said: "And are Munkar and Nakīr a fact?" He replied, "Yes, by Allāh, besides Whom none is worthy of worship! They sat me down and asked me, saying to me, "Who is your Lord? What is your Religion? And who is your Prophet?" I began to wave my beard, which was white with dust and I said: "Is a person such as myself to be asked? I am Yazīd Ibn Hārūn Al-Wāsiṭī and I lived as the most knowledgeable of people in the world for sixty years." On hearing this, one of them said: "He has spoken the truth. He is Yazīd Ibn Hārūn. Sleep the sleep of a newlywed and let there be no fear upon you after today." Then one of them said: "Did you record on the authority of Harīz Ibn 'Uthmān?" I replied, "Yes; and he was trustworthy in matters of ḥadīth." He (the angel) said: "Trustworthy, but he hated 'Alī (*raḍiyAllāhu 'anhu*)—may Allāh, (the Almighty, the All-Powerful)[378] hate him."[379]

[378] This is from manuscript (B).

=

217. I read to Abū Bakr Al-Barqānī, on the authority of Ibrāhim Ibn Muḥammad Ibn Yaḥyā Al-Naysābūrī, who said that he was informed by Muḥammad Ibn Isḥāq Al-Thaqafī, who said that he was told by ʿAlī Ibn Aḥmad Al-Raqqī, who said that he was informed by Al-Ṣawwāq, who said that he was told by Zakariyya Ibn ʿAdiyy, who said that he saw Ibn Al-Mubārak in a dream and he asked him:

> "How did Allāh treat you?" He said: "He forgave me due to my travelling (in pursuit of ḥadīth)."[380]

Abū Saʿd Al-Malīnī imparted to us that he was told by ʿAbdullāh Ibn ʿAdiyy, who said that he was told by Aḥmad Ibn Ḥafṣ, who said that he was told by Aḥmad Ibn Saʿīd Al-Dārimī, who said that he heard Al-ʿAlā' saying that a man informed him that he saw ʿAbdullāh Ibn Al-Mubārak in a dream and he asked him how Allāh had treated him. He replied:

> "He forgave me due to my travelling in [pursuit of] ḥadīth."[381]

219. We were informed by Muḥammad Ibn Aḥmad Ibn Rizq Al-Bazzār, who said that he was informed by ʿUthmān Ibn Aḥmad Al-Daqqāq.

---

[379] Its chain of narrators is *ṭalif* (bad, broken, damaged).

In it is ʿAbdullāh Ibn Al-Ḥārith Al-Sanʿānī and he is a fabricator. Ibn Ḥibbān said of him, "Shaikh Dajjal. He narrated on the authority of ʿAbdu'l-Razzāq amazing (i.e. unbelievable) things from the people of Iraq, fabricating aḥādīth and attributing them to them." Abū Nuʿaym said: "He transmitted fabrications; he is nothing." Ibn Al-Sam'ani said: "He used to fabricate aḥadīth."

[380] Its chain of narrators is ḥasan.

ʿAlī Ibn Aḥmad Ibn Surayj Al-Ṣawwāq was mentioned by Al-Khaṭīb in his *'Tārīkh'* (11/315) and he said: "I know nothing but good regarding his status." The remainder of the men in the chain of narrators are trustworthy and Ḥuffāẓ, aside from Zakariyyā Ibn ʿAdiyy, who is trustworthy.

[381] I do not know who Al-ʿAlā' is. Al-Dārimī did not mention his name in his works.

And we were informed by Muḥammad Ibn Al-Ḥusayn Al-Qaṭṭān, who said that he was told by Ismāʿīl Ibn Muḥammad Al-Ṣaffar, who said that they were told by Jaʿfar Ibn Muḥammad Al-Ṣaʿigh, who said that he was told by Abū Muʿāwiyah Al-Ghallabī, who said that he was told by Abū Bahr Al-Bakrawī, who reported on the authority of one of their companions who used to seek knowledge of ḥadīth and then he died. Abū Bahr saw him in a dream and he asked him what had happened to him. He replied:

> "He (Allāh) forgave me." Abū Bahr asked, "Due to what?" He replied, "Due to my pursuit of ḥadīth."[382]

220. We were informed by Aḥmad Ibn Muḥammad Ibn Ghālib Al-Khawārizmī, who said that he was informed by Muḥammad Ibn Al-ʿAbbās Al-Khazzāz, who said that he was told by ʿUbaydullāh Ibn ʿAbdu'l-Raḥmān Al-Sukūnī,[383] who said that he was told by Muḥammad Ibn Ḥujjah, who said that he heard Muḥammad Ibn Al-Khalīl—who is one of our companions, and one of the best of people—say that he saw Sulaymān Al-Shazakūnī after his death and he was in a good situation, so he said to him:

> "O Abū Ayyūb! How has Allāh treated you?" He replied, "He has forgiven me." I asked, "Due to what?" He said: "Due to the ḥadīth."[384]

221. A letter was written to Abū Muḥammad ʿAbdu'l-Raḥmān Ibn ʿUthmān Al-Dimashqī in which it was mentioned that Abū'l-

---

[382] Its chain of narrators is weak; this is due to the weakness of Al-Bakrawī.

[383] This is how it appears in manuscript (A), while in manuscript (B) it says *'Al-Sukkarī'*.

[384] Its chain of narrators is weak.

In it is Muḥammad Ibn Ḥujjah, Abū Bakr Al-Bazzāz, whose biography was given by Al-Khaṭīb in *'Tārīkh Baghdād'* (2/296) and he did not record any criticism or praise of him therein.

Ḥasan[385] Aḥmad Ibn Ja'far Al-Ṣaydalānī Al-Baghdādī informed them in Damascus that he was told by Al-Ḥusayn Ibn 'Ubaydillāh Al-Abzārī, who said that he was told by Ḥubaysh Ibn Mubashshir, who said that he saw Yaḥyā Ibn Ma'īn ina dream and he asked him how Allāh had treated him. He replied:

> "He smoothed the way for me between two gates of Paradise." Then he raised his sleeve and brought out a scroll and he said: "I only attained what I attained due to this (i.e. his recording of ḥadīth)."[386]

222. I read to Abū Bakr Al-Barqānī, on the authority of Ibrāhīm Ibn Muḥammad Al-Naysābūrī, who said that he was informed by Muḥammad Ibn Isḥāq Al-Thaqafī, who said that he heard Muḥammad Ibn Aḥmad Ibn Bint Mu'āwiyah Ibn 'Amr, who said that he heard Abū Isḥāq Ibn Ibrāhīm, the *mustamillī* of Abū Hamām saying that he saw Abū Hamām in a dream and there was a ring of connected lamps on his head. He said:

> "O Abū Hamām! What are these lamps?" He replied, "I was given this[387] because of the ḥadīth regarding intercession, this because of the ḥadīth regarding Al-*Ḥawḍ*..."[388] and he continued to mention things."[389]

---

[385] This is how it appears in manuscript (A), which is the correct version, while in manuscript (B), it says: 'Abū'l-Ḥusayn'.

[386] It is fabricated.

In its chain is Al-Ḥusayn Ibn 'Ubaydillāh Al-Abzārī, who is a liar, as we mentioned earlier.

[387] This is how it appears in manuscript (A), while in manuscript (B), it says: "I was given it".

[388] *Al-Ḥawḍ*: The pool known as *Al-Kawthar*, promised to the Prophet (ﷺ) by Allāh in the Hereafter.See *Sūrah Al-Kawthar* (108):1

[389] It is authentic up to Abū Isḥāq Ibn Ibrāhīm.

Muḥammad Ibn Aḥmad is Ibn Al-Naḍr, for whom a biography is given in *'Tārīkh Baghdād'* (1/364) and he is trustworthy.

223. We were informed by ʿAlī Ibn Al-Ḥusayn Ibn Dawmā Al-Naʿālī, who said that he was told by Bakkār Ibn Aḥmad Ibn Bakkār Al-Muqrī' by dictation, who said that he was informed by Aḥmad Ibn Muḥammad Ibn Shāhīn, who said that he was told by Muḥammad Ibn Kurdūs, who said that he was told by ʿAlī Ibn Ādam Al-Kharrāṭ, the freed slave of ʿUmar Ibn Al-Khaṭṭāb (*raḍiyAllāhu ʿanhu*), who said that he was told by Sufyān Ibn ʿUyaynah, who said that he was told by Khalaf, the companion of Al-Khalqān, who said:

> "I had a friend with whom I used to study ḥadīth and he died.Then I saw him in a dream and he was wearing new green garments in which he roamed around. I said to him, "Did you not study ḥadīth with me? So what is this I see?" He said: "I used to record ḥadīth with you and I did not see any ḥadīth in which mention was made of the name of Muḥammad (ﷺ) except that I wrote below it: '(ﷺ)" (may the blessings and peace of Allāh be upon him). Because of this, my Lord [the Almighty, the All-Powerful][390] granted me what you see upon me."[391]

---

[390] This is from manuscript (A).

[391] I did not find any biographies for Aḥmad Ibn Muḥammad Ibn Shāhīn, Muḥammad Ibn Kurdūs and ʿAlī Ibn Ādam. It should not be thought that Ibn Kurdūs is the same person whose biography was given by Ibn Ḥibbān in *'Al-Thiqāt'* and by Ibn Abū Ḥātim in *'Al-Thiqāt'*, since the former came earlier and the latter, for whom a biography exists, came later.

The tradition was narrated by the author in *'Al-Jamiʿ'* (#565 and #566) via two routes in succession:

The first is from the narration of Aḥmad Ibn Mūsā Ibn Isḥāq Al-Anṣārī, who said that he was told by Sulaymān Ibn Muḥammad Ibn Mardas Al-Anṣārī—a native of Baṣrah from the son of ʿAbdu'l-ʿAzīz Ibn Suhayb—who said that he was told by ʿAlī Ibn Qāḍim, who said that he was told by Sufyān Ibn ʿUyaynah... and he quoted it in a mawqoof form, without any connection and in an abbreviated form.

I say: Aḥmad Ibn Mūsā Al-Anṣārī is trustworthy and a biography is given for him in *'Tārīkh Baghdād'*, while ʿAlī Ibn Qāḍim is weak. As for Sulaymān, he is unknown. =

Shaikh Abū Bakr [Al-Ḥāfiẓ][392] said: [I say:][393] Reports have been transmitted from the Messenger of Allāh (ﷺ) which prove this tradition regarding the ḥadīth.

224. We were told it by 'Isā Ibn Ghassān Al-Baṣrī by dictation and he said that he was told by Abū'l-'Abbās Muḥammad Ibn Aḥmad Ibn Abū Ghassān Al-Daqqāq, who said that he was told by 'Abdullāh Ibn Muḥammad Al-Khumrī, who said that he was told by Muḥammad Ibn Mahdī Ibn Hilāl, who said that he was told by Muḥammad Ibn Yazīd Ibn Khunays, who said that he was told by 'Abdu'l-Raḥmān Ibn Muḥammad Al-Thaqafī, who reported on the authority of 'Abdu'l-Raḥmān Ibn Hurmuz, who reported on the authority of Abū Hurayrah (*raḍiyAllāhu 'anhu*), who said that the Messenger of Allāh (ﷺ) said:

> "Whoever wrote in his book (ﷺ) (may the blessings and peace of Allāh be upon him), the angels will continue ask forgiveness for him (i.e. as long as it remains in his book)."[394]

225. I was told by Abū Ṣāliḥ Aḥmad Ibn 'Abdu'l-Mālik Al-Mu'azzin, who said that he heard Abū 'Abdullāh Al-Ḥusayn Ibn Al-Ḥusayn Ibn Muḥammad Ibn Aḥmad Al-Ḥalabī, in Damascus,

=

The second is from the narration of Muḥammad Ibn 'Abdullāh Ibn Muḥammad Al-Kūfī, who said that he was told by Aḥmad Ibn Muḥammad Ibn 'Abdu'l- Khāliq, who said that he was told by Al-Ḥusayn Ibn 'Alī Ibn Yazīd Al-Sada'ī, who said that he was told by a Shaikh—whom he named—on the authority of Khālid, the companion of Khalqan.

I say: This chain of narrators is talif and it is quite possible that it is fabricated and stolen, for in it is Muḥammad Ibn 'Abdullāh Al-Kūfī, who is a liar, described as being a fabricator and of stealing (*asanīd*). See his biography in *'Tārīkh Baghdād'* (5/467).

[392] This is from manuscript (A).

[393] This is from manuscript (B).

[394] It is fabricated.

This has been written about previously (#60).

who said that he heard Aḥmad Ibn 'Aṭā' Al-Rawzabārī saying that he heard Abū Ṣāliḥ 'Abdullāh Ibn Ṣāliḥ Al-Ṣūfī saying that one of the companions of ḥadīth was seen in a dream and it was said [to him]:

> "How did Allāh [the Almighty, the All-Powerful][395] treat you?" He replied, "He forgave me." It was asked, "Due to what?" He answered, "Because of the prayers I invoked on the Messenger of Allāh (ﷺ) in my books."[396]

[395] This is from manuscript (B).

[396] Its chain of narrators is weak.

In it is Aḥmad Ibn 'Aṭā' Al-Rawzabārī , who is one of the Shaikhs of the Ṣūfīs and his narrations are weak. Ibn 'Āsakir said: "He narrated incorrect aḥādīth that contained monstrous errors, and I have not found any biography for his Shaikh. It should not be imagined that he is the scribe of Al-Layth, for the person in the sanad came later than Al-Layth's scribe. And Allāh knows better.

CHAPTER FIFTY-TWO

Mention of Some Traditions That Might be Problematic for Those Who Hear Them and Elucidation of the Ambiguity Regarding Their Objectives and Their Meanings

226. I was informed by Muḥammad Ibn Al-Ḥusayn Ibn Al-Faḍl Al-Qaṭṭān, who said that he was informed by Daʿlaj Ibn Aḥmad, who said that he was informed by Aḥmad Ibn ʿAlī Al-Ubār, who said that he was told by Abū ʿAmmār—Al-Ḥusayn Ibn Ḥurayth—who said that he heard Al-Faḍl Ibn Mūsā, who reported on the authority of Al-Fuḍayl that he said that Al-Mughīrah said:

> "No one studies this ḥadīth except that his prayer is reduced."[397]

[397] The men in the isnād are trustworthy, except that it appears to be *munqaṭiʿ* between Al-Faḍl Ibn Mūsā Al-Mirwāzī and Al-Fuḍayl, for Al-Fuḍayl was not mentioned among Al-Faḍl's Shaikhs.

227. We were informed by Aḥmad Ibn Muḥammad Ibn Ghālib Al-Khawārizmī, who said that it was recited to Abū Isḥāq Al-Muzakkī while he was listening and Abū'l-Ḥasan Ibn Aḥmad Ibn Zuhayr told them that he was told by Yūsuf Ibn 'Isā Al-Mirwazī, who said that he was told by Al-Faḍl Ibn Mūsā Al-Sīnānī, who said that Mughīrah said..." and he quoted something similar, except that he did not mention Fuḍayl in the *isnād*.[398]

Shaikh Abū Bakr [Al-Ḥāfiẓ] said: "These words emanated from Mughīrah and he intended them with regard to his own situation; and it is likely that he used to perform many voluntary prayers and so if he exerted himself in the pursuit of ḥadīth by travelling to faraway places,[399] this would reduce the number of voluntary prayers he could offer and so Mughīrah said this, but if he had thought deeply[400] about it, he would have realised that his striving in pursuit of ḥadīth was better than his [voluntary] prayers."

228. I was informed by Al-Ḥusayn Ibn 'Alī Al-Ṭanājirī, who said that he was told by 'Umar Ibn Aḥmad Lawā'iẓ.

We were informed by 'Ubaydullāh Ibn Aḥmad Al-Ṣayrafī, who said that he was told by Aḥmad Ibn 'Imrān, who both said that they were told by 'Abdu'l-Ghāfir Ibn Salāmah ['Umar added: Al-Ḥimṣī],

---

398 Its chain of narrators is *mu'ḍal* (having more than one consecutive narrators missing from the chain).

The two chains are acceptable up to Al-Faḍl Ibn Mūsā, who sometimes narrated it in a mursal form on the authority of Al-Fuḍayl and sometimes narrated it in a *mu'ḍal* form, in the manner of a quotation from Al-Mughīrah, leaving out Al-Fuḍayl and the narrator connecting him to Al-Fuḍayl.

399 In manuscript (A) it says *"place"*.

400 In manuscript (A) it says *"am'an al-naḍr"*, while in manuscript (B) it says *"am'am al-naḍr"*, but both expressions carry the same meaning.

then they both agreed that Abū Thawbān Mazdādh[401] Ibn Jamīl said ʻAmr Ibn Ismāʻīl asked a man from among the companions of ḥadīth, Al-Mu'afa Ibn ʻImrān: "O Abū ʻImrān! What thing is most beloved to you? That I should pray or that I should record ḥadīth?"He replied:

> "Writing a single ḥadīth is more beloved to me than standing for a whole night in prayer." [402]

229. It was imparted to us by Abū Saʻd Al-Malīnī, who said that he was informed by ʻAbdullāh Ibn ʻAdiyy Al-Ḥāfiẓ, who said that he was told by Abū'l-Khuṣayb Aḥmad Ibn Al-Mustanīr Al-Maṣīṣī, who said that he heard ʻAbdah saying that he heard Ibn Al-Mubārak saying:

> "If I thought that [voluntary] prayer was better than ḥadīth, I would not relate ḥadīth to you."[403]

230. Al-Qāḍī Abū Bakr Al-Ḥayrī[404] and Abū Saʻīd Al-Ṣayrafī informed us that they were told by Abū'l-ʻAbbās Muḥammad Ibn Yaʻqūb Al-Aṣamm, who said that he heard Al-Rabīʻ Ibn Sulaymān saying that he heard Al-Shāfiʻī saying:

> "Seeking knowledge is better than offering voluntary prayers." And he narrated something similar to the saying of Mughīrah on the authority of Shuʻbah Ibn

[401] This is how it appears in manuscript (A), while in manuscript (B) it says Mazdad.

[402] Its chain of narrators is weak.

The status of Mazdād, or it was also said: Izdād and Yazdād Ibn Jamīl is unknown and we spoke about him previously.

The tradition was also narrated Ibn ʻAbdu'l-Barr in *'Jamiʻ Bayān Al-ʻIlm'* (1/24), by way of Mazdād.

[403] The men in the chain of narrators are trustworthy, aside from Ibn ʻAdiyy's Shaikh, for whom I have not found a biography.

[404] In manuscript (A) it says *'Al-Khabarī'*.

=

Al-Ḥajjāj.[405]

231. We were informed by Abū'l-Ḥasan Muḥammad Ibn Aḥmad Ibn Rizq Al-Bazzāz, who said that he was told by 'Uthmān Ibn Aḥmad Al-Daqqāq, who said that he was told by Al-Ḥasan Ibn Mukram, who said that he was told by Abū'l-Walīd, who said...

And we were informed by Aḥmad Ibn Muḥammad Ibn Ghālib Al-Faqīh, who said that it was recited to Isḥāq Al-Na'ālī, while he was listening, that they were told by Abū Khalīfah, who said that he heard Abū'l-Walīd saying that he heard Shu'bah saying:

> "Verily, this ḥadīth will divert you away from the remembrance of Allāh and from prayer. So will you desist?"[406]

Abū Khalīfah said: "Shu'bah (may Allāh have mercy on him) intended by this to say that his people were losing the opportunity to perform [good] deeds by listening to his words and preoccupying themselves with them, for ḥadīth does not distract a person from the remembrance of Allāh; rather, it guides him to Allāh's Command," and he went on to expand on the subject.

232. I was told by Al-Ḥasan[407] Ibn Abū Ṭālib, who said that he was told by 'Abdu'l-Wāḥid Ibn 'Alī Al-Liyḥānī, who said that he

---

[405] Its chain of narrators is authentic.
The tradition was narrated by Al-Bayhaqī in *'Al-Madkhal'* (#474), by Abū Nu'aym (9/119) and by Ibn 'Abdu'l-Barr (1/25) by various routes on the authority of Al-Rabī'.

[406] Its chain of narrators is authentic.
Abū Khalīfah is Al-Faḍl Ibn Al-Ḥabbāb Al-Baṣrī, Abū'l-Walīd is Al-Ṭayālisī and Al-Barqānī's Shaikh is Isḥāq Ibn Muḥammad Ibn Isḥāq. Abū Ya'qūb Al-Na'ālī is trustworthy and dependable and a biography is given for him in *'Tārīkh Baghdād'* (6/400-401).

[407] In manuscript (A) it says 'Al-Ḥusayn'.

was told by ʿAbdullāh Ibn Sulaymān Ibn ʿIsā Al-Qāḍī, who said that he was told by Isḥāq Ibn Ibrāhim Ibn Hānī', who said that he heard Abū ʿAbdullāh—Aḥmad Ibn Ḥanbal—being asked about the words of Shuʿbah: "Verily, this ḥadīth will divert you away from the remembrance of Allāh and from prayer. So will you desist?" And he said: "It is possible that Shuʿbah was fasting and that when he sought ḥadīth and strove earnestly to that end, he became weak and unable to fast, or that he wished to perform some [other] good deed, but was unable to do so, because of his pursuit of ḥadīth and that this was his meaning."

[I say]:[408] It is not permissible for anyone to say that Shuʿbah hindered people from seeking knowledge of ḥadīth. How could he, when he himself used to do that? So much so, that he was known as the Commander of the Faithful in ḥadīth? All of that was due to his pursuit of it and his preoccupation with it and he continued to seek [knowledge of] it for the whole of his life, being engaged in collecting ḥadīth until the day he died—and he did not busy himself with anything else. He would record from those younger than he in years and those below him in *isnād.* And he was the most careful of the companions of ḥadīth in reporting what he heard and the best of them regarding his thoroughness and exactitude in memorising it.

233. We were informed by ʿUbaydullāh Ibn Aḥmad Al-Ṣayrafī and Ḥamzah Ibn Muḥammad Ibn Ṭāhir Al-Daqqāq, who both said that they were informed by Aḥmad Ibn Ibrāhim Ibn Al-Ḥasan, who said that he was told by ʿAbdullāh Ibn Muḥammad Al-Baghawī, who said that he was told by ʿAbbās—Ibn Muḥammad— who said that he was told by Abū Bakr Ibn Abū'l-Aswad, who said that

[408] This is from manuscript (B).

ʿAbdu'l-Raḥmān said that Sufyān used to say:

> "Shuʿbah was the Commander of the Faithful in ḥadīth."[409]

234. We were informed by Muḥammad Ibn Aḥmad Ibn Rizq, who said that he was informed by Aḥmad Ibn [Isḥāq][410] Al-Bandār, who said that he was told by ʿAlī Ibn Aḥmad Ibn Al-Naḍr, who said that he heard Muḥammad Ibn ʿAbdu'l-Raḥmān Ibn Sahm, who said that he heard Baqiyyah Ibn Al-Walīd, who said that he heard Shuʿbah Ibn Al-Ḥajjāj saying:

> "Verily, I memorise ḥadīth and when something escapes me, I become ill."[411]

235. We were informed by Muḥammad Ibn Al-Ḥusayn Al-Qaṭṭān, who said that he was informed[412] by ʿAbdullāh Ibn Jaʿfar Ibn Darastawayh Al-Fārisī, who said that he was told by

Yaʿqūb Ibn Sufyān, who said that he was told by Mujahid Ibn

[409] Its chain of narrators is authentic.

ʿAbdu'l-Raḥmān is Ibn Mahdī and ʿAbbās Ibn Muḥammad is Al-Dawrī.

The tradition was narrated by Ibn Abū Ḥātim in *'Muqaddimah Al-Jarḥ wa'l-Taʿdīl'* (p. 126), on the authority of his father, who said that he was told by Abū Bakr Ibn Abū'l-Aswad...

The author also narrated it in his *'Tārīkh'* (9/259) from another source, on the authority of Al-Thawrī.

[410] This is from manuscript (B).

[411] Its chain of narrators is weak.

A biography was given for Muḥammad Ibn ʿAbdu'l-Raḥmān Ibn Sahm by Ibn Abū Ḥātim in *'Al-Jarḥ wa'l-Taʿdīl'* (2/3/315) and he did not mention any criticism or praise of him in it. As for Ibn Ḥibbān, he mentioned him in *'Al-Thiqāt'* (9/87), saying, "Possibly he used to make mistakes."

And ʿAlī Ibn Aḥmad Ibn Al-Naḍr was declared weak by Al-Dāraquṭnī, as stated in *'Tārīkh Baghdād'* (11/316).

[412] This is from manuscript (B).

Mūsā, who said that he was told by Abū Kāmil Muẓaffar Ibn Mudrik, who said that a ḥadīth was mentioned to Al-Shuʿbah which he had not heard and he said:

"Let us appraise it!"[413]

236. We were informed by Ibrāhim Ibn Mukhallad Al-Qāḍī, who said that he was told by Abū ʿAbdullāh Muḥammad Ibn Aḥmad Ibrāhīm Al-Ḥakīmī, who said that he was told by Muḥammad Ibn Al-ʿAbbās Al-Khurasānī, who said that he heard ʿĀṣim—Ibn ʿAlī—saying that he was told by the brother of Al-Ḥasan Ibn ʿAlī, who said that Shuʿbah said to him:

> "O Ḥasan! It is possible that Qays Ibn Al-Rabīʿ informed me of the ḥadīth of Abū Ḥusayn and I hope that the ceiling might fall on me and that it might kill him and me."[414]

237. We were told that by Abū Saʿd Al-Malīnī, who said that he was informed by ʿAbdullāh Ibn ʿAdiyy Al-Ayyūb, who said that he was told by his father, who said that he was told by ʿAlī Ibn ʿĀṣim, who said that Shuʿbah went to Khālid Al-Ḥadhā' and said:

> "O Abū Munāzil! Do you have aḥādīth that you can

[413] Its chain of narrators is authentic as far as Muẓaffar Ibn Mudrik.

Shuʿbah was not mentioned among his Shaikhs. Ibn Darastawayh is trustworthy and those who declared him to be weak are not correct, as is made clear in his biography in '*Tārīkh Baghdād*' (9/428).

[414] Its chain of narrators is weak.

Al-Ḥasan Ibn ʿAlī is Ibn ʿĀṣim Al-Wasiṭī, of whom Ibn Maʿīn said: "He is nothing." And in his parlance, that is a severe criticism. Ibn Al-Madīnī said: "I saw him, but I did not record anything from him." As for Abū Ḥātim, he said: "His status is one of truthfulness." Ibn ʿAdiyy said: "His aḥadīth are sound and I hope that there is no objection to him."

I say: It is more likely that he is weak.

relate to me?" But Khālid was in poor health and so he said to him, "I am in pain." He replied, "It is only one." And so he related it to him and when he had finished, he said: "Die, if you wish."[415]

[415] Its chain of narrators is weak.

In it is 'Alī Ibn 'Āṣim Ibn Suhayb and he frequently made mistakes. He used to re-ported on the authority of Khālid Al-Ḥadhā' and others and he would misquote them. Yazīd Ibn Zurai' said: "I met 'Alī Ibn 'Āṣim in Al-Baṣrah when Khālid Al-Ḥadhā' was still alive and he informed me of some things on the authority of Khālid and so I asked him (i.e. Khālid) about them and he rejected them all."

CHAPTER FIFTY-THREE

A Tradition of Sufyān Al-Thawrī

238. We were informed by Abū Sa'īd Muḥammad Ibn Mūsā Al-Ṣayrafī, who said that he was told by Abū'l-'Abbās Muḥammad Ibn Ya'qūb Al-Aṣamm, who said that he was told by Muḥammad Ibn Isḥāq Al-Ṣāghanī, who said that he was told by 'Alī Ibn Qāḍim...

We were informed by Muḥammad Ibn Al-Ḥusayn Ibn Al-Faḍl Al-Qaṭṭān, who said that he was told by 'Alī Ibn 'Abdu'l-Raḥmān Al-Kūfī, who said that he was told by Aḥmad Ibn Ḥāzim, who said that he heard 'Alī Ibn Qādim saying that he heard Sufyān Al-Thawrī that he said:

> "I wished that I had not embarked on anything of it (i.e. ḥadīth) and I wished that I could be free [from it],[416] nothing upon me and nothing for me."[417] The wording is that of Ibn Al-Faḍl.

[416] This is from manuscript (B).

[417] Its chain of narrators is weak.

In it is 'Alī Ibn Qādim, who is weak, especially when he narrates on the authority of Al-Thawrī.

=

239. We were informed by Al-Qāḍī Abū Bakr Aḥmad Ibn Al-Ḥasan Al-Ḥarshī, who said that he was told by Muḥammad Ibn Ya'qūb Al-Aṣamm, who said that he was told by Al-Khiḍr Ibn Ubān Al-Hashimī, who said that he was told by Muḥammad Ibn Bishr, who said that he heard Sufyān Al-Thawrī:

> "I wish that I could be completely free from it (i.e. ḥadīh)."[418]

Abū Bakr Al-Khaṭīb (may Allāh have mercy on him) said: Sufyān Al-Thawrī only said this due to fear for himself that he would not fulfil the requirements of ḥadīth and act upon them and he feared that it would be a proof against him, as in the following:

240. We were informed by Abū'l-Ḥasan Aḥmad Ibn Muḥammad Ibn Aḥmad Ibn Mūsā Ibn Hārūn Ibn Al-Salṭ Al-Ahwāzī, who said that he was told by Muḥammad Ibn Mukhallad Al-'Aṭṭār, who said that he was told by Mūsā—Ibn Hārūn—who said that he was told by Muḥammad—Ibn Na'īm Al-Hayṣam—that he said that he saw Bishr Ibn Al-Ḥārith and he had been to visit a companion of ḥadīth and Bishr said to them:

> "What is this I see with you that you are showing?" They

=

However, it was narrated by Ibn Abū Ḥātim in *'Muqaddimah Al-Jahr'* (p. 61) by way of Al-Firyābī and Qubaysah, on the authority of Al-Thawrī—and its chain of narrators is authentic.

He narrated it (p. 62) by way of 'Isā Ibn Muḥammad Al-Naḥḥās, who said that Ḍhamrah (i.e. Ibn Rabī'ah) said: "I heard Sufyān..." and he quoted it without the first portion, but added to it: "Today, I am seeking knowledge—and for what is it?"

[418] Its chain of narrators is weak, but the tradition is authentic.

In it is Al-Khiḍr Ibn Ubān Al-Hashimī; a biography is given for him in *'Al-Lisān'* (2/487) and he was declared weak by Al-Ḥākim and others and Al-Dāraquṭnī spoke of him (i.e. negatively). See what has preceded.

replied, "O Abū Naṣr! We are acquiring knowledge, in the hope that Allāh will benefit us thereby one day." He said: "You know that it is incumbent upon you to pay *zakah* on it, just as it is incumbent upon any of you, if he possesses two hundred *dirhāms*, to pay five *dirhāms*. Likewise, if one of you hears two hundred aḥādīth, then he must act upon five of them. If he does not, then see what this will cause to you on the morrow."[419]

241. We were informed by Muḥammad Ibn Aḥmad Ibn Rizq, who said that he was told by Abū 'Alī Ibn Al-Ṣawwāf, who said that he was told via dictation by Maḥmūd Abū Muḥammad Al-Mirwāzī, who said that he was told by Abū Mu'ādh Al-Jarūd Ibn Mu'ādh Tirmidhī, who said that he was told by 'Umar, who reported on the authority of Mālik Ibn Maghūl, who said that he heard Al-Sha'bī saying:

"I wish that I had not learnt anything of this knowledge."[420]

He said: "Al-Sha'bī only said that due to fear that he would not fulfil its obligations or the gratitude that such knowledge entails."

242. We were told by Abū Ṭālib Yaḥyā Ibn 'Alī Ibn Al-Ṭayyib Al-Daskarī, who said that he was told by Abū Bakr Ibn Al-Muqrī', in Aṣbāhanī, who said that he was told by Bakr Ibn Muḥammad

[419] Its chain of narrators is weak, but the tradition is authentic.
In it is Muḥammad Ibn Na'īm Al-Ḥaysam, whose biography is given by Al-Khaṭīb in his *'Tārīkh'* (3/321) and he did not mention either praise or criticism of him. He narrated reports on the authority of Bishr Ibn Al-Ḥārith. But it was narrated by Al-Ḥasan Ibn 'Amr Al-Shī'ī, who reported it on the authority of Bishr.
The author narrated it in his *'Tārīkh'* (7/69) and its chain of narrators is authentic.
It also has another chain of narrators from Abū Nu'aym in *'Al-Ḥilyah'* (8/47).

[420] I have not found anyone among the Shaikhs of Mālik Ibn Maghūl who is known as 'Umar. Only 'Amr Ibn Marzūq and 'Amr Ibn Al-Haytham narrated on his authority. As for Jarīd, I have not found any biography for him.

Al-Maṣīṣī, who said that he was told by Ibrāhīm Ibn Sa'īd, who said that he heard Abū Qutn 'Amr Ibn Al-Haytham say that Al-Shu'bah said:

> "I am not entrusted with anything which I fear will cause me to be admitted to the Fire more than it (i.e. ḥadīth)."[421]

And Ibn 'Awn said: "I wish that I could escape completely from it."

243. We were informed by Abū 'Abdullāh Al-Ḥusayn Ibn 'Umar Ibn Burhān Al-Ghazal, the righteous Shaikh, who said that he was told by 'Abdu'l-Bāqī Ibn Qāni' [Al-Qāḍī],[422] who said that he was told by Abū Ghālib 'Alī Ibn Aḥmad, who said that he was told by Yazīd Ibn 'Abdu'l-Raḥīm[423] Ibn Muṣ'ab, who said that he heard his father say that he heard Sufyān Al-Thawrī saying:

> "Whoever increases in knowledge also increases in pain; and if I did not have knowledge, it would have eased my sadness."[424]

244. I was informed[425] by Al-Qāḍī Abū Bakr Aḥmad Ibn Al-

---

[421] I have not found any biography for Bakr Ibn Muḥammad Al-Maṣīṣī.

[422] This is from manuscript (B).

[423] This is how it appears in manuscript (A) and manuscript (B), but the correct name is 'Abdu'l-Raḥmān, as is made clear in *'Al-Ḥilyah'*.

[424] Its chain of narrators is weak.

In it is Abū Ghālib 'Alī Ibn Aḥmad Ibn Al-Naḍr Al-Azdi, who was declared weak by Al-Dāraquṭnī and he was also mentioned by Salāmah Al-Andalusī, who said: "He is trustworthy." I say: Al-Daraquṭni is more knowledgeable with regard to him, because Abū Ghālib was a Baghdādi Shaikh. Yazīd Ibn 'Abdu'l-Raḥmān Ibn Muṣ'ab is truthful;a biography is given for him in *'Al-Jarḥ wa'l-Ta'dīl'* (2/4/277), but his father's status is unknown; he is one of the men in *'Al-Tahẓīb'*.

The tradition was included by Abū Nu'aym in *'Al-Ḥilyah'* (6/363).

[425] In manuscript (B) it says: *"We were informed"*.

Ḥasan Al-Ḥarshī, who said that he was told by Abū'l-'Abbās Muḥammad Ibn Ya'qūb Al-Aṣamm, who said that he was told by 'Abdullāh Ibn Hilāl Ibn Al-Furat, who said that he was told by Aḥmad—Ibn Abū'l-Hawarī—who said that he was told by Muḥammad Ibn Na'īm Al-Mawsilī, who reported on the authority of Al-Mu'afa Ibn 'Imrān, who said that he heard Sufyān— Ibn Sa'īd Al-Thawrī—who said:

> "I wished that every ḥadīth in my breast and every ḥadīth that men have memorised on my authority were erased from my breast and from their breasts." I said: "O Abū 'Abdullāh, bearer of correct knowledge and bearer of the clear Sunnah, which you have explained! Do you wish that they be erased from your breast and the breasts of the men?" He replied: "Be silent! What will inform you [of my situation], should I wish not to stand on the Day of Resurrection and be questioned about every gathering I attended and about every ḥadīth I have related?"[426]

Sufyān made clear in this ḥadīth the reason why he feared for himself; and it has been said that Sufyān only feared for himself from ḥadīth and wished that he had not embarked on [the study of] it because love of *isnād* and craving for the narration had overcome his heart to such a degree that he used to relate on the authority of weak narrators and those whose narrations should not be cited as proof. When the name of a person from among them

[426] 'Abdullāh Ibn Hilāl Ibn Al-Furat is Al-Dawmī, mistakenly written as Al-Rūmī in Ibn Abū Ḥātim's work, *'Al-Jarḥ wa'l-Ta'dīl'* (2/2/193), where he cited a biography for him. He said that his father was asked about him and he said: "He is truthful." As for Muḥammad Ibn Al-Mawsilī, I have not found any biography for him and Abū Zakariyya Al-Mawsili did not mention him in *'Tārīkh Al-Mawsil'*. It is likely that he is the same person as Muḥammad Ibn Na'īm Al-Ḥaysam, the person who narrated on the authority of Bishr Ibn Al-Ḥārith, who is from the same tabaqah (stage or level of narrators) and whom we discussed previously.

was well known, he would mention him by his agnomen, thereby committing *tadlīs*. So he feared for himself due to this action. And a group from among the Imāms and scholars have expressed their disapproval of *tadlīs*.

245. I was informed by 'Ubaydullāh Ibn Abū'l-Fatḥ Al-Fārisī, who said that he was informed by Muḥammad Ibn Al-Muẓaffar, who said that he was told by 'Abdullāh Ibn Muḥammad Ibn Ja'far Al-Qizwīnī, in Egypt, who said that he was told by Abū Zur'ah 'Ubaydullāh Ibn 'Abdu'l-Karīm, who said that Musaddad told him that Yaḥyā said to him:

> "Sufyān Al-Thawrī was overcome by his craving for ḥadīth."[427]

246. We were informed by Al-Ḥasan[428] Ibn Abū Bakr, who said that he was told by Muḥammad Ibn 'Alī Ibn Al-Haytham Al-Muqrī', who said that he was told by Yazīd Al-Badā', who said that he heard 'Ubaydullāh Ibn 'Umar, who said that he heard Yaḥyā Ibn Sa'īd, who said:

> "I do not fear anything for Sufyān except his love for ḥadīth."[429]

247. We were informed by Muḥammad Ibn Aḥmad Ibn Rizq,

[427] Its chain of narrators is extremely weak.
In it is 'Abdullāh Ibn Muḥammad Ibn Ja'far Al-Qizwīnī, who is a liar and is accused (of fabricating aḥādīth). Al-Dāraquṭnī said: "He is a liar; he wrote a book on the Sunan of Al-Shāfi'ī and in it there are more than two hundred aḥādīth, none of which was related by Al-Shāfi'ī." He also said: "Al-Qizwīnī fabricated in the manuscript of 'Amr Ibn Al-Hārith more than a hundred aḥādīth." See his biography in *'Al-Lisān'* (3/425).

[428] In manuscript (A) it says: *'Al-Ḥusayn'*.

[429] Its chain of narrators is authentic.
Yazīd Al-Badā' is Ibn Al-Haytham Ibn Tahmān, in Baghdād, who is trustworthy. A biography is given for him in *'Tārīkh Baghdād'* (14/349). 'Ubaydullāh Ibn 'Umar is Al-Qawarīrī.

who said that he was informed by Ja'far Ibn Muḥammad Ibn Nuṣayr Al-Khaldī, who said that he was told by Muḥammad Ibn 'Abdullāh Ibn Sulaymān Al-Ḥaḍrī, who said that he was told by Aḥmad Ibn Sinan, who said that he was told by 'Abdu'l-Raḥmān Ibn Mahdī, who said: "We would be with Sufyān and it was as if he had been summoned for his last reckoning. We would not dare speak a word to him, but then we would mention a ḥadīth." [He said: [430] "...then that humility would be dispelled and nothing remain except *'Ḥaddathana... waḥaddathana...'* ('We were told... and we were told...']."[431]

248. We were informed by Muḥammad Ibn Al-Ḥusayn Ibn Al-Faḍl Al-Qaṭṭān, who said that he was informed by Abdullah Ibn Ja'far Ibn Darāstawayh, who said that he was told by Ya'qūb Ibn Sufyān, who said that he was told by Abū Sa'īd Al-Ashajj, who said that he was told by Ibn Yaman, who said that he heard Sufyān saying:

> "The *fitnah* (trial, temptation) of ḥadīth is more severe than the *fitnah* of gold and silver." [432]

249. We were informed by Ibn Al-Faḍl, who said that he was informed by Ibn Darastawayh, who said that he was told by Ya'qūb Ibn Sufyān, who said that he was told by Aḥmad Ibn Al-Khalīl, who said that he heard Abū Nūḥ Qurād, who said that Shu'bah said:

[430] This is from manuscript (B).

[431] Its chain of narrators is authentic.

Al-Hadhramī is Al-Ḥāfiẓ Al-Kabīr Mutayyin.

The tradition was also narrated by Abū Nu'aym in *'Al-Ḥilyah'* (6/371), by way of Mutayyin.

[432] Its chain of narrators is weak.

In it is Yaḥyā Ibn Yaman, who is weak, especially when he narrates on the authority of Al-Thawrī; and we have spoken of him previously.

The tradition was narrated by Abū Nu'aym in *'Al-Ḥilyah'* (6/363), by way of Ibn Yaman.

"The best of men is Sufyān, were it not that he collects [aḥādīth] indiscriminately (i.e. from all of the people)."[433]

250. I was informed by ʿUbaydullāh Ibn Abū'l-Fatḥ, who said that he was informed by Muḥammad Ibn Al-Muẓaffar, who said that he was told by ʿAbdullāh Ibn Muḥammad Ibn Jaʿfar, who said that he was told by Abū Ismāʿīl Tirmidhī, who said that he quoted the words of Sufyān Al-Thawrī to Muḥammad Ibn ʿAbdullāh Ibn Numayr:

"I do not fear anything for myself except ḥadīth." He asked, "For what reason did he say that?" He [Abū Ismāʿīl] said: "Because he used to relate from weak narrators."[434]

[433] Its chain of narrators is authentic.

Aḥmad Ibn Al-Khalīl is Abū ʿAlī Al-Tājir, a native of Baghdād, who took up residence in Naysabūr, he is trustworthy; Qurad is a nickname, and his full name was ʿAbdu'l-Raḥmān Ibn Ghazwān; he is trustworthy and one of the men from *'Al-Tahzīb'*.

[434] Its chain of narrators is extremely weak.

In it is ʿAbdullāh Ibn Muḥammad Ibn Jaʿfar Al-Qizwīnī, who is a liar and was accused (of fabricating aḥādīth); and we spoke of him previously.

CHAPTER FIFTY-FOUR

Traditions Related from Mughīrah Ibn Miqsam Al-Ḍhabbī

251. I was informed by Muḥammad Ibn Al-Ḥusayn [Ibn Al-Faḍl][435] Al-Qaṭṭān, who said that he was informed by Da'laj Ibn Aḥmad, who said that he was informed by Aḥmad Ibn 'Alī Al-Ubār, who said that he was told by 'Awn Ibn Salām, who said that he was told by 'Abthar, who said that he heard Mughīrah saying:

> "Murrah was the best of people who learn ḥadīth, then he became the worst of people who learn ḥadīh. If I were to face what I have previously experienced, I would not have related ḥadīth."[436]

252. We were informed by Muḥammad Ibn Aḥmad Ibn Rizq, who said that he was informed by Muḥammad Ibn Al-Ḥasan Ibn Ziyād Al-Naqqāsh, who said that he was told by Abū Aḥmad

[435] This is from manuscript (B).

[436] Its chain of narrators is authentic.

Muḥammad Ibn ʿAbdūs, who said that he was told by Abū Maʿmar, who said that he was told by ʿAbthar, who said that he heard Mughīrah saying:

> "If I were to face what I have previously experienced, I would not have related ḥadīth." [437]

Shaikh Abū Bakr [Al-Ḥāfiẓ][438] said:

> "Seekers of knowledge are at (different) levels. It might be that a writer of ḥadīth may come to the scholar and he will not spend a long time learning (from him), and he will treat him with his customary good manners. So Mughīrah—and Allāh knows better—saw some of those people in his gatherings and witnessed their bad behaviour and reprehensible manners, which made him angry and so he spoke these words. And gatherings of learning are seldom free of such people as we have described. We ask Allāh to bless us with good manners and to grant us that we act upon our knowledge, through His Bounty and His Mercy."

253. We were informed by Ibrāhīm Ibn Mukhallad Al-Qāḍī, who said that he was told by Abū Bakr Muḥammad Ibn ʿAbdullāh Ibn Ṣāliḥ Al-Abhārī, who said that he heard Ibn Abū Dāwūd saying that he heard ʿIsā Ibn Ḥammād Zaghbah, who said that he heard Al-Layth Ibn Saʿd saying—when he had observed the Companions of Ḥadīth (*Aṣḥāb al-Ḥadīth*) and seen something (negative) from them—and so he said:

> "What is this? You are more in need of a small amount

[437] Its chain of narrators is extremely weak.
This is because in it is Al-Naqqāsh, who is accused (of fabricating ḥadīth). See his biography in *'Al-Lisān'* (5/149). But the tradition is authentic, due to the previous narration.
[438] This is from manuscript (A).

> of good manners than you are of a great deal of knowledge."[439]

254. We were informed by Muḥammad Ibn Aḥmad Ibn Rizq, who said that he was told by Abū 'Alī Ibn Al-Ṣawwāf, who said that he was told by 'Abbās Ibn Aḥmad Al-Washā', who said that he was told by Surayj, who said that he was told by Sufyān, who said that 'Ubaydullāh Ibn 'Umar looked at the companions of ḥadīth and their crowding and he said:

> "You have dishonoured knowledge and taken away its light; and if you and I were to have met 'Umar Ibn Al-Khaṭṭāb, he would have inflicted a painful beating on us." [440]

[439] Its chain of narrators is authentic.

[440] Its chain of narrators is weak.

In it is 'Abbās Ibn Aḥmad Ibn Al-Ḥasan Al-Washā'; Al-Khaṭīb gave a biography for him in his *'Tārīkh'* (12/151) and he said, "He was one of the Shaikhs of the righteous."

I say: This does not necessarily mean that he was trustworthy, for righteousness is one thing, but preciseness is another. And Allāh knows better.

As for 'Ubaydullāh Ibn 'Umar, he is Al-'Amrī.

CHAPTER FIFTY-FIVE

Traditions from Sufyān Al-Thawrī

255. We were informed by Al-Qāḍī Abū Bakr Aḥmad Ibn Al-Ḥasan Al-Ḥarshī, who said that he was told by Al-ʿAbbās Muḥammad Ibn Yaʿqūb Al-Aṣamm, who said that he was told by Al-Khiḍr Ibn Ubbān Al-Hashimī, who said that he as told by Muḥammad Ibn Bishr, who said that he heard Sufyān saying:

> "If this was from goodness, it would have decreased, as goodness decreases (i.e. ḥadīth)."[441]

256. I was informed by Muḥammad Ibn Al-Ḥusayn Ibn Al-Faḍl Al-Qaṭṭān, who said that he was informed by Daʿlaj Ibn Aḥmad, who said that he was informed by Aḥmad Ibn ʿAlī Al-Ubār, who said that he was told by ʿAlī Ibn Ḥajr, who said that he heard Khalaf Ibn Khalīfah saying that he heard Sufyān Ibn Saʿīd

[441] Its chain of narrators is weak.
In it is Al-Khiḍr Ibn Ubbān and we have spoken of him previously when we dealt with no. (#239).

saying:

> "I see every kind of goodness diminishing and this ḥadīth is increasing, so I think that if it were a cause of goodness, it would also diminish."[442]

[Abū Bakr said][443]: One of the people took these words and arranged them into a poem: Abū Bakr Aḥmad Ibn Muḥammad Ibn Ghālib Al-Khawārizmī recited to us, without naming the person who said it:

"I observe that much of the goodness in this world
is decreasing,
And it diminishes greatly while the ḥadīth is increasing,
So if it was good, then it would be like all goodness,
But the devil of the ḥadīth increases,
And Ibn Ma'īn has a saying regarding the men,
He will be asked about them while the angels bear witness,
And if he is truthful, he will have the ruling of backbiting,
While if it is a lie, then the accounting will be severe."

Shaikh Abū Bakr [Al-Ḥāfiẓ][444] said: "The matter is not as the

[442] Its chain of narrators is ḥasan.

If 'Alī Ibn Ḥajr hearing from Khalaf was before he began to mix things up—and there has been (negative) talk regarding Khalaf's memory—then his reports fall from the level of Ḥasan. And Allāh knows better.

The tradition was also narrated by Abū Nu'aym (6/369) by way of 'Abdu'l-Razzāq, who reported something similar on the authority of Al-Thawrī.

It also contains the Shaikh of Abū Nu'aym, Ibrāhīm Ibn 'Abdullāh Ibn Isḥāq Al-Aṣbāhanī, who has a blameless record. A biography is given for him in *'Akhbar Aṣbāhan'* (10/201) and Al-Khaṭīb also gave a biography for him in *'Tārīkh Baghdād'* (12/82-83).

[443] This is from manuscript (B).

[444] This is from manuscript (A).

poet claims, i.e. that the scholars' clarification of the status of narrators is backbiting; rather, it is advice. And in exposing them, they have a great reward, due to them revealing their status—and it is not permissible for them to conceal them."

257. I was informed by 'Alī Ibn Aḥmad Al-Razzāz, who said that he was informed by 'Alī Ibn Muḥammad Ibn Sa'īd Al-Mawsilī, who said that he was told by Abul Wajīh Ṣāliḥ Ibn Mūsā, who said that he was told by Aḥmad Ibn Ḥanbal, who said that he was told by 'Affān, who said that he was told by Yaḥyā Ibn Sa'īd, who said that he asked Shu'bah, Sufyān Ibn Sa'īd. Sufyān Ibn 'Uyainah and Mālik Ibn Anas about a man who is not weak and is not accused [of fabrication] and all of them said:

"Make clear his status."[445]

258. Abū Muḥammad 'Abdu'l-Raḥmān Ibn 'Uthmān Al-Dimashqī wrote to me and Muḥammad Ibn Yūsuf Al-Naysabūrī told me of it, saying that Abul Maymūn 'Abdu'l-Raḥmān Ibn 'Abdullāh Al-Bajlī informed them, saying that he was informed by Abū Zur'ah—'Abdu'l-Raḥmān Ibn 'Amr Al-Naṣrī—who said that he heard Abū Mashar being asked about a man who made mistakes, misconstrued things and misrepresented things, and he said, "Make clear his status." I said to Abū Mashar, "Do you consider that to be backbiting?" He replied, "No."[446]

---

[445] Its chain of narrators is *talif.*

In it is 'Alī Ibn Muḥammad Ibn Sa'īd Al-Mawsilī, whose biography was given by Al-Khaṭīb in *'Tārīkh Baghdād'* (12/82-83) and he transmitted on the authority of Abū Nu'aym and Muḥammad Ibn Al-Muẓaffar that they declared him to be a liar.

[446] Its chain of narrators is authentic.

'Abdu'l-Raḥmān Ibn 'Uthmān is 'Abdu'l-Raḥmān Ibn Abū Naṣr, the virtuous Shaikh, who is trustworthy and reliable and a leading scholar. A biography is given for him in *'Al-Siyār'* (17/366). Al-Dhahabi also provided a biography for 'Abdu'l-Raḥmān Al-Bajlī in *'Al-Siyār'* (15/533) and he said, "The Shaikh, Imām and trustworthy and reliable author."

The tradition was also narrated by the author in *'Al-Kifāyah'* (p. 63).

Shaikh Abū Bakr said: "We have discussed this in full in our well known book entitled *'Al-Kifāyah'* and there is no need for us to repeat it in this book. So let us return to the discussion regarding the meaning of the first section and we say: Al-Thawrī was referring in his aforementioned words to aḥādīth that are *gharā'ib*[447] and those that are *manākīr*,[448] and not including those that are *ma'rūfah*[449] or those that are *mashhūrah*.[450] This is because the traditions that are *shazzāh*[451] and the aḥādīth that are *munkarah* are too many to enumerate. So Al-Thawrī considered that there was no good in them, since they contradict the narrations of trustworthy reporters and scholars of *fiqh* act upon them. And it has been reported on the authority of a number of scholars besides Al-Thawrī that it is disliked to preoccupy oneself with them or to spend time studying them.

259. We were informed by Abū Ḥāzim 'Umar Ibn Aḥmad Al-'Abdawī, who said that he was informed by Muḥammad Ibn 'Abdullāh Ibn Ibrāhīm Al-Sulayṭī, who said that he was told by Ja'far Ibn Muḥammad Ibn Al-Ḥusayn, better known as Al-Turkī,[452] who said that he was told by Yaḥyā Ibn Yaḥyā, who said that he was informed by Muḥammad Ibn Jābir, who reported on the authority

---

[447] *Gharā'ib*: Plural of *gharīb*, i.e. a narration which is transmitted at some point in its isnād by a single narrator. If at the beginning of the *isnād*, it is known as *gharīb mutlaq* and if at any other point in the *isnād*, it is known as *gharīb nisbī*.

[448] *Manakīr*: Plural of munkar, i.e. a narration by a weak narration that contradicts what been authentically reported by someone trustworthy.

[449] *Ma'rūfah*: plural of *ma'rūf*, i.e. a narration transmitted by a trustworthy reporter, which contradicts what has been narrated by a weak reporter.

[450] *Mashhūrah*: Plural of *mashhūr*, i.e. a narration that has been transmitted by three or more narrators at each level of its *isnād*, without reaching the level of mutawatir (narrated by so many people that it is inconceivable that that they collaborated to propagate a lie).

[451] *Shazzāh*: Plural of shāzz, i.e. something narrated by an acceptable reporter which contradicts what has been narrated by someone more reliable.

[452] This is how it appears in manuscript (A), while in manuscript (B) and in *'Al-Kifāyah'* it says *'Al-Turk'*.

of Al-Aʿmash, who reported on the authority of Ibrāhīm, who said:

> "They used to dislike speech that was *gharīb* and ḥadīth that was *gharīb*."[453]

260. I recited to Muḥammad Ibn Al-Ḥusayn Al-Qaṭṭān, who reported on the authority of Daʿlaj Ibn Aḥmad, who said that he was told by Mūsā Ibn Hārūn, who said that he was told by Bishr Ibn Al-Walīd, who said that he heard Abū Yūsuf saying:

> "Do not recite many *aḥādīth* that are *gharībah*, which the jurists did not produce, for the last state of their bearer is that he is branded a liar."[454]

261. We were told verbally by ʿAbdu'l-ʿAzīz Ibn Abu'l-Ḥasan

[453] Its chain of narrators is weak, but it is authentic due to similar narrations.

Muḥammad Ibn Jābir is Ibn Sayyār; Yaḥyā Ibn Yaḥyā was mentioned in his biography in *'Tahzīb Al-Kamal'* (24/565) as being among those who narrated on his authority. As for Ibn Jābir, he is weak; he used to write aḥādīth in his books and he mix things up in them.

The tradition was also narrated by the author in *'Al-Kifāyah'* (p. 171) with the same chain of narrators.

And Al-Ramāhurmuzī narrated it in *'Al-Muḥaddith Al-Fāsil'* (#774), on the authority of Musaddad, who said that he was told by Muḥammad Ibn Jābir, who narrated it and it was authentically reported on the authority of Ibrāhīm, who said: "They used to dislike when they gathered, that a man should narrate the ahsan of his ḥadīth or the ahsan of what he had."

It was also narrated by Al-Ramāhurmuzī (#765 and #766) and by the author in *'Al-Jāmiʿ'* (2/101) by various routes on the authority of Ibn ʿAwn, who reported on the authority of Ibrāhīm and its chain of narrators is authentic. And what is meant by ahsan here is the *gharīb*.

[454] Its chain of narrators is ḥasan.

We have previously discussed Bishr Ibn Al-Walīd when we dealt with narration no. 2. And Mūsā Ibn Hārūn is Ibn ʿAbdullāh Ibn Marwān, who is trustworthy, a Ḥāfiẓ and a scholar.

The tradition was narrated by Al-Ramāhurmuzī (#769), who said that he was told by Jaʿfar Al-Firyābī, who said that he was told by Bishr Ibn Al-Walīd, who said that he heard Abū Yūsuf saying: "Whoever followed the *gharīb* from the ḥadīth is a liar."

And something similar to the last part of it was narrated; see tradition no. (#2).

Al-Qarmīsīnī, who said that he was informed by 'Abdullāh Ibn Mūsā Al-Hashimī, who said that he was told by Ibn Badīna, who said that he heard Al-Mirwadhī saying that he heard Aḥmad Ibn Ḥanbal saying:

> "They have abandoned ḥadīth and they have devoted themselves to *al-gharā'ib*; how little is their understanding!"[455]

Abū Bakr said, "It is not permissible to believe that Al-Thawrī meant by his aforementioned words authentic aḥādīth and the well-known *Sunan*; how could that be permissible when it is he who said:

262. I was informed by Abū'l-Qāsim Al-Azharī, who said that he was told by 'Ubaydullāh Ibn Aḥmad Al-Muqrī', who said that he was told by Al-Ḥusayn Ibn Ismā'īl, who said that he was told by Muḥammad Ibn 'Amr Ibn Ḥannān, who said that he was told by Baqīyyah, who said that he was told by 'Abdu'l-Raḥmān Ibn Khālid, who reported on the authority of Sufyān Al-Thawrī that he said:

> "Study ḥadīth much, for it is a weapon."[456]

---

[455] Its chain of narrators is weak.

In it is 'Abdullāh Ibn Mūsā Al-Hashimī, who was declared trustworthy by Al-'Atīqī and Abū'l-Ḥasan Ibn Al-Furāt. And it is as if they did not take any position on his status. Ibn Abū'l-Fawāris said, "There was a degree of leniency and lack of strictness in him." And Al-Azharī said, "He was weak," while Al-Barqānī said, "He is weak."

I say: This is a clear criticism and is indefensible.

The tradition was also narrated by the author in *'Al-Kifāyah'* (p. 172).

[456] It is unclear to me who 'Abdu'l-Raḥmān Ibn Khalid is and he was not mentioned among the Shaikhs of Baqīyyah, nor among those who narrated on the authority of Al-Thawrī. So it is not unlikely that he was one of the unknown Shaikhs of Baqīyyah, or that he committed *tadlīs*. The remainder of the men in the chain of narrators are authoritative.

263. We were informed by Muḥammad Ibn Aḥmad Ibn Rizq, who said that he was told by Muḥammad Ibn 'Umar Al-Ḥāfiẓ, who said that he was told by 'Abdullāh Ibn Bishr, who said that he was told by Zayd Ibn Akhzam, who said that he was told by Ibn Zaid—which is how it is written in my book, on the authority of Ibn Rizq, but the correct version is Ibn Dāwūd—who said that he heard Al-Thawrī saying:

> "It is incumbent upon a man to compel his son to study ḥadīth." He added, "For he will be asked about it." [457]

264. We were informed by 'Alī Ibn Abū 'Alī Al-Baṣrī, who said that he was told by Aḥmad Ibn Ibrāhīm Ibn Al-Ḥasan, who said that he was told by 'Abdullāh Ibn Muḥammad Ibn 'Abdu'l-'Azīz, who said that he was told by Abū Ya'qūb Isḥāq Ibn Abū Isra'īl, who said that he heard Yaḥyā Ibn Yaman, who said that he heard Sufyān saying:

> "I know of nothing through which Allāh, [the Almighty, the All-Powerful][458] is sought." A person said to him, "What if they seek it without an intention?" He replied, "Their seeking of it is the intention."[459]

265. We were informed by Muḥammad Ibn Aḥmad Ibn Rizq, who said that he was informed by 'Uthmān Ibn Aḥmad Al-Daqqāq,

---

[457] Its chain of narrators is *munkar*.

Muḥammad Ibn 'Umar Al-Ḥāfiẓ is Al-Ja'ābī, and there is discussion (among scholars) regarding him. And we have spoken previously about the tradition in no. 129.

The tradition was also narrated by Abū Nu'aym in *'Al-Ḥilyah'* (6/364) by way of Al-Ja'ābī.

[458] This is from manuscript (B).

Its chain of narrators is weak, but it (the text) is authentic.

In it is Yaḥyā Ibn Al-Yaman, and we have spoken previously of him.

[459] The tradition, with authentic chains of narrators, was mentioned previously. See nos. 159-161).

who said that he was told by Ja'far Ibn Muḥammad Ibn Shākir Al-Zāhid Al-Ṣā'igh, who said that he was told by Abū Mu'āwiyah Al-Ghallabī, who said that he was told by Wakī', who said that he heard Sufyān saying:

> "We know of no deed better than seeking knowledge and ḥadīth for one who has a good intention."[460]

266. I was informed by Muḥammad Ibn Al-Ḥusayn Al-Qaṭṭān, who said that he was informed by Da'laj Ibn Aḥmad, who said that he was informed by Aḥmad Ibn 'Alī Al-Ubār, who said that he was told by Aḥmad Ibn Hashim, who said that he was told by Ḍhamrah, who said that Sufyān Al-Thawrī was relating ḥadīth in 'Asqalān and Ṣūr and as he began speaking to them, he declared:

> "The springs have gushed forth. The springs have gushed forth..." impressed by himself. And sometimes a man might relate ḥadīth and say: "This is better for you than your governorship of 'Asqalān and Ṣūr."

[460] It is authentic.
We previously quoted something similar in no. 160.

CHAPTER FIFTY-SIX

A Tradition of Mālik Ibn Anas and ʿAbdullāh Ibn Idrīs

267. We were informed by Abū Bakr Aḥmad Ibn Muḥammad Ibn Ghālib Al-Faqīh, who said that he recited it to ʿAlī Ibn Aḥmad Al-Barqānī,[461] who said that Muḥammad Ibn Aḥmad Ibn Masʿūd told them, who said that Muḥammad Ibn Idrīs—Abū Ḥātim Al-Razī—who said that he heard ʿAlī Ibn Muḥammad Al-Ṭanāfisī, who said that ʿAbdullāh Ibn Idrīs said regarding learning many aḥādīth:

> "We used to say that learning many aḥādīth was madness."[462]

Al-Ṭanāfisī said, "This is true."

Abū Ḥātim said, "And Abū'l-Ṭāhir Ibn Al-Sarḥ said, "I heard Ibn Wahb mention on the authority of Malik that he said:

---

[461] In manuscript (B) it says 'Al-Baznani'.

[462] Its chain of narrators is authentic.

> "The more a person learns ḥadīth, the more successful he will be."

The Shaikh, Al-Ḥāfiẓ[463] said:

> "And it has been memorised on the authority of 'Abdu'l-Razzāq Ibn Hamām regarding learning many aḥādīth something close to this meaning."

268. We were informed by Muḥammad Ibn 'Umar Ibn Ja'far Al-Ḥarfī, who said that he was informed by Aḥmad Ibn Ja'far Al-Khatlī, who said that he was told by Aḥmad Ibn 'Alī Al-Ubār, who said that he was told by 'Abdu'l-Raḥmān Ibn Bishr Al-Naysabūrī, who said that he heard 'Abdu'l-Razzāq saying:

> "We used to think that [learning] many aḥādīth was good, but it is bad, all of it."[464]

The Shaikh, Al-Ḥāfiẓ[465] said: "All of this speech is similar to the speech of Al-Thawrī, regarding the censure of aḥādīth that are *shaẓẓāh* and the meaning of them is the same. Malik, Ibn Idrīs and others only disliked learning many chains of narrators that are *gharībah* and routes that are rejected, such as the *asānīd* of the ḥadīth of the bird,[466] the routes of the ḥadīth of *al-mighfar* (the helmet),[467] performing *ghusl* on Friday and the ḥadīth regarding

[463] In manuscript (B) it says, *"Abū Bakr said..."*

[464] Its chain of narrators is authentic.

[465] In manuscript (B) it says, *"Abū Bakr said..."*

[466] This refers to a ḥadīth narrated by Al-Tirmidhī and others on the authority of Anas Ibn Malik (*raḍiyAllāhu 'anhu*), who said: "There was a bird with the Prophet (ﷺ), so he said: 'O Allāh! Send to me the most beloved of Your creatures to eat this bird with me.' Then 'Alī came and ate with him'."

[467] It was reported on the authority of Anas Ibn Mālik that he said, "In the year of the conquest of Makkah, the Prophet (ﷺ) entered Makkah wearing a helmet on his head."

the taking away of knowledge,[468] the ḥadīth: "Verily, the people of the highest degrees..."[469] the ḥadīth: "Whoever lied against me..."[470] the ḥadīth: "There is no marriage except with a guardian..."[471] and other *aḥādīth* whose routes are followed by the Companions of Ḥadīth (*Aṣḥāb al-Ḥadīth*)... and they memorise them and study them, while it is likely that any of them knows not any authentic ḥadīth; and you will see him quoting routes that are *gharībah* and chains of narrators that are astonishing, most of which are fabricated and the bulk of which are manufactured and from which no benefit is derived, and they spend their lives in pursuit of them. And this weakness has removed most of the students of ḥadīth in our time from understanding them and from being able to derive rulings from them.

And the jurists of our time have done as they have done and followed their path, rejecting the hearing of the *Sunan* from the scholars of ḥadīth and preoccupying themselves with the written works of the philosophers—and both groups have strayed from what should concern them and embarked upon that which does not benefit."

269. We were informed by Abū Bakr Al-Barqānī, who said that

[468] It was reported on the authority of 'Abdullāh Ibn 'Amr Ibn Al-'Āṣ (*raḍiyAllāhu 'anhumā*), who said, "I heard the Messenger of Allāh (ﷺ) saying, 'Allāh does not take away knowledge by taking it away from (the hearts of) the people, but He takes it away by the death of the religious learned men till none of the (religious learned men) remains, then people will take as their leaders ignorant persons who,when consulted, will give their verdict without knowledge. So they will go astray and will lead the people astray."

[469] "The Messenger of Allāh (ﷺ) said: 'The people of the highest degrees of Paradise will be seen by those beneath them as a rising star is seen on the horizon. Abū Bakr and 'Umar will be among them, and how blessed they are!'."

[470] It was reported on the authority of Jābir (*raḍiyAllāhu 'anhu*) that the Messenger of Allāh (ﷺ) said, "Whoever tells lies about me deliberately, let him take his place in the Fire."

[471] It was reported on the authority of Abū Mūsā (*raḍiyAllāhu 'anhu*) that the Messenger of Allāh (ﷺ) said: "There is no marriage except with a guardian."

he was told by Ya'qūb Ibn Mūsā Al-Ardabīlī, who said that he was told by Aḥmad Ibn Ṭāhir Ibn Al-Najm, who said that he was told by Sa'īd Ibn 'Amr Al-Barzā'ī, who said that he heard Abū Zur'ah—Al-Rāzī—who said that Abū Thawr wrote to him:

> "This matter will continue to be with your companions unless and until they divert themselves from it by preoccupying themselves with the accumulation of a number of narrators: "Whoever deliberately lied against me..." and these people become predominant."[472]

[472] Its chain of narrators is authentic.

CHAPTER FIFTY-SEVEN

Traditions of Sulaymān Ibn Mahrān Al-Aʿmash

270. I was informed by Al-Qāḍī Abū Bakr Aḥmad Ibn Al-Ḥasan Ibn [Aḥmad][473] Al-Ḥarshī, who said that he was told by Abū'l-ʿAbbās Muḥammad Ibn Yaʿqūb Al-Aṣamm, who said that he was told by Ibrāhīm Ibn Sulaymān Al-Burullusī, who said that he was told by Yūsuf Ibn Yaʿqūb Al-Ṣaffār, who said that he heard Abū Muʿāwiyah saying that Al-Aʿmash said:

> "That I should give charity with a small piece of bread is more beloved to me than that I should relate seventy aḥādīth." He (Abū Muʿāwiyah) said, "I mentioned this to Abū Usāmah and he said that he heard Al-Aʿmash saying that."[474]

271. I was informed by Muḥammad Ibn Al-Ḥusayn Al-Qaṭṭān,

[473] This is from manuscript (B).

[474] Its chain of narrators is authentic.

The author's Shaikh is Al-Ḥayrī, Al-Naysabūrī, Al-Ḥāfiẓ, whose biography is given in *'Al-Siyār'*.

who said that he was informed by Da'laj Ibn Aḥmad, who said that he was informed by Aḥmad Ibn 'Alī Al-Ubār, who said that he was told by 'Alī Ibn Khashram, who said that he heard Ḥafṣ Ibn Ghiyāth, who said that it was said to Al-A'mash:

> "Will you not relate ḥadīth to us?" He replied, "That I should give charity with a basket (of dates) or a loaf of bread is more beloved to me than that I should relate ten aḥādīth to you."[475]

272. We were informed by Abū'l-Fatḥ Hilal Ibn Muḥammad Ibn Ja'far Al-Ḥaffār, who said that he was informed by Ismā'īl Ibn Muḥammad Al-Ṣaffār, who said that he was told by Ibrāhīm Ibn Al-Walīd Al-Jashshāsh, who said that he was told by Aḥmad Ibn Yūnus Al-Kūfī, who said that he was told by Abū Bakr Ibn 'Ayyāsh, who reported on the authority of Al-A'mash that he said:

> "There is no people in the world more wicked than the companions of ḥadīth."

Abū Bakr said, "I rejected this until I saw from them what I know."[476]

273. We were informed by Aḥmad Ibn Muḥammad Ibn Ghālib Al-Khawārizmī, who said that he heard Abū'l-Qāsim Al-Anbadūnī[477] saying that it was recited to Abū 'Alī Al-Ḥasan Ibn Muḥammad Ibn 'Abthār[478] Al-Baghdādī, who said that they were told by Al-Qawarīrī, who said that Yazīd Ibn Zurai' said to him

[475] Its chain of narrators is authentic.

[476] Its chains of narrators is authentic.

[477] This is how it is written in manuscript (A), while in manuscript (B) it says: Al-Anbadhūnī.

[478] This is how it is written in manuscript (A), while in manuscript (B) it says: 'Anbar, and that is the correct version.

that Al-Aʿmash said:

> "If I had dogs, I would send them against the companions of ḥadīth."[479]

274. We were informed by Muḥammad Ibn Aḥmad Ibn Zarq, who said that he was informed by ʿUthmān Ibn Aḥmad Ad-Daqqāq, who said that he was told by ʿAbdu'l-Malik Ibn Muḥammad, who said that he was told by Abū Bishr Ibn Sulayṭ, who said that he heard ʿAbdullāh Ibn Dāwūd saying that he heard Al-Aʿmash saying:

> "If this door was left for the companions of ḥadīth, they would steal its iron."[480]

The Shaikh, Abū Bakr [Al-Ḥāfiẓ][481] said: "Al-Aʿmash was ill-natured, rude, niggardly with ḥadīth, harsh in narration and his traditions in this are well known to the scholars. They include:

275. We were informed by Abū'l-Ḥasan Aḥmad Ibn Muḥammad Ibn Aḥmad Ibn Al-Salṭ Al-Ahwāzī, who said that he was informed by Muḥammad Ibn Mukhallad Al-ʿAṭṭār, who said that he was told by ʿAlī Ibn Sahl, who said that he was told by ʿAffān, who said that

[479] Its chain of narrators is weak.

In it is Al-Ḥasan Ibn Muḥammad Ibn ʿAnbār Abū ʿAlī Al-Baghdādī Al-Washā', who was declared weak by Ibn ʿAdiyy and he quoted a false ḥadīth that he narrated, saying, "If Ibn ʿAnbār did not do it deliberately, then it is probable that he included one ḥadīth in another. He was also declared weak by Ibn Qāniʿ and Al-Dāraqutnī said, "They (the scholars) discussed him with regard to his hearing (narrations)." As for Al-Barqānī, he declared him to be trustworthy, but he was unaware of his true status.

[480] Its chain of narrators is weak.

In it is Abū Qilabah Ibn Al-Raqashī ʿAbdu'l-Mālik Ibn Muḥammad and he is truthful, but had a poor memory.

[481] This is from manuscript (A).

he was told by Abū ʿAwānah, who said:

> "Raqabah Ibn Maṣqalah came to Al-Aʿmash and he asked him about something and he frowned and Raqabah said to him: 'By Allāh, I did not know that you were continually scowling, quickly tired and scorned the rights of *al-zuwwār* (visitors).[482] It is as if you are sniffing mustard seeds when you are asked for wisdom'."[483]

276. We were informed by Aḥmad Ibn Muḥammad Ibn Ghālib, who said that he recited to Abū'l-Ḥasan Al-Karāʿī, who said that Abū Ḥāmid Aḥmad Ibn ʿAlī Al-Kashmīhanī said that he heard ʿAlī Ibn Khashram, who said that he heard ʿIsā Ibn Yūnus saying that they went out with a funeral procession and a man from among the companions of ḥadīth was leading Al-Aʿmash, and when they returned from the funeral, he deviated from the road with him until the landscape became desert, then he said to him, "O Abū Muḥammad! Do you know where you are? You are in such-and-such a graveyard. By Allāh, I will not return you until you have filled my writing tablets with ḥadīth." He said, "Write." And when he had filled the tablets, he took them from him, then he took Al-Aʿmash by the hand and led him and when they entered Al-Kūfah, he met one of his acquaintances and he gave the tablets to him. Then when he had taken Al-Aʿmash to his door, he clung to him and said, "Take the tablets from the sinner." He (ʿIsā) said, "O Abū Muḥammad! They have gone." When he despaired of him, he said, "All that I related to you is lies." The young man (ʿIsā) said, "You are more knowledgeable of Allāh than to lie."[484]

---

[482] In manuscript (A) it says: *'al-zawr'* (visiting).

[483] Its chain of narrators is authentic.

ʿAlī Ibn Sahl is Ibn Al-Mughīrah and ʿAffān is Ibn Muslim.

[484] I have not found any biography for Al-Barqānī's Shaikh, or for his Shaikh's Shaikh.

277. I was informed by Abū'l-Qāsim Al-Azharī, who said that he was told by 'Umar Ibn Aḥmad Al-Wā'iẓ, who said that he was told by 'Abdullāh Ibn Sulaymān, who said that he was told by Aḥmad Ibn Ḥarb Al-Ṭā'ī, who said that he heard Muḥammad Ibn 'Ubayd saying:

> "Al-A'mash would not let anyone sit beside him and if a person sat, he would cease his recitation of ḥadīth and stand up. There was a man with them whom he found annoying and he came and sat beside him, thinking that Al-A'mash would not know (due to his poor eyesight), but Al-A'mash realised and began to clear his throat and expectorate on him. But the man remained silent, fearful that he would cease reciting the ḥadīth."[485]

278. I was informed by Muḥammad Ibn Al-Ḥusayn Al-Qaṭṭān, who said that he was informed by Da'laj Ibn Aḥmad, who said that he was informed by Aḥmad Ibn 'Alī Al-Ubār, who said that he was told by Al-Ḥasan Ibn 'Alī, who said that he was told by Abū Usāmah, who said that Ḥafṣ Ibn Ghiyāth asked Al-A'mash about the *isnād* of a ḥadīth and he took him by the throat and pressed him against a wall, saying: "This is its *isnād*—its support."[486]

279. We were informed by Riḍwān Ibn Muḥammad Al-Daynūrī, who said that he heard Abū Bakr Ibn Lal, in Hamazān, saying that he heard Al-Khalīl Ibn 'Abdullāh saying that he heard 'Alī Ibn Ṣāliḥ saying that he heard 'Abdullāh Ibn Muḥammad Al-Rāzī saying that he was informed by Jarīr, who said that they went to Al-A'mash and he had a dog which used to harm the companions

[485] Its chain of narrators is authentic.
'Abdullāh Ibn Sulaymān is Abū Bakr Ibn Abū Dāwūd, 'Umar Ibn Aḥmad is Ibn Shahīn and Muḥammad Ibn 'Ubayd is Al-Ṭanāfisī.

[486] Its chain of narrators is authentic.

of ḥadīth. He said:

> "We went to him one day and found that it had died and so we went into his house and when he saw us, he wept and said, "The one who ordered good and forbade evil has died.""[487]

The Shaikh, Al-Ḥāfiẓ said:[488] "The traditions of Al-Aʿmash bearing this meaning are extremely numerous, but aside from his ill-nature, he was trustworthy in ḥadīth, fair in his narrations, precise in [relating] what he heard and accurate in what he memorised, and the people journeyed to him and flocked to hear him. So it might be that the companions of ḥadīth requested him to relate to them and he refused them because they were rude in their requests and he wearied of their requests, became angry with them and received them with rebuke and censure, until his initial outburst was over, his anger had dissipated and annoyance was replaced by reconciliation and censure by praise.

280. We were informed by Muḥammad Ibn Aḥmad Ibn Rizq, who said that he was informed by Jaʿfar Al-Khaldī, who said that he was told by Muḥammad Ibn ʿAbdullāh Ibn Sulaymān, who said that he was told by Ismāʿīl Ibn Bahrām, who said that he was told by Muḥammad Ibn ʿUbayd, who reported on the authority of Al-Aʿmash that he said:

> "I would love when I see a Shaikh who does not write

[487] Its chain of narrators is weak.

Al-Khalīl Ibn ʿAbdullāh is Al-Khalīlī, the author of *'Al-Irshad'* and his Shaikh is ʿAlī Ibn Ṣāliḥ, who is ʿAlī Ibn Aḥmad Ibn Ṣāliḥ, the Shaikh of the (Qur'ān) Reciters. Al-Khalīlī gave a biography for him in *'Al-Irshad'* (3/745), but he did not state anything in it that would prove his status as a narrator. Al-Ḥāfiẓ Al-Dhahabī also transmitted a biography for him in *'Al-Siyār'* (16/410).

[488] This is in manuscript (B); in manuscript (A) it says: *'Abū Bakr said...'*

ḥadīth, to slap him."[489]

281. I was informed by Aḥmad Ibn Muḥammad Ibn Isḥāq Al-Muqrī', who said that he was informed by 'Umar Ibn Ibrāhīm Ibn Kathīr, who said that he was told by Abū Bakr Aḥmad Ibn Al-Qāsim, the brother of Abū'l-Layth [Al-Farā'iḍī],[490] who said that he was told by Abū Hamām, who said that he was told by Abū Mu'āwiyah Al-Ḍarīr, who said that he heard Sulaymān Al-A'mash saying:

> "Whoever does not study ḥadīth, I wish to beat him with my shoes."[491]

282. I was informed by Al-Qāḍī Abū Naṣr Aḥmad Ibn Al-Ḥusayn Al-Daynūrī, who said that he was told by Abū Bakr Aḥmad Ibn Muḥammad Ibn Isḥāq Al-Sunnī Al-Ḥāfiẓ, who said that he was told by 'Alī Ibn Aḥmad Al-Jurjānī, who said that he heard Al-A'mash saying:

> "If I was a grocer, you would deem me of little value and were it not for these aḥādīth, we would certainly be on a par with the grocers."[492]

---

[489] Its chain of narrators is authentic.

Muḥammad Ibn 'Abdullāh Ibn Sulaymān is Al-Ḥaḍramī, the Ḥāfiẓ known as Muṭayyan.

[490] This is from manuscript (B).

[491] Its chain of narrators is ḥasan.

The author's Shaikh is Abū Manṣūr Al-Muqrī', who is known as Manṣūr Al-Ḥabbāl, who is trustworthy; a biography is given for him in *'Tārīkh Baghdād'* (4/393). 'Umar Ibn Ibrāhīm is Ibn Aḥmad Ibn Kathīr, who is trustworthy. Aḥmad Ibn Al-Qāsim is Ibn Naṣr Ibn Ziyād, who was described as trustworthy by Al-Khaṭīb in his *'Tārīkh'* (4/352). Abū Hamam is Al-Walīd Ibn Shujā', who is trustworthy, there was some discussion regarding his memory; however, his aḥādīth are still at the level of Ḥasan. And Allāh knows better.

[492] Its chain of narrators is weak, but an authentic version with a similar wording has been reported.

Aḥmad Ibn 'Alī is Ibn 'Imrān, for whom a biography is given in no. 4 of *'Tārīkh* =

283. We were informed by ʿAlī Ibn Aḥmad Al-Razzāz, who said that he was told by Muḥammad Ibn Aḥmad Ibn Ibrāhīm Al-Aṣbāhanī, who said that he was told by Abū Bakr Muḥammad Ibn Al-Ḥasan Ibn Aḥmad Ibn Muḥammad Ibn Al-Ḥasan Ibn Ḥafṣ Al-Hamadhānī, who said that he was told by Aḥmad Ibn Mahdī, who said that he was told by Al-Furāt Ibn Maḥbūb, who said that he heard Abū Bakr Ibn ʿAyyāsh saying:

"Al-Aʿmash continued to learn ḥadīth until he died."[493]

284. I was informed by Muḥammad Ibn Al-Ḥusayn Ibn Al-Faḍl, who said that he was informed by Daʿlaj Ibn Aḥmad...

And we were informed by Ibn Al-Faḍl and Al-Ḥasan Ibn Abū Bakr, who both said that Abū Sahl Aḥmad Ibn Muḥammad Ibn ʿAbdullāh Ibn Ziyād Al-Qaṭṭān informed them that Abū Sahl said that he was told by Daʿlaj, who said that he was informed by

=

Jurjān', but there is nothing in it to indicate his status. ʿAlī Ibn Aḥmad Al-Jurjānī is most likely the person for whom a biography is given by Al-Dhahabī in *'Al-Siyār'* (17/22), in *'Al-Mīzān'* (3/112) and by Ibn Ḥajr in *'Al-Lisān'* (4/225). Al-Ḥākim, however, declared him weak, saying, "He appears to speculate and so he was abandoned. And he related to us surprising things on the authority of Al-Muṣʿabī."

His death and that of Ibn Al-Sunnī were close and so the narration of Ibn Al-Sunnī on his authority is uncertain: if it is he that is in the chain (*sanad*), then the *sanad* is extremely weak. And Allāh knows better.

There is disagreement pertaining to this tradition, with regard to ʿAbdu'l-Razzāq:

It was narrated by Al-Khaṭīb in *'Tārīkh Baghdād'* (9/6) with an authentic chain of narrators, up to ʿAbdu'l-Razzāq, who said that he was informed by Ibn ʿUyaynah, who said that he saw Al-Aʿmash wearing a sheepskin inside-out and an outer garment whose threads hung down to his legs and he said, "Do you consider that had I not acquired knowledge, who would come to me?! If I were a grocer, the people would demean me and not buy from me."

[493] Its chain of narrators is weak. The status of Al-Furāt Ibn Maḥbūb is unknown. Ibn Abū Ḥātim gave a biography for him in *'Al-Jarḥ wal-Ta'dīl'* (2/3/80), but he mentioned neither criticism nor praise of him in it.

Aḥmad Ibn ʿAlī Ibn Al-Ubār, who said that he was told by Abū Nuʿaym Al-Ḥalabī, who said that he was told by ʿAṭā' Ibn Muslim Al-Ḥalabī, who said that when Al-Aʿmash became angry with the companions of ḥadīth, he said: "I will not relate ḥadīth to you, nor show you any respect and nor do you deserve it. No sign of it is visible upon you." But they continued to entreat him until he was pleased [with them] and he said:

> "Blessings and honour! And how many are you among the people! By Allāh, verily, you are dearer to me than red gold."[494]

---

[494] Its chain of narrators is ḥasan.

Abū Nuʿaym Al-Ḥalabī is 'Ubayd Ibn Hisham and he his truthful, though he changed towards the end of his life and he suggested things that were not from his ḥadīth, as a result of which, a number of the scholars declared him to be weak.

I say: There is no objection to this report of his, for it is from the printed manuscripts. As for ʿAṭā' Ibn Muslim Al-Ḥalabī, there is weakness in him, but it does not harm this tradition, as he is its narrator.

CHAPTER FIFTY-EIGHT

Abū Bakr said: "A similar action to this was related on the authority of Abū Bakr Ibn ʿAyyāsh:

285. We were informed by Abū Bakr Al-Barqānī, who said that he was informed by Muḥammad Ibn ʿAbdullāh[495] Ibn Khumayrawayh Al-Harawī, who said that he was informed by Al-Ḥusayn Ibn Idrīs, who said that Ibn ʿAmmār said that he heard Abū Bakr Ibn ʿAyyāsh saying:

> "The companions of ḥadīth are the worst of creation, they are shameless, they are such-and-such..." and he applied several insulting epithets to them, then he became silent, after which he said: "These are the companions of ḥadīth; they are the best of people, they are such-and-such." He (Ibn ʿAyyāsh) said to him: "What thing is apparent to you in them?" He replied,

[495] In manuscript (A) it says: ʿUbaydullāh.

> "Verily, a man among them keeps company with me to hear ḥadīth and he remains with me until he has heard it, then if he wishes, he leaves and he says: 'I was told by Abū Bakr Ibn 'Ayyāsh...' Then who can say: 'You did not hear him'?"[496]

286. I was informed by Abū 'Alī 'Abdu'l-Raḥmān Ibn Muḥammad Ibn Faḍalah Al-Naysabūrī Al-Ḥāfiẓ, in Al-Rai, who said that he was informed by Ibrāhīm Ibn Aḥmad Al-Mustamilli, in Balkh, who said that he heard Muḥammad Ibn Ḥāmid Abū 'Āmir, who said that he heard 'Isā Ibn 'Abdu'l-Raḥmān saying that he heard Muḥammad Ibn Hisham Al-'Absī[497] saying:

> "When we went to Abū Bakr Ibn 'Ayyāsh and he was in a cheerful disposition, he would say to us when he saw us: '[They are] the best people on the face of the earth, giving life to the Sunnah of the Prophet (ﷺ).' But if he saw us when he was not in a good mood, he would say: '[They are] the worst people on the face of the earth, disobeying their fathers and mothers and abandoning prayers in congregation'."[498]

The Shaikh said: Abū Bakr was stern with regard to ḥadīth.

287. We were informed by Al-Ḥasan Ibn Abū Bakr, who said that he was informed by Muḥammad Ibn Al-Ḥasan Ibn Ziyād Al-Naqqāsh, who said that he heard Yūsuf Ibn Al-Ḥusayn, who said that he heard Aḥmad Ibn Abū'l-Hawarī, who said that he arrived in Al-Kūfah and he met Abū Bakr Ibn 'Ayyāsh and said to him:

---

496 Its chain of narrators is authentic.

Ibn Khumayrawaih and Al-Ḥusayn Ibn Idrīs are both trustworthy. A biography was given for them both by Al-Dhahabī in *'Al-Siyār'* (16/311 and 14/113).

497 In manuscript (A) it says: Al-'Aishī.

498 I have not found any biographies for Muḥammad Ibn Hamid and 'Isā Ibn 'Abdu'l-Raḥmān.

> "Relate ḥadīth to me, for I am a stranger." He replied, "The people of my city have more right than you." He said, "I am from Al-Shām." He replied, "That is farther for you."[499]

288. I was told by 'Abdu'l-'Azīz Ibn Abū'l-Ḥasan Al-Qarmīsīnī, who said that he was told by Muḥammad Ibn Aḥmad Al-Mufīd, who said that he was told by Al-Ḥasan Ibn Ismā'īl Al-Rab'ī, who said that he was told by Al-Akhnasī, who said that he heard Abū Bakr Ibn 'Ayyāsh saying:

> "If I knew that any of you was seeking this knowledge to become more pious, I would come to his house in order to relate ḥadīth to him. Do you consider that I would disapprove of what I have done for you? Verily, I know that you are its people, and if you were to abandon it, it would disappear."[500]

Abū Bakr said: "And among the most extreme reports of Abū Bakr Ibn 'Ayyāsh regarding the companions of ḥadīth is:

---

[499] Its chain of narrators is talif.

This is because Al-Naqqāsh is accused (of fabrication); and we have discussed him previously.

[500] Its chain of narrators is extremely weak.

In it is Muḥammad Ibn Aḥmad Ibn Ya'qūb Al-Jurjā'ī, who is a weak ḥadīth narrator. He related aḥādīth that are *munkarah* and he reported on the authority of unknown narrators. Al-Bajī said, "I rejected *asanid* that he claimed (to be authentic)." Al-Khaṭīb also declared him to be weak, as did Al-Dhahabī, due to the great number of his narrations. As for his Shaikh, I have not found any biography for him, so it is likely that he is one of the obscure people from whom he narrated. As for Al-Akhnas, he is Aḥmad Ibn 'Imrān; Al-Sam'ānī mentioned his narration in *'Al-Ansab'* (1/98), on the authority of Abū Bakr Ibn 'Ayyāsh and Al-Dhahabī gave a biography for him in *'Al-Mīzān'* and he said, "Al-Bukharī said, 'They (the scholars) spoke (negatively) about him, but they said his name was Muḥammad'." Al-Sam'ānī added to Al-Bukharī's statement, saying, "(His) aḥādīth on the authority of Abū Bakr Ibn 'Ayyāsh are *munkarah*." And Abū Zur'ah said, "They (the scholars) abandoned him." And Abū Ḥātim also abandoned him.

289. We were informed by Abū Manṣūr Muḥammad Ibn 'Isā Ibn 'Abdu'l-'Azīz Al-Hamazānī, who said that he was told by Ṣāliḥ Ibn Aḥmad Al-Ḥāfiẓ, who said that he was informed by Aḥmad Ibn Muḥammad Al-Muqrī', by way of recitation, who said that he was told by Muḥammad Ibn 'Abdu'l-Ghaffār, who said that he visited Aḥmad Ibn Badīl Al-Kūfī and the companions of ḥadīth were all around him, and they mentioned his sternness, upon which he said, "And how would it be if you saw Abū Bakr Ibn 'Ayyāsh?" They asked, "How was he?" He said, "I visited him with Abū Kurayb and Yaḥyā Ibn Ādam and with them was So-and-so Al-Hashimī, and they asked him to relate ten aḥādīth to them, but he said, 'No, not even two ḥadīths!' They said, 'Will you not then relate to us [even] two ḥadīths?' He said, 'Not even half a ḥadīth.' They said, 'Then [even] half a ḥadīth?' He replied, 'Select, if you will, an *isnād*, and if you will, a ḥadīth.' He [the narrator] said, 'Yaḥyā Ibn Ādam said, 'Our Shaikh said, 'O Abū Bakr! You are an isnād with us, so give.' Abū Bakr replied, 'The Messenger of Allāh (ﷺ) said...' and he quoted a ḥadīth.[501]

290. We were informed on the authority of Aḥmad Ibn Muḥammad Ibn Ghālib, who said that he recited to Abū'l-Ḥasan Al-Maḥmūdī, that Muḥammad Ibn 'Alī Al-Ḥāfiẓ told them that he was told by Abū'l-Dardā', who reported on the authority of one of his companions that he said that it was said to Abū Bakr Ibn 'Ayyāsh, "Relate ḥadīth to us." He replied, "I will not do so." They said, "[Not even] one ḥadīth?" He said, "Mughīrah told us

[501] I have not found any biography for this person, Muḥammad Ibn 'Abdu'l-Ghaffār, nor was he mentioned among the students of Yaḥyā Ibn Ādam, nor among the students of Abū Bakr Ibn 'Ayyāsh.

Aḥmad Ibn Muḥammad Al-Muqrī' is Ibn Aws Al-Hamazānī, whose biography was given by Al-Dhahabī in *'Al-Siyār'* (15/388) and he quoted his narration on the authority of Aḥmad Ibn Badīl.

So his narration of this incident is through a person who witnessed it. And Allāh knows better.

that he saw Al-Sha'bī overturning an earthenware wine jug."[502]

[Abū Bakr said][503]: "Observe Abū Bakr's sternness when the companions of ḥadīth annoyed him and they asked him to relate to them a single ḥadīth, and how he related something to them in which there was no good and no benefit for the hearers. But a saying has been reported on the authority of Abū Bakr that shows clearly the virtue of the companions of ḥadīth."

291. I was told on the authority of 'Abdu'l-'Azīz Ibn Ja'far Al-Faqīh, who said that he was told by Abū Bakr Al-Khallāl, who said that he was informed by Muḥammad Ibn Idrīs, who said that he heard Ḥamzah Ibn Sa'īd Al-Mirwazī, who said that he heard Abū Bakr Ibn 'Ayyāsh, who struck the shoulder of Yaḥyā Ibn Ādam and said:

> "Woe to you, o Yaḥyā! Are there any people in the world who are better than the companions of ḥadīth?!"[504]

292. I was told by Abū Ṭālib Yaḥyā Ibn 'Alī [Ibn Al-Ṭayyib][505] Al-Daskarī, who said that he was told by Ḍirār Ibn Rāfi' Al-Harawī, who said that he heard Abū Bakr Muḥammad Ibn Aḥmad saying that he was told by Muḥammad Ibn 'Abdān, who said that he was told by Sa'īd Ibn Yaḥyā Ibn Al-Azhar, who said that he heard Abū Bakr Ibn 'Ayyāsh saying:

> "I have not seen a people better than the companions

[502] Its chain of narrators is weak.
This is due to the unknown status of the person who narrated on the authority of Abū Bakr Ibn 'Ayyāsh.
[503] This is from manuscript (B).
[504] (This is) authentic.
Even though the author's sanad is *munqaṭi'*, it has been mentioned previously (#87 and #88) with an authentic chain of narrators.
[505] This is from manuscript (B).

> of ḥadīth; one of them will regularly visit to speak with me and if he wishes to say, 'I heard Abū Bakr Ibn 'Ayyāsh...' he may do so."[506]

293. We were informed by Abū Nu'aym Al-Ḥāfiẓ, who said that he was told by 'Abdullāh Ibn Muḥammad Ibn Ja'far, who said that he was told by Ibrāhīm Ibn Muḥammad Ibn Al-Ḥasan, who said that he was told by Hannād Ibn Al-Sirrī, who said that Abū Bakr Ibn 'Ayyāsh set out one day and he found the companions of ḥadīth at his door and he said:

> "These are the best of people; if they wish, they may return and say: 'We have heard...'."[507]

[Abū Bakr said][508]: "We have mentioned in this book of ours the virtue of ḥadīth and its people, who specialise in memorisation and transmission and we have sufficiently dealt with the topic to the degree that there is no need to repeat it here.

And I will mention [in my book],[509] after this [if Allāh wills],[510]

---

[506] Its chain of narrators is weak.

In it is Ḍirār Ibn Rāfi' ; he was mentioned by the author in his *'Tārīkh'* (9/345), but he did not mention any criticism or praise of him.

[507] Its chain of narrators is authentic.

And Abū Nu'aym's Shaikh is the father of Al-Shaikh Ibn Ḥayyān, whose Shaikh is Ibn Mutawayh. And Allāh knows better.

[508] This is from manuscript (B).

[509] This is from manuscript (A).

[510] This is from manuscript (B).

The verifier said: The person in need of the Pardon of his Lord, the Most Beneficent, the Most Merciful:

"The verification of the third section of this valuable book—and thereby the completion of the whole book—was completed in the afternoon of Tuesday, the 14th of Jumād Al-Thani in the year 1416 A. H.

The revision of the proof manuscript was completed after the fajr prayer on 11th of Ramadhan in the year 1416 A. H.

All praise and thanks be to Allāh, the Lord of the worlds.

and in a separate book entitled: *'Akhlāq Al-Rāwī wa Ādāb Al-Wāʿī'* what is incumbent upon them, what is recommended from them and what is disliked for them, and this knowledge is indispensible for any of the companions of ḥadīth.

We ask help from Allāh to achieve what we are striving for and for protection from error and inaccuracy therein. Verily, He is able to do all things.

This is the end of the book: *'Sharaf Aṣḥāb al-Ḥadīth'*

May Allāh be praised in the manner befitting Him and may He send His Blessings on the best of His creation, Muḥammad, the Prophet And upon all of his Family and Companions And upon the Tabiʿūn and those that came after them

And may the Blessings and Peace of Allāh be upon our Prophet, Muḥammad and upon all of his family and Companions.

THE SECOND TREATISE

The Faithful Counsel

being a translation of his

Naṣiḥātu Ahlu'l-Ḥadīth

by al-Ḥāfiẓ Abū Bakr Aḥmad Ibn 'Alī al-Khaṭīb al-Baghdādī

INTRODUCTION

With the Name of Allāh, the All-Merciful, the Most Merciful

Al-Khaṭīb Abū Bakr Aḥmad Ibn 'Alī Ibn Thābit Al-Ḥāfiẓ (may Allāh, Most High have mercy on him) said: I have written this book for the follower of ḥadīth in particular, but also for others. My words are advice to him and to others and it is to stay away from the one who is content to remain ignorant and have no thoughts or ideas that would cause him to become attached to the people of virtue and instead preoccupies himself with things that take up most of his time and waste most of his life, keeping him away from the books of the ḥadīth of the Messenger of Allāh (ﷺ), from collecting them and acquiring the knowledge that Allāh has ordained upon him, such as the lawful (*ḥalāl*) and unlawful (*ḥarām*)—both the specific (*khāṣ*) and the general (*'ām*) —including the obligatory (*farḍ*), the recommended (*mandūb*), the *mubah* (permitted) and the prohibited (*ḥaẓr*), the that which abrogates (*nāsikh*) and the that which has been abrogated (*mansūkh*) and other such knowledge before the opportunity to attain it has been lost.

* *Naṣiḥa Ahlu'l-Ḥadīth* by al-Ḥāfiẓ Abū Bakr Aḥmad Ibn 'Alī al-Khaṭīb al-Baghdādī, explanation and checking of the aḥādīth and verification by 'Amr 'Abdu'l-Mun'im Salīm

CHAPTER ONE

1. We were informed by Abul Ḥasan Muḥammad Ibn Aḥmad Ibn Rizqawayh, who said that he was told by Muḥammad Ibn Aḥmad Ibn Isḥāq Ibn Ibrāhīm Al-Sarkhasī, who said that he was told by Muḥammad Ibn Al-Mundhir Al-Harawī, who said that he was told by Al-Ḥasan Ibn 'Amir Al-Naṣībī, who said that he heard Aḥmad Ibn Ṣāliḥ saying that Al-Shāfi'ī said:

> "Acquire knowledge while you are still young, before you become a leader, for once you become a leader, there is no way to acquire knowledge."[512]

---

[512] Its chain of narrators is weak.

It was narrated by Al-Bayhaqī in *'Manāqib Al-Shāfi'ī'* (2/142) by way of Muḥammad Ibn Al-Mundhir Ibn Sa'īd (who is Al-Harawī), with the author's chain of narrators.

I say: And its *sanad* is weak, because I have not found any biography for this person, Al-Ḥasan Ibn 'Āmir. A biography was given for Muḥammad Ibn Al-Mundhir by Ibn Ḥibbān in *'Al-Thiqāt'* (9/94) and he said, "He used to make mistakes sometimes."

Al-Bayhaqī narrated it with a different wording, following the first narration and he said: "We were informed by Abū Sa'd Al-Malīnī, who said that he was informed by Abū Aḥmad Ibn Ṣāliḥ, who said that Al-Shāfi'ī said to him, 'O Abū Ja'far! Worship before =

....

=
you become old, for when you become old, you will not be able to worship'."

Al-Bayhaqī said, "This is how I found it and it was marked 'authentic', but the first narration is more authentic."

I say: The men in the *sanad* of the second (narration) are trustworthy, except Ibn 'Adiyy's Shaikh, for whom I have not found any biography.

And it has been authentically reported on the authority of 'Umar (*raḍiyAllāhu 'anhu*) that he said, "Study Islamic Jurisprudence before you become leaders."

And the *takhrīj* of it will given shortly.

And the meaning of that is: When a seeker of knowledge becomes a leader or chief, this prevents him from acquiring knowledge. How could it be otherwise, when leadership and chieftainship entail so many responsibilities. This is from one aspect; from another aspect, he could be affected by the view of the general populace—or those who have no understanding of knowledge—towards him, for they might hold him in high esteem and listen and obey him without question, which could cause him to become arrogant and neglect to ask others from among the scholars about questions and rulings that vex him.

And censure of being a leader before acquiring knowledge has been authentically reported from the *Salaf*—may Allāh be pleased with them all—and regarding that, there is a report on the authority of 'Alī (*raḍiyAllāhu 'anhu*):

It has been reported on the authority of Sa'īd Ibn Abū'l-Ḥasan that he met Abū Yaḥyā Al-Mu'arqab and he asked him who had said to him, "Do they know me? Do they know me?" He added, "I am he." He said, "I do not know that you are he." He insisted, "I am he. 'Alī Ibn Abū Ṭālib (*raḍiyAllāhu 'anhu*) passed by me when I was relating (something) in Al-Kūfah and he said to me, 'Who are you?' I replied, 'I am Abū Yaḥyā'." He said, "You are not Abū Yaḥyā, yet you said, 'Do they know me? Do they know me'?" Then he said, "Do you know the *nasikh* (that which abrogates) from the *mansūkh* (that which is abrogated)?" He replied, "No." He said, "Then you are destroyed and you will cause others to be destroyed." He said, "After that, I did not relate anything to anyone. Does that satisfy you, Sa'īd?"

It was narrated by Al-Ḥāzimī in *'Al-I'tibār'* (p. 3) from this source.

It was also narrated by Ibn Abū Shaybah (5/290), by Abū Khaythamah in *'Al-'Ilm'* (#40), by Ibn Abū 'Asim in *'Al-Muzakkir'* (#14) and by Al-Bayhaqī in *'Al-Madkhal'* (#184) from another source.

And its chain of narrators is authentic.

If this censure pertains to such stories as these, and if 'Alī (*raḍiyAllāhu 'anhu*) made it a condition for the storyteller to have knowledge of *al-nasikh* and *al-mansūkh* , then what may be said of one who issues legal rulings and teachings when he is an ignorant person or one who pretends to possess knowledge?

And if he falsely claims to possess knowledge in order to seek leadership and rank, then he is guilty of the sin of tadlees and as such, the saying of the Prophet (ﷺ) in the two authentic compilations of Al-Bukhārī and Muslim, on the authority of Asmā' (may
=

2. We were informed by 'Ubaydullāh Ibn Abū'l-Fatḥ Al-Fārisī, who said that he was informed by 'Umar Ibn Aḥmad Ibn 'Uthmān Al-Wā'iẓ, who said that he was told by Mūsā Ibn 'Ubaydillah Ibn Yaḥyā, who said that he was told by 'Abdullāh Ibn Abū Sa'd, who said that he was told by Abū Muḥammad[513] Al-Mirwazī, who said that it was said:

> "The potter's clay only accepts an imprint when it is still moist." [i.e. knowledge should be acquired in one's early years].[514]

=

Allāh be pleased with her) is applicable to him: "The one who creates a false impression of receiving what he has not been given, is like one who wears two garments of falsehood."

This is because he is impersonating a scholar, when he is not one of them, so he has deceived the general public and so he is described as a liar and a purveyor of falsehood, in which there is no virtue for himself and he also misguides others.

And among the things mentioned that warn against seeking leadership before acquiring knowledge is the following:

This was mentioned by Al-Dhahabī (may Allāh have mercy on him) in the biography of the great Ḥāfiẓ, Abū'l-Qāsim Ibn 'Asākir in *'Al-Siyār'* (20/565); he said: "Abū'l-Muwāhib said, 'Ibn 'Asākir said to me, 'When I resolved to study ḥadīth, by Allāh, what caused me to do that was not love of leadership and command; rather, I said: When I relate all that I have heard, what is the benefit in me following it? So I sought guidance from Allāh and I sought permission from the leading Shaikhs and the leaders of the city and I visited them, and all of them said, 'And who has more right to do this than you?' Then I began that in the year 33 AH.'."

[513] This is how it was written in the two manuscripts, but the most likely case is that it is an error and that it should be Abū Aḥmad.

[514] Its chain of narrators is authentic up to Al-Mirwazī.

A biography is given for the author's Shaikh in *'Tārīkh Baghdād'* (10/385) and he said of him, "He was one of those who narrated numerous aḥādīth, both in his books and via oral transmission... and he also collected them in a trustworthy and faithful manner, with truthfulness and sincerity, following correct practices and sound beliefs and continually studying the Qur'ān."

His Shaikh's Shaikh was Al-Ḥāfiẓ Ibn Shāhīn (may Allāh have mercy on him).

Mūsā Ibn 'Ubaydillāh is the Ibn Yaḥyā Ibn Khaqān, whose father was the Vizier of Ja'far Al-Mutawakkil 'Alā' Allāh. Al-Khaṭīb said in his *'Tārīkh'* (13/59), "He was trustworthy, devout and he was one of *Ahl Al-Sunnah*."

=

3. He said: "And it has been reported on the authority of the Commander of the Faithful, 'Umar Ibn Al-Khaṭṭāb (*raḍiyAllāhu 'anhu*) that he said:

"Acquire knowledge before you seek leadership."[515]

=

And carved on his signet ring was: *"Follow the Sunan..."*.

His Shaikh was 'Abdullāh Ibn Abū Sa'd Al-Warrāq, who was trustworthy, transmitted traditions and was a man of letters, as mentioned by Al-Khaṭīb (10/26).

And it is most likely in my opinion, that Abū Muḥammad Al-Mirwazī is a miswriting of Abū Aḥmad Al-Mirwazī, for Al-Khaṭīb stated in the biography of 'Abdullāh Ibn Abū Sa'd that among his Shaikhs was Al-Ḥusayn Ibn Muḥammad Al-Mirwazī is Abū Aḥmad Al-Ḥāfiẓ.

And in it there is proof of the preferability of acquiring learning during one's youth and the importance of teaching memorisation of the Qur'ān and listening (to *aḥādīth*) from a young age. This is due to the limited amount of things that preoccupy them at this age and the lack of worries or distractions.

Moreover, as the student advances in years, the number of distractions increases for him and so it might be that they divert him from the acquisition of knowledge or reduce his zeal for it. If he marries and sires children, he might abandon the acquisition of knowledge due the necessity to earn a living, or at best, he might reduce his studies a great deal and devote himself more to his marital and parental duties.

For this reason, the scholars have encouraged diligence and endeavour during childhood hours and the days of youth.

Badruddīn Ibn Jama'ah said regarding the required manners of the student, in his book *'Tazkirah Al-Sāmi' wa'l-Mutakallim'* (p. 70): "He should embark during his youth on the acquisition of knowledge and he should not be misled by the deception of procrastination and expectation."

As for the words: "...that is, that it is incumbent to seek knowledge during one's tender years," it is most likely that this is the saying of Al-Khaṭīb and from his explanation.

[515] This is an authentic narration on the authority of 'Umar Ibn Al-Khaṭṭāb (*raḍiyAllāhu 'anhu*).

And the author (may Allāh have mercy on him) placed the text of this tradition before the *isnād* and that is a permissible action, according to the experts in the field. Al-Dhahabī said in *'Al-Mūqiẓah'* (p. 52), "It is permissible for a text that the narrator has heard to be placed before the isnād and vice versa, so that he says, "The Messenger of Allāh (ﷺ) said, 'Regret is (equivalent to) repentance.' We were informed of this by So-and-so, on the authority of So-and-so."

The tradition was also narrated by Abū Khaythamah in *'Al-'Ilm'* (111), by Al-Dārimī (#250), by Ibn 'Abdu'l-Barr in *'Jami' Bayān Al-'Ilm Wa Faḍlihi'* (1/86) by way

=

We were informed of it by 'Alī Ibn Muḥammad Ibn 'Abdullāh Al-Mu'addil, who said that he was informed by Ismā'īl Ibn Muḥammad Al-Ṣaffār, who said that he was told by Sa'dān Ibn Naṣr, who said that he was told by Wakī', who reported on the authority of Ibn 'Awn...

And we were informed by Muḥammad Ibn Aḥmad Ibn Rizq, who said that he was informed by 'Uthmān Ibn Aḥmad Al-Daqqāq, who said that he was told by Ḥanbal Ibn Isḥāq, who said that he was told by Bakkār Ibn Muḥammad, who said that he was told by 'Abdullāh Ibn 'Awn...

And we were informed by Al-Ḥasan Ibn Abū Bakr, who informed us that Abū Sahl Aḥmad Ibn Muḥammad Ibn 'Abdullāh Ibn Ziyād Al-Qaṭṭān, who said that he was told by Muḥammad Ibn Ghālib Ibn Ḥarb...

And we were informed by Abū'l-Faraj Muḥammad Ibn 'Umar Ibn Muḥammad Al-Jaṣṣāṣ, who said that he was informed by Aḥmad Ibn Yūsuf Ibn Khallad Al-'Aṭṭār, who said that he was

=

of Muḥammad Ibn Sīrīn, who reported on the authority of Al-Aḥnaf Ibn Qays, who reported on the authority of 'Umar (*raḍiyAllāhu 'anhu*).

And the tradition's *isnād* is authentic, for Al-Bukhārī asserted its authenticity, reporting it in a mu'allaq form in his *'Ṣaḥīḥ'* (*'Al-'Ilm'* [Knowledge], in the Chapter: 'The Joy of Knowledge and Wisdom'). And this entails it being regarded as authentic.

And it was explained by Abū 'Ubayd in a manner that we shall set forth shortly, while in *'Al-Fatḥ'*, Shamr Al-Lughawī explained the word *'tasawwud'* as meaning marriage, (as opposed to leadership); he said: "This is because when he marries, he becomes the leader of his family, especially if he has children."

Al-Shāfi'ī said, "If a young man becomes a leader, much knowledge will elude him."

In the last narration, by way of Al-Ḥasan:

Aḥmad Ibn Isḥāq Ibn Nīkhab; this is how Ibn Makūla determined it in *'Al-Ikmal'* (7/438) and he said, "The first letter (of his name) is noon, after it comes *ya'*... then the letter kha'."

And in *'Tārīkh Baghdād'* (4/35), it was written as 'Banjab' (i.e. Punjab).

informed by Aḥmad Ibn ʿAlī—he is Al-Khazzāz—who said that they were told by Hawzah, who reported on the authority of Ibn ʿAwn...[516]

And we were informed by Al-Ḥasan Ibn Abū'l-Ḥasan, who said that he was informed by Abū Bakr Muḥammad Ibn Jaʿfar Ibn Muḥammad Al-Ādamī Al-Qarī', who said that he was told by Muḥammad Ibn Al-Qāsim, the freed slave of Bani Hāshim, who said that he was told by Azhar, who reported on the authority of Ibn ʿAwn, who reported on the authority of Muḥammad, who reported on the authority of Al-Aḥnāf...

And in the ḥadīth of Wakīʿ and Bakkār, on the authority of Ibn Sīrīn, who reported on the authority of Al-Aḥnaf Ibn Qays that he said that ʿUmar Ibn Al-Khaṭṭāb (*raḍiyAllāhu ʿanhu*) said:

> "Acquire knowledge before you seek leadership."

We were informed by Al-Ḥasan Ibn Abū Bakr, who said that he was informed by Aḥmad Ibn Isḥāq Ibn Nīkhab Al-Ṭayyibī, who said that he was told by Muḥammad Ibn Yūnus Al-Qurashi, who said that he was told by Azhar, who said that he was told by Ibn ʿAwn, who reported on the authority of Ibn ʿAwn, who reported on the authority of Al-Ḥasan, who reported on the authority of Al-Aḥnāf Ibn Qays, who said that ʿUmar Ibn Al-Khaṭṭāb (*raḍiyAllāhu ʿanhu*) said:

> "Acquire knowledge before you seek leadership."

This is how he said it: "On the authority of Al-Ḥasan," but the correct version is: "On the authority of Ibn Sīrīn..." as we quoted it at the start. And Allāh knows better.

---

[516] In both manuscripts it says Hawzah Ibn ʿAwn, but this is a misspelling.

4. We were informed by Abū'l-Ḥasan Aḥmad Ibn 'Alī Ibn Al-Ḥasan Al-Badā', who said that he was informed by Da'laj Ibn Aḥmad, who said that he was told by 'Alī Ibn 'Abdu'l-'Azīz: "Abū 'Ubayd said regarding the ḥadīth of 'Umar (*raḍiyAllāhu 'anhu*):

> "Acquire knowledge before you seek leadership.": "Acquire knowledge under supervision while you are you still young, before you become a leader or a chief, for if you do not learn before that, you will be embarrassed to learn after you become older and you will remain ignorant, learning from the young—and that will cause you to feel reviled and disparaged. And this is similar to the ḥadīth of 'Abdullāh: "The people will continue be in a good state as long as they acquire knowledge from their elders, and if it comes to them from their *'aṣāghir'*, they will be ruined."[517]

---

[517] This saying of Abū 'Ubayd was mentioned in *'Gharīb Al-Ḥadīth'* (2/94).

And the saying of Ibn Al-Mubārak was mentioned by Nu'aym Ibn Ḥammād on his authority, as reported in *'Al-Zuhd'* (in the margin on page 281), where he said: "The knowledge came to them from their young, i.e. the innovators. As for elders narrating on the authority of the young, then, no."

Abū 'Ubayd gave a third explanation for *'al-aṣāghir'*, saying: My opinion regarding *'al-aṣāghir'* is that it means that knowledge is taken from those who came after the Companions of the Prophet (ﷺ) and this is given preference over the opinions of the Companions (*raḍiyAllāhu 'anhum*) and their knowledge and this is taking knowledge from *'al-aṣāghir'* but I do not consider that 'Abdullāh meant anything except this.

I say: And on what was the explanation of *'al-aṣāghir'* based? Taking from these three types of people is objectionable and it is not permissible to take from the innovator.

It was reported on the authority of 'A'ishah (may Allāh be pleased with her) that she said: "The Messenger of Allāh recited this verse: 'It is He Who has sent down to you the Book. In it are verses that are entirely clear, they are the foundations of the Book; and others not entirely clear. So as for those in whose hearts there is a deviation (from the truth) they follow (only) that which is not entirely clear thereof, seeking *al-fitnah*, and seeking its *ta'wīl* (hidden meanings).' [*Al-'Imrān* (3):7]."

She said that the Messenger of Allāh said: "So if you see those who follow thereof that which is not entirely clear, then they are those whom Allāh has named (as having deviated [from the Truth]), so beware of them." (Narrated by Al-Bukhārī (3/110), by Muslim (4/2053), by Abū Dāwūd (#4598) and by Al-Tirmidhī (#2993), by way of =

....

=

'Abdullāh Ibn Abū Mulaykah, who reported on the authority of Al-Qāsim, who reported on the authority of 'A'ishah (*raḍiyAllāhu 'anhā*).

And it was reported on the authority of Al-Ḥasan Al-Baṣrī and Ibn Sīrīn that they said: "Do not sit with people of heretical tendencies and do not argue with them, nor listen to them."

This was narrated by Al-Dārimī (1/121), by Al-Lalakā'ī in *'Sharḥ Usūl Al-I'tiqad'* (1/133), by Ibn Baṭṭah in *'Al-Ibānah'* (#458) with an authentic chain of narrators—and according to Al-Lalaka'i, it is from the sayings of Al-Ḥasan alone.

And it was reported on the authority of Abū Qilabah (may Allāh have mercy on him) that he said: "Do not sit with people of heretical tendencies and do not argue with them, for I do not feel assured that they will not immerse you in their misguidance or cause you to doubt what you know."

It was narrated by Al-Dārimī (1/120) and by Al-Ājurī (p. 56), by Ibn Wadhdhah (#125) with an authentic chain of narrators.

And it was reported on the authority of Ibn Sīrīn that he said, "This knowledge is (of) Religion, so be careful from whom you take your Religion."

It was narrated by Muslim in the foreword of his *'Ṣaḥīḥ'* (1/14) with an authentic chain of narrators.

In it (the foreword) it was also reported on his authority with a ḥasan chain of narrators. He said, "They did not use to ask about the *isnād*, but when the *fitnah* occurred, they said, 'Name your men (i.e. narrators) and the people of the Sunnah will look (at them) and their ḥadīth will be accepted; and the innovators will be identified and their ḥadīth will not be accepted'."

Likewise, it is not permissible to take from one who came after the Companions of the Prophet (ﷺ) and to give preference to his saying over the saying of one of the Companions (*raḍiyAllāhu 'anhum*).

Accepting the saying of a Companion (*raḍiyAllāhu 'anhum*) or his ruling is (tantamount to) accepting the Sunnah, according to the saying of the Prophet (ﷺ), as reported in the well-known and authentic ḥadīth of Al-'Irbadh Ibn Sariyah: "It is incumbent upon you to accept my Sunnah and the Sunnah of the rightly guided Caliphs." (Narrated by Abū Dāwūd and Al-Tirmidhī).

And Imam Aḥmad cited this ḥadīth as proof in *'Masa'il Abū Dāwūd'* (p. 276) that the saying or deed of a Companion (*raḍiyAllāhu 'anhum*) is from the Sunan; and he said, "Following means that a man follows what has been reported from the Prophet (ﷺ) and from the Companions (*raḍiyAllāhu 'anhum*), then regarding what came from after the Tabi'oon, he is free to choose."

And regarding the matter of the permissibility of paying *zakah al-fitr* in money, instead of in grains (lentils, rice etc.), Imām Aḥmad rejected what was cited as evidence by those who claimed that it is permissible, based on the saying of 'Umar Ibn 'Abdu'l-'Azīz and Al-Ḥasan, which they gave precedence to, over the saying of Ibn 'Umar (*raḍiyAllāhu 'anhumā*).

=

Abū ʿUbayd said, "And regarding *'al-aṣāghir'* there is a different explanation which was conveyed to me on the authority of Ibn Al-Mubārak, who interpreted *'al-aṣāghir'* as referring to the innovators and that it did not refer to age.

5. We were informed by ʿAbdu'l-Mālik Ibn Muḥammad Ibn ʿAbdullāh Al-Wāʿiẓ, who said that he was informed by ʿUmar Ibn Muḥammad Ibn Aḥmad Al-Jamḥī, who said that he was told by ʿAlī Ibn ʿAbdu'l-ʿAzīz, who said that he was told by Muḥammad Ibn ʿAmmār Al-Mawṣilī, who said that he was told by ʿAfīf Ibn Sālim, who reported on the authority of Ibn Lahīʿah, who reported on the authority if Bakr Ibn Sawādah, who reported on the authority of Abū Umayyah Al-Jamḥī (*raḍiyAllāhu ʿanhu*) that he said that the Messenger of Allāh (ﷺ) was asked about the Signs of the Hour and he said:

> "Verily, among its Signs is that knowledge will be sought from *al-aṣāghir*."[518]

=

As for accepting something on the authority of a younger person whose qualification is incomplete, it is not permissible—neither according to Islāmic Law, nor to commonsense—and Allāh knows better.

[518] Its chain of narrators is *mursal.*

It was narrated by Ibn Al-Mubārak in *'Al-Zuhd'* (#61): We were informed by ʿAbdullāh Ibn Lahīʿah, who said that he was told by Bakr Ibn Sawādah, who reported on the authority of Abū Umayyah Al-Lakhmī (or Al-Jamḥī) in a *marfūʿ* form.

And from his source: Al-Lalakā'ī reported in *'Sharḥ Usūl Al-I'tiqad'* (#102) and Ibn ʿAbdu'l-Barr reported in *'Jamiʿ Bayān Al-'Ilm wa Faḍlihi'* (1/157).

And it was narrated by Ibn ʿAbdu'l-Barr (also) by way of ʿAfīf Ibn Sālim.

I say: This chain of narrators is ḥasan up to Abū Umayyah and the tradition is from the narration of Ibn Al-Mubārak, on the authority of Ibn Lahīʿah; and Ibn Lahīʿah made clear in it that he heard it, so the suspicion of confusion disappears, as does the suspicion of *tadlīs.*

However, there is a difference of opinion regarding whether or not this person, Abū Umayyah was a Companion or not. He is not Ṣafwān Ibn Umayyah, so the chain of narrators is mursal. And Allāh knows better. It is strengthened by the following tradition of Ibn Masʿūd (*raḍiyAllāhu ʿanhu*).

6. And 'Alī said: We were informed by Muslim Ibn Ibrāhīm, who said that he was informed by Shu'bah, who reported on the authority of Abū Isḥāq, who reported on the authority of Sa'īd Ibn Wahb, who reported on the authority of 'Abdullāh, who said:

> "The people will continue to be in a good situation as long as they take knowledge from their elders, from those among them who are trustworthy and from their scholars. But if they take from their sighār or their wicked people, they will be destroyed."[519]

7. We were informed by Abū'l-Ḥasan Muḥammad Ibn 'Abdu'l-Wāḥid Ibn Muḥammad Ibn Ja'far, who said that he was informed by Abū 'Umar Muḥammad Ibn Al-'Abbās Al-Khazzāz, who said that he was informed by 'Ubaydullāh Ibn 'Abdu'l-Raḥmān Al-Sukkarī, who reported on the authority of 'Abdullāh Ibn Muslim

[519] This is authentic.

It was narrated by Ibn Al-Mubārak in *'Al-Zuhd'* (#815), by 'Abdu'l-Razzāq in *'Al-Muṣannaf'* (#20446 and #20483), by Ibn 'Adiyy in *'Al-Kamil'* (1/164) and by Ibn 'Abdu'l-Barr (1/158) by way of Abū Isḥāq.

And the second report of 'Abdu'l-Razzāq, something similar was narrated.

I say: Abū Isḥāq is a *mudallis*, however, Shu'bah narrated it on his authority, but he does not narrate on the authority of those of his Shaikhs to whom tadlees was attributed, unless it was confirmed that he had heard directly from them. He was mentioned by Al-Ḥāfiẓ in *'Al-Fatḥ'* and I have not encountered anything that indicates his status.

Then I found after that the virtuous brother, who is the verifier of Dar Al-Manar's printing and he referred to this saying in the book *'Al-Nakt'* (2/631).

As for the author's saying: "'Alī said..."

That is, with the previous chain of narrators, so it is *muttasil* (connected), not *mu'allaq*, as might be wrongly inferred. And it is a permissible action, for there are a number of such actions in the authentic compilations of Al-Bukhārī and Muslim.

As for his saying: *"their ṣighār"*, the aforementioned three possible meanings are implied by it. Abū 'Ubayd's opinion is supported by the second narration reported by 'Abdu'l-Razzāq in *'Al-Muṣannaf'*: We were informed by Mu'ammar, who reported on the authority Abū Isḥāq, who reported on the authority of Sa'īd Ibn Wahb, who said that he heard 'Abdullāh Ibn Mas'ūd (*raḍiyAllāhu 'anhu*) saying, "The people will continue to be righteous and devout as long as knowledge comes to them from the Companions of Muḥammad (ﷺ) and from their elders; if it comes to them from their *asaghir*, they will be destroyed."

Ibn Qutaybah Al-Daynūrī, who said that he asked about what was intended by his saying:

> "The people will continue to be in a good state as long as they take knowledge from their elders."[520]

[He said that] the people will continue to be in a good state as long their scholars are their *mashayikh*—their elders—and they are not their juniors, because an elder person is no longer in the enjoyment and passion of youth, along with the hastiness and foolishness that often accompany it, for he has gained experience and his knowledge is not tainted by doubt, nor is he overcome by whim or caprice, he is not swayed by greed and Satan does not cause him to commit the errors of youth. And with age comes dignity, honour and respect. As for the young person, he is often afflicted by those things from which an older person is protected. And if he is afflicted by them and he gives a legal opinion, he is destroyed and he destroys [others].

[520] Its chain of narrators is ḥasan.

A biography was given for the author's Shaikh in *'Tārīkh Baghdād'* (2/361), in which he said, "He was truthful." And his Shaikh is Abū 'Umar Ibn Hayawayh Muḥammad Ibn Al-'Abbās Ibn Muḥammad Ibn Zakariyya, who is trustworthy; he heard from many sources and he narrated large works. As for 'Ubaydullāh Al-Sukkarī, a biography is given for him in *'Al-Tārīkh'* (10/351), in which Al-Khaṭīb said, "...and he was trustworthy."

CHAPTER TWO

Al-Khaṭīb said: "A person should not be content to be a narrator, or a transmitter of ḥadīth only:

8. For we were informed by Abū Nu'aym Al-Ḥāfiẓ Ibrāhīm Ibn 'Abdullāh Al-Mu'addil, who said that he was informed by Aḥmad Ibn 'Alī Al-Anṣārī [who was born in Aṣbāhan], who said that he was informed by Abū'l-Ṣalt Al-Harawī, who said that he was informed by 'Alī Ibn Mūsā Al-Riḍā, who reported on the authority of his father, who reported on the authority of his grandfather, who reported on the authority of his parents that the Messenger of Allāh (ﷺ) said:

> "Be knowledgeable and be not [simply] narrators; a ḥadīth whose jurisprudence you understand is better than a thousand aḥādīth that you narrate."[521]

---

[521] This tradition is fabricated.

In it is Abū'l-Ṣalt Al-Harawī and he is a liar, who narrated a fabricated manuscript on =

9. We were informed by Aḥmad Ibn Abū Jaʿfar Al-Qaṭīʿī, who said that he was informed by ʿAlī Ibn ʿAbdu'l-ʿAzīz Al-Barzaʿī, who said that he was told by ʿAbdu'l-Raḥmān Ibn Abū Ḥāṭim, who said, "In my book it was reported on the authority of Al-Rabīʿ Ibn Sulaymān that he said that he heard Al-Shāfiʿi saying, when a person who acquires knowledge haphazardly was mentioned:

> "'This [person] is like a person collecting wood by night, preparing a bundle of firewood and carrying it, and there may be a viper in it and it bites him—and he is unaware of it'."[522]

Al-Rabīʿ said: "It means those who do not ask about where

=

the authority of ʿAlī Al-Riḍā. He has been discussed at length in my book, *'Al-Naqd Al-Sarīh li-Ajwibah Al-Ḥāfiẓ Ibn Ḥajr 'Ala Aḥādīth Al-Maṣabīh'* (p. 107). As for ʿAlī Ibn Mūsā Al-Riḍā, Ibn Ṭāhir said of him, "He narrated odd things on the authority of his father."

Al-Ḥāfiẓ Al-Dhahabī commented on him in *'Al-Mīzān'* (3/158), saying, "The matter only pertains to the reliability of the *sanad* up to him. If not, then the man has been lied against and he did not lie against his grandfather, Jaʿfar Al-Ṣādiq."

The tradition was reported by Abū Nuʿaym in *'Akhbār Aṣbāhan'* (1/138), with the aforementioned chain of narrators.

And a biography was given for Aḥmad Ibn ʿAlī Al-Anṣārī by Abū Nuʿaym, but he did not mention any criticism or praise of him in it.

[522] This is authentic.

The saying of Ibn Abū Ḥāṭim: "In my book it was reported on the authority of Al-Rabīʿ..." leaves open the possibility that he was given permission to transmit it or that he wrote it or that he memorised it.

Al-Bayhaqī narrated it with a connected chain of narrators in *'Manāqib Al-Shāfiʿī'* (2/143): We were informed by Abū ʿAbdullāh Al-Ḥāfiẓ, who said that he heard Abul ʿAbbās Muḥammad Ibn Yaʿqūb saying that he heard Al-Rabīʿ Ibn Sulaymān..." and he quoted it.

Al-Bayhaqī also narrated it by way of Ibn Abū Ḥāṭim.

It was also recorded by Ibn Abū Ḥāṭim in *'Manāqib Al-Shāfiʿī'* (p. 100).

And it is also possible that its meaning is: "Whoever sought knowledge, not in order to act upon it, but only to acquire some worldly gain from it, it would be a cause for his punishment in the Hereafter, even though the acquisition of knowledge is itself beneficial for those who desire salvation and to act upon it.

the evidence is from."

10. We were informed by Abū'l-Ḥasan Aḥmad Ibn Muḥammad Ibn Aḥmad Al-ʿAtīqī, who said that he was informed by Abū Muslim Muḥammad Ibn Aḥmad Ibn ʿAlī Al-Kātib Al-Muʿabbir, who said that he was informed by Abū Bakr Muḥammad Ibn Al-Ḥasan Ibn Durayd, who said:

> "Some of them asked when will learning be harmful?" He replied: "If innate disposition lessens and narration increases."[523]

11. We were informed by Al-Qāḍī Abū'l-ʿAlā' Muḥammad Ibn ʿAlī Al-Wāsiṭī, who said that he was informed by Abū'l-Ḥasan Muḥammad Ibn Jaʿfar Al-Tamīmī Al-Kūfī, who said that Abū'l-ʿAbbās Ibn ʿUqdah said to him one day, when a man asked him about a ḥadīth:

> "Decrease these aḥādīth, for they are of not benefit except to one who understands their meaning."[524]

---

[523] Its chain of narrators is ḥasan up to Ibn Durayd.

A biography was given for the author's Shaikh in *'Tārīkh Baghdād'* (4/379) and he said, "I wrote on his authority and he was truthful." And Ibn Makūla said in Al-Dhahabī's *'Siyār'* (17/603), "He was trustworthy and painstaking and he understood what he had."

Al-Dhahabī said, "It is he of whom Al-Khaṭīb says, "We were informed by Aḥmad Ibn Abū Jaʿfar Al-Qatīʿī..."

That is, he and the narrator of the previous tradition are one.

And Abū Muslim Al-Kātib used to mix things up, while Al-Dāraquṭnī said regarding Ibn Durayd, "They (i.e. the scholars) spoke of him (negatively) and he was a poet and a scholar of language."

[524] Its chain of narrators is weak.

This is because a biography was given for the author's Shaikh in *'Tārīkh Baghdād'* (3/95) and his status not a praiseworthy one, though he collected (aḥādīth) and sought (knowledge), for Al-Khaṭīb mentioned things about his status that are disparaging, which is why, when Al-Dhahabī transmitted it in *'Al-Mīzān'* (3/654), he said, "(It is) weak."

And this saying of Ibn ʿUqdah is strengthened by the tradition of the Commander =

....

=

of the Faithful, 'Alī Ibn Abū Ṭālib (*raḍiyAllāhu 'anhu*): O people! Do you wish that Allāh and His Messenger (*raḍiyAllāhu 'anhu*) be belied? Relate to the people that which they know and leave that which they reject."

It was narrated by Al-Bukhārī in his *'Ṣaḥīḥ'* (*'Al-Fatḥ'* 1/182), by Al-Bayhaqī in *'Al-Madkhal'* (#601) by way of Ma'rūf Ibn Kharbūz, who reported on the authority of Abū'l-Ṭufayl, who reported on the authority of 'Alī.

This is a serious matter and it is of great consequence for one who does not appreciate its significance, and verily, it is the concealment of knowledge, for it is not permissible to conceal it, unless it is thought that revealing it would cause a *fitnah*.

This is proven by the ḥadīth of the Prophet (ﷺ), who said to Mu'ādh Ibn Jabal (*raḍiyAllāhu 'anhu*), "No one testifies sincerely from his heart that none has the right to be worshipped but Allāh and Muḥammad is His slave and Messenger, except that Allāh will safeguard him from the Fire." He (Mu'ādh [*raḍiyAllāhu 'anhu*]) said, "O Messenger of Allāh! Shall I not then inform people of it, so that they may have glad tidings?" He (ﷺ) replied, "Then they will rely on it alone (and thus give up good works altogether)." Mu'ādh (*raḍiyAllāhu 'anhu*) disclosed this ḥadīth at the time of his death, to avoid the sin of concealment." (Narrated by Al-Bukhārī and Muslim).

Ibn Al-Ṣalah said in *'Sharḥ Ṣaḥīḥ Muslim'* (p. 185): "Mu'ādh (*raḍiyAllāhu 'anhu*) revealed this on his deathbed due to fear of committing a sin, even though the Prophet (ﷺ) forbade him from informing the people of it. In my opinion, the intent of this was that he forbade him from giving the glad tidings to the people out of fear that it would reach those who had no expertise and no knowledge and that they would be misled and depend on it, but in spite of this, the Prophet (ﷺ) informed specifically one who was safe from being misled and dependence on it from among the people possessing knowledge of the true state of affairs. He informed Mu'ādh (*raḍiyAllāhu 'anhu*) of it and Mu'ādh (*raḍiyAllāhu 'anhu*) followed this course of action and he only informed those whom he deemed to be possessed of understanding - and that was out of fear that by withholding it, he would be guilty of sin.

Something similar was reported on the authority of 'Ubādah Ibn Al-Ṣāmit (*raḍiyAllāhu 'anhu*) in Muslim's *'Ṣaḥīḥ'*; Al-Nawawī said in his *'Sharḥ'* (1/194): "Al-Qāḍī 'Iyāḍ (may Allāh have mercy on him) said, "In it there is evidence that he concealed that which he feared might be harmful and cause a *fitnah* and which might not be understood by every mind. This refers to aḥādīth that do not entail action and do not involve legal punishments." He said, "And there are numerous examples of a ḥadīth that does not entail action and which do not call for anything essential being abandoned when it is feared that the minds of the general populace may not understand it, or it is feared that it will cause harm to the person relating it or to the one who hears it—especially when it relates to information regarding the hypocrites, authority or specifying a people who have been described in

=

Yaḥyā Ibn Sulaymān narrated on the authority of Ibn Wahb that he said that he heard Mālik saying: "Many of these aḥādīth are misguidance; some aḥādīth have emanated from me each of for which I wish that I had been beaten with two stripes of a whip, and that I had not related them."

=

a negative manner, or the censure of others and their being cursed."

I say: Also included in this category is the relating of the *mutashabih* (that which is unclear), as reported in the story of Ṣabīgh Al-'Iraqī and 'Umar Ibn Al-Khaṭṭāb's chastisement of him—even though there is some (negative) discussion regarding its chain of narrators.

Similar to them are the aḥādīth regarding Allāh's Attributes, which are not understood by the minds of the common folk, along with the aḥādīth about rebelling against the ruler and any others the mention of which might cause corruption or evil.

Al-Ḥāfiẓ said in *'Al-Fatḥ'* (1/182): "Among those who rejected the transmission of ḥadīth to some and not to others was Imām Aḥmad, such as the aḥādīth whose apparent meaning seems to endorse rebellion against the ruler, while Imām Mālik said likewise regarding the aḥādīth pertaining to Allāh's Attributes, as did Abū Yūsuf regarding *al-gharā'ib* (who said, "Whoever seeks them will be deemed a liar.").

And before them, Abū Hurayrah (*raḍiyAllāhu 'anhu*)—as we mentioned earlier from him said the same thing regarding types of knowledge—and he confirmed that what is meant is the fitan (corruptions, evils) that may befall.

Something similar was reported on the authority of Hudhayfah and it was reported on the authority of Al-Ḥasan that he rejected the transmission of the ḥadīth of Anas (*raḍiyAllāhu 'anhu*) by Al-Ḥajjāj, concerning the story of the people of the tribe of 'Uraynah, because he used it as a proof for the permissibility of transgressing the limits with regard to bloodshed, based on his weak interpretation. And the general rule regarding that is that the apparent meaning of the ḥadīth strengthens the innovation, but the apparent meaning is not what was originally intended; in this case, it is required that a person who fears to act upon the apparent meaning should refrain from doing so."

As for the saying of Mālik transmitted on the authority of Ibn 'Uqdah: "Many of these aḥādīth are misguidance," it means that they could be the cause of misguidance for one whose intellect does not have the capacity to understand it, such as one who is deluded by the aḥādīth whose apparent meaning is the permissibility of rebelling against the ruler and he is misled by his false understanding of them and as a result, he then goes on to consider that unleashing the sword against the Muslim *ummah* is permissible. Or one who rejects aḥādīth or Qur'ānic verses pertaining to Allāh's Divine Attributes, due to his inability to understand them and his inability to reconcile them with verses and aḥādīth whose meaning is clear... and so on, not because they are misguidance in themselves—may Allāh protect us from such an idea - and that meaning is clear from what we have mentioned.

CHAPTER THREE

12. We were informed by 'Abdu'l-Mālik Ibn Muḥammad, who reported on the authority of 'Umar Ibn Muḥammad Al-Jamḥī,[525] who said that he was informed by 'Alī Ibn 'Abdu'l-'Azīz, who said that he was informed by Abū Nu'aym: Al-Faḍl Ibn Dakīn, who reported on the authority of Sa'd Ibn Aws Al-'Absī Al-Kātib, who reported on the authority of Bilāl Ibn Yaḥyā, who said that 'Umar (*raḍiyAllāhu 'anhu*) said:

> "I have come to know when [something is] beneficial for the people and when [it] is harmful to them: when jurisprudence comes from *Al-saghīr* and it is rejected by *al-kabīr* (it is harmful) and when jurisprudence comes from *al-kabīr* and he is followed by *al-saghīr* and they

[525] In both manuscripts it says: We were informed by 'Abdu'l-Mālik Ibn Muḥammad Ibn 'Umar Ibn Muḥammad Al-Jamḥī, but the correct version is seen in tradition no. 5.

And the author's Shaikh is 'Abdu'l-Mālik Ibn Muḥammad Ibn 'Abdullāh Ibn Bashāran Al-Ḥāfiẓ, whose biography is given in *'Al-Tārīkh'* (10/433).

are both guided (it is beneficial)."[526]

So if success comes to him from Allāh, the Almighty, the All-Powerful and he asks the jurist (*faqīh*) a question, he cannot be assured that there is someone present who knows it and so he blames him for his inability when he is in the prime of life, if he has been neglectful in his education, and at that point, he will become despondent and regret his former neglect.

---

[526] Its chain of narrators is *mursal.*

It is not known that Bilāl Ibn Yaḥyā Al-ʿAbsī heard from ʿUmar (*raḍiyAllāhu ʿanhu*), which would enable a ruling of *ittisāl* (i.e. a connected chain of narrators), in particular, since he has narrations on the authority of some of the Companions (*raḍiyAllāhu ʿanhum*) and he did not hear from them.

The tradition was also narrated by Ibn ʿAbdu'l-Barr in *'Jamiʿ Bayān Al-ʿIlm wa Faḍlihi'* (1/158), from two sources on the authority of Abū Nuʿaym, one of them from the narration of ʿAlī Ibn ʿAbdu'l-ʿAzīz and the other from the narration of Muḥammad Ibn Ismāʿīl Al-Tirmidhī.

And the matter pertaining to this subject is taking from *Al-ṣaghīr* if he is a scholar and the narration of one of higher status from one of lower status, which is permissible; indeed, it is preferred, such as the narration of Imām Al-Bukhārī on the authority of Al-Tirmidhī, who was a student and graduate of his. And the evidence from the Sunnah is the ḥadīth of Anas Ibn Mālik (*raḍiyAllāhu ʿanhu*), in which it is stated that the Messenger of Allāh (ﷺ) said to Ubayy (*raḍiyAllāhu ʿanhu*), "Verily, Allāh has commanded me to recite (the Qur'ān) to you." (Narrated by Al-Bukhārī and Muslim).

And the ḥadīth of Ibn Masʿūd (*raḍiyAllāhu ʿanhu*), who said, "The Messenger of Allāh (ﷺ) said to me, "Recite the Qur'ān to me." (Narrated by Al-Bukhārī and Muslim).

Ibn Jamāʿah said (p. 29): "A number from among the *Salaf* benefited from their students by hearing aḥādīth that they did not have. Al-Humaydī—who was a student of Al-Shāfiʿī—said, "I accompanied Al-Shāfiʿī from Makkah to Egypt and I was benefiting from the (juristic) issues discussed, while he was benefiting from aḥādīth from me."

And Aḥmad Ibn Ḥanbal said, "Al-Shāfiʿi said to us, 'You are more knowledgeable regarding ḥadīth than we. So if a ḥadīth is authentic in your view, tell us, so that I may act upon it'."

And narrations reported from a number of the Companions (*raḍiyAllāhu ʿanhum*) on the authority of the Tabi'ūn are authentic.

And more profound than all of that is the recitation of the Messenger of Allāh (ﷺ) to Ubayy (*raḍiyAllāhu ʿanhu*) and they (i.e. the scholars) said, "Among the benefits of it is that it is not forbidden for one of higher status to take from one of lower status."

13. I was told by Abū Ṭāhir Muḥammad Ibn Aḥmad Ibn 'Alī Al-Ashnānī, who said that he was informed by Aḥmad Ibn Isḥāq Al-Nahawāndī, who said that he was informed by Al-Ḥasan Ibn 'Abdu'l-Raḥmān Ibn Khallād, who said that he was informed by 'Abdullāh Ibn Aḥmad Ibn Ma'dān, who said that he was informed by Aḥmad Ibn Ḥarb Al-Mawṣilī, who said that he heard Muḥammad Ibn 'Ubayd saying:

> "A man with an abundant beard came to Al-A'mash and he asked him a question about young men which they might memorise and Al-A'mash turned to us and said: "Look at his beard: it bears four thousand aḥādīth and he is asking about young men."[527]

[527] Its chain of narrators is weak.

The author's Shaikh is trustworthy; a biography is given for him in *'Tārīkh Baghdād'* (1/324). Aḥmad Ibn Isḥāq Al-Nahawāndī is Abū 'Abdullāh Al-Baṣrī Al-Qāḍī; Al-Khaṭīb said in his *'Tārīkh'* (4/36), "He was trustworthy; he studied Shāfi'ī Jurisprudence from Al-Qāḍī Abū Ḥāmid Al-Mirwazī." His Shaikh was Al-Ramāhurmuzī, the author of the book: *'Al-Muḥaddith Al-Fāsil bain Al-Rāwī wa'l-Wā'ī'*.

Al-Ramāhurmuzi's Shaikh was 'Abdullāh Ibn Aḥmad Ibn Ma'dān Al-Ghazza'; this was the lineage attributed to him by Al-Mizzī in *'Tahẓīb Al-Kamāl'* (1/289) and he was one of the students of Aḥmad Ibn Ḥarb Al-Mawsilī, but I did not found any biography for him, except in Al-Sam'ānī's book *'Al-Ansāb'* (4/289) and he mentioned that he narrated on the authority of some of the Shaikhs and that Al-Ramāhurmuzī narrated from him.

CHAPTER FOUR

And it should be known that studying many books of ḥadīth and narrations does not make a man into a jurist; he will only become a jurist by deriving the meanings and careful study of them.

14. I was told by Muḥammad Ibn Aḥmad Ibn Al-Ashnānī, who said that he was informed by Aḥmad Ibn Isḥāq Al-Nahāwandī, who said that he was informed by Al-Ḥasan Ibn ʿAbdu'l-Raḥmān, who said that he was told by Aḥmad Ibn Muḥammad Ibn Suhayl Al-Faqīh, who said that he was informed by Muḥammad Ibn Ismāʿīl Abū ʿAbdullāh Al-Aṣbāhanī in Makkah, who said that he was informed by Muṣʿab Al-Zubayrī, who said that he heard Mālik Ibn Anas, who said to his nephews—Abū Bakr and Ismāʿīl, the two sons of Abū Uways:

> "I see that you love this subject and study it." They said, "Yes." He said, "If you like to benefit from it and for Allāh to benefit you by it, then acquire less (*aḥādīth*)

and study them."[528]

15. We were informed by Muḥammad Ibn Al-Ḥusayn Al-Qaṭṭān, who said that were informed by ʿAbdullāh Ibn Isḥāq Ibn Ibrāhīm Al-Baghawī, who said that he was informed by Aḥmad Ibn Al-Sirrī, who said that he was informed by Sahl Ibn Zanjalah, who said that he was informed by Sufyān, who reported on the authority of Ismāʿīl Ibn Umayyah, who reported on the authority of Al-Aʿmash that he said:

---

[528] I have not found any biography for Al-Ramāhurmuzī's Shaikh, or for his Shaikh.

The tradition was narrated by Al-Ramāhurmuzī in *'Al-Muḥaddith Al-Fāsil'* (p. 241-242).

It should not be thought that what is intended by the author's words: "And it should be known that studying many books of ḥadīth... etc." is a prohibition of studying narrations; there is only an encouragement in it to study the meanings of the aḥādīth, to go to great lengths to acquire the jurisprudence from it and to give priority to this over increasing one's acquisition of sources for the ḥadīth, or *al-gharā'ib*, which would lead to a person giving priority to that over the acquisition of jurisprudence from the ḥadīth, learning its meanings and its rulings. It should not be thought that understanding the ḥadīth and its meaning refers to seeking the opinions of the followers of a *madhhab*, especially the later ones. It only means studying the *fiqh* of the Qur'ān and Sunnah and the rulings that they prove.

Imam Aḥmād (may Allāh have mercy on him) censured the studying of the opinions of men and the abandonment of confirmed *Sunan*.

ʿUthmān Ibn Saʿīd Al-Dārimī transmitted from him the words: "Do not look at the books of Abū ʿUbayd, nor the writings of Isḥāq, nor Sufyān, nor Al-Shāfiʿī, nor Mālik, but instead you should refer to the original source (i.e. the Qur'ān and Sunnah)."

It should not be thought that he was belittling the status of these scholars—may Allāh protect us from that—and how could he do so, when he has commended a number of them. What he intended by that was only was to close the door on seeking the opinions of men and dependence on them, giving them priority over the Book (of Allāh) and the Sunnah, even when they contradict an authentic proof, as is the case with the later adherents of the schools of Islamic Jurisprudence.

And whoever said that the people of ḥadīth are ignorant is in error; rather, they are the narrators and spreaders of blessings. Among them are those who are only narrators—and this is not a denunciation of them, for if they did not bear the burden of the *Sunan* and the traditions and the acquisition of them—whether they are confirmed or not—many *Sunan* and numerous traditions would be lost to the Muslims in every time and place. So maligning them is a characteristic of the innovators.

> "When I heard ḥadīth, I said: If I sit in a room, I may deliver legal verdicts to the people." He added, "So I sat in a room and the first question they asked me I did not know [the answer to] it!"[529]

16. We were informed by Muḥammad Ibn Aḥmad Ibn 'Alī Al-Daqqāq, who said that he was informed by Aḥmad Ibn Isḥāq Al-Nahawāndī, who said that he was informed by Ibn Khallād, who said that he was informed by Abū 'Umar Aḥmad Ibn Muḥammad Ibn Suhayl, who said that he was told by a man from among the scholars, whose name he mentioned, though Ibn Khallād said, "I forget his name," that he said:

> "A woman stood in a gathering in which Yaḥyā Ibn Ma'īn, Abū Khaythamah and Khalaf Ibn Sālim were present and they were reminding each other of ḥadīth, and [she said,] "I heard them saying, 'The Messenger of Allāh (ﷺ) said... it was narrated by So-and-so and no one but So-and-so transmitted it.' So I asked them about whether the menstruating woman may take part in the washing of a dead body, when she is the washer, but not one of them answered.Then they began to look at each other and as Abū Thawr approached and they said to her, 'You should approach.' So I turned towards him as he came near to me and I asked him and he said, 'Wash the dead, in accordance with the ḥadīth of Al-Qāsim, on the authority of 'A'ishah (*raḍiyAllāhu 'anhuā*), who reported that the Prophet (ﷺ) said to her, 'Your menses is not in your hand,' and her saying: 'I used to part the hair of the Prophet (ﷺ) with water when I was menstruating.' Abū Thawr said, 'So if she

[529] Its chain of narrators is weak.
In it is 'Abdullāh Ibn Isḥāq Al-Baghawī, of whom Al-Dāraquṭnī said, "There is leen (i.e. a lack of strictness) in him.

parted the hair of the living, then the dead have more right to it.' They said, 'Yes, it was narrated by So-and-so and So-and-so told us of it, and they know it from such-and-such a source.' And they became engrossed with the sources, upon which the woman said, 'Where were you until now?!'[530]

[530] This story is extremely *munkar*.

In it is the Shaikh of Al-Ramāhurmuzī's Shaikh, who is unknown. In addition, Ibn Ma'īn and Abū Khaythamah were too knowledgeable to have not known the answer to a question such as this.

The amazing thing is a group from among those who claim to have knowledge have taken this story as a proof with which to malign the companions of ḥadīth. But how far from the truth is this and what has the ground to do with the Pleiades? They bore the knowledge of the Messenger of Allāh (ﷺ) and they transmitted it and defended it from the falsifications of the liars, the calumnies of the rumourmongers and the fabrications of the forgers.

Yes, we do not deny that some of the people of ḥadīth concerned themselves only with the narration, but this does not detract from their status, nor does it diminish their good work. In addition, among the numerous scholars who possess understanding of the Book (of Allāh) and the Sunnah, they are a minority.

This is Imām Aḥmad (may Allāh have mercy on him), the Commander of the Faithful in Ḥadīth, a leading jurist, founder of the (Ḥanbalī) school of jurisprudence, whose legal opinion is given priority over that of others, due to what is known of his vast learning in the field of traditions, narrations and understanding (of them), in acceptance and rejection. So may Allāh reward the people of ḥadīth, for they are like the pearl in the necklace and the head on a body.

CHAPTER FIVE

He [Al-Khaṭīb] said, "The tongues of the transgressors only hastened to malign the Scholars of Ḥadīth because of their ignorance of *Usūl Al-Fiqh* (Principles of Islāmic Jurisprudence) and their proofs from among the Sunan, coupled with their lack of knowledge of context. But when a Companion of Ḥadīth (*Aṣḥāb al-Ḥadīth*) possesses understanding, their tongues are silenced and his status is magnified in the hearts and minds and those who maligned him are struck with fear.

17. Muḥammad Ibn ʿAbdullāh Al-Ḥannāʾī imparted to us that he was informed by Jaʿfar Ibn Muḥammad Ibn Nuṣayr Al-Khaldi, who said that he was informed by ʿAbdullāh Ibn Jābir Al-Ṭarsūsī, who said that he was informed by Muḥammad Ibn Al-ʿArjī Al-ʿAskarī, who said that he heard Muslim Al-Jarmī saying that he heard Wakee' saying:

> "I was met by Abū Ḥanīfah and he said to me, 'If

> you gave up the writing of ḥadīth and studied Islāmic Jurisprudence, would that not be better?' I said, 'Does not ḥadīth encompass all of Islāmic Jurisprudence?' He asked, 'What do you say regarding a woman who claims to be pregnant, but her husband denies paternity?' I said, 'I was told by 'Abbād Ibn Manṣūr, who reported on the authority of 'Ikrimah, who reported on the authority of Ibn 'Abbās (*raḍiyAllāhu 'anhumā*) that the Prophet (ﷺ) made *li'an* between them, due to the pregnancy.'

Then he left me and whenever he saw me on the path after that, he would take another path." [531]

18. I was informed by Al-Ḥasan Ibn Muḥammad Ibn Al-Ḥasan Al-Khallāl, who said that he was informed by Muḥammad Ibn Al-'Abbās Al-Khazzāz, who said that he was informed by Abū Bakr Ibn Abū Dāwūd, who said that he was informed by 'Alī Ibn Khashram, who said that he heard Wakī' saying on more than one occasion:

> "O young men! Acquire understanding the jurisprudence of ḥadīth, for if you understand the jurisprudence of ḥadīth, you will not be defeated by the people

[531] Muslim Al-Ḥarbī is Muslim Ibn Abū Muslim 'Abdu'l-Raḥmān Al-Jarmī; his biography is given by Al-Khaṭīb in *'Tārīkh Baghdād'* (13/100) and he said, "He was trustworthy." He was also mentioned by Ibn Ḥibbān in *'Al-Thiqāt'* (9/158), and he said, "Possibly he made mistakes."

And I have not found any biography for 'Abdullāh Ibn Jābir Al-Ṭarsūsī and Muḥammad Ibn Al-'Arjī Al-'Askarī.

[532] Its chain of narrators is authentic.

Muḥammad Ibn Al-'Abbās Al-Khazzāz is Abū 'Umar Ibn Ḥayawayh.

And the saying of Wakī': "O young men! Acquire understanding the jurisprudence of ḥadīth..." means that if you learn their meanings and what benefits can be derived from them, such as rulings and (the answers to *fiqh*) questions, you will not be defeated =

of opinion."[532]

19. We were informed by Al-Ḥasan Ibn Al-Ḥusayn Ibn Al-ʿAbbās Al-Naʿālī, who said that he was informed by Abū Bakr Aḥmad Ibn Jaʿfar Ibn Muḥammad Ibn Silm Al-Khatlī, who said that he was informed by Aḥmad Ibn ʿAlī Al-Ubbār, who said that he was informed by ʿAlī Ibn[533] Khashram Al-Mirwazī, who said that he heard Wakīʿ saying to the Companions of Ḥadīth:

> "If you study the *fiqh* of *ḥadīth* and learn it, you will not be defeated by the adherents of opinion. Abū Ḥanīfah does not express an opinion regarding anything.... except that we narrate something regarding it."

=

by the people of opinion, for you will only rule based on the Sunnah of the Prophet (ﷺ), while they will rule based on qiyas (analogy) and the musings of their minds, without citing evidence from aḥādīth or traditions.

533 Its chain of narrators is weak.

A biography of the author's Shaikh is given in *'Tārīkh Baghdād'* (7/3), in which he said, "We wrote about him and he heard many narrations, however he spoiled his reputation by reporting things as if he had heard them personally, when he had not."

And the meaning of the tradition is that whenever Abū Ḥanīfah delivered a *fatwa* (legal ruling) in any matter based on his opinion, the people of ḥadīth would narrate something related to it; so a *fatwa* based on a tradition is more worthy to be acted upon.

Arriving at the truth through opinion does not make a person from the people of the Sunnah, until he abandons opinion and arrives at it based on the Sunnah and regarding this meaning Imām Aḥmad said in *'Risalah 'Abdūs Ibn Mālik Al-'Aṭṭār'*, "...and from the indispensible Sunnah, which, whoever abandoned any aspect of it and did not accept it or believe in it, he will not be from its followers..." then he mentioned some things from it, including: "That he does not argue or debate with anyone or learn disputation, for debating regarding *Qadar* (Divine Foreordainment), dreams, the (meanings of) the Qur'ān and the Sunnah is detested and prohibited. Such a person, even if he arrives at the Sunnah through his philosophising, will not be considered to be from the people of the Sunnah until he abandons disputation and believes in the traditions."

And regarding this meaning, the Imām of the Ḥanbalī jurists during his time, Abū Muḥammad Al-Barbaharī said in *'Sharḥ Al-Sunnah'* (p. 24): "Debate, argument, disputation and quarrelling are an innovation which impairs the heart, even if the perpetrator arrives at the truth and his conclusion concurs with the Sunnah.

CHAPTER SIX

He (may Allāh have mercy on him) said: "It is essential for the one studying Islāmic Jurisprudence to have a teacher from whom he learns, to whom he refers for explanations of things that he does not understand, from whom he can study the ways of *ijtihād*[534] and the means of distinguishing between what is correct and what is false.

20. We were informed by Abū'l-Fatḥ 'Abdu'l-Karīm Ibn Muḥammad Ibn Aḥmad Ibn Al-Qāsim Al-Muḥamilī, who said that he was informed by 'Umar Ibn Aḥmad Ibn 'Uthmān Al-Marūrūzī, who said that he was informed by Al-Ḥusayn Ibn Aḥmad Ibn Ṣadāqah, who said that he was informed by Aḥmad Ibn Abū Khaythāmah, who said that he was informed by Sulaymān Ibn Abū Shaikh, who said that he was informed by one of the people of Kūfah, who said:

---

[534] Independent judgment in a legal or theological question, based on the interpretation and application of the four *Usūl* (Qur'ān, Sunnah, *Qiyās* and *Ijmā'*).

> "Abū Ḥanīfah (may Allāh have mercy on him) was asked about a study circle in the *masjid* in which they are studying Islāmic Jurisprudence and he said: 'Does it have a head (i.e. a leader)?' They said, 'No.' He said, 'These people will never have knowledge (of Islamic Jurisprudence).'"[535]

21. We were informed by Al-Ḥasan Ibn Abū Ṭālib, who said that he was informed by ʿAlī Ibn ʿAmr Al-Ḥarīrī, who said that ʿAlī Ibn Muḥammad Ibn Kās Al-Nakhaʿī told them that he was informed by Ibrāhīm Ibn Isḥāq Al-Zuhrī, who said that he was informed by Abū Nuʿaym, who said:

> "I passed by Zafar and he was wrapped in a cloak, and he said, 'O Aḥwal![536] Come, and I will sift your aḥādīth for you.' So I showed him what I had heard and he said, 'This may be accepted, this may not be accepted, this here abrogates and this is abrogated.'"[537]

22. We were told by Muḥammad Ibn ʿAlī Al-Ṣūrī via dictation, who said that he was informed by ʿAbdu'l-Raḥmān Ibn ʿUmar Al-Miṣrī, who said that he was informed by Muḥammad Ibn

[535] Its chain of narrators is weak.

This is due to the unknown status of the narrators on the authority of Abū Ḥanīfah.

And the subject of the chapter is: learning from Shaikhs and abandoning study from manuscripts (i.e. books).

Al-Shāfiʿī (may Allāh have mercy on him) said, "Whoever learnt *fiqh* from the depths of books (i.e. purely from books) will be deprived of the rulings."

And some of them (i.e. the scholars) said, "Among the greatest of trials is a Shaikh of books."

This was quoted by Ibn Jamāʿah (p. 87).

Details of this question can be found in our book *'Al-Subul Al-Nājiʿah li-Ṭalab Al-ʿUlūm Al-Nāfiʿah'*.

[536] *Aḥwal*: Squint-eyed.

[537] Its chain of narrators is authentic.

The author's Shaikh is Al-Ḥasan Ibn Muḥammad Al-Khallāl.

Aḥmad Ibn ʿAbdullāh Ibn Warkān Al-ʿĀmirī, who said that he was informed by Ibrāhīm Ibn Abū Dāwūd, who said that he was informed by ʿAlī Ibn Maʿbad, who said that he was informed by ʿUbaydullāh Ibn ʿAmr, who said:

> "A man came to Al-Aʿmash and asked him about a certain matter while Abū Ḥanīfah was sitting there. Al-Aʿmash said, 'O Nuʿmān! Speak about it.' So he answered and Al-Aʿmash said, 'From where did say this?' He replied, 'From your ḥadīth, which you related to us.' He answered, 'Yes, we are apothecaries, and you are physicians."[538]

23. We were informed by Al-Qāḍī Abū ʿAbdullāh Al-Ḥusayn Ibn ʿAlī Al-Ṣaymarī, who said that he was informed by ʿAbdullāh Ibn Muḥammad Al-Shāhid, who said that he was informed by Mukarram Ibn Aḥmad, who said that he was informed by Aḥmad Ibn ʿAṭiyyah...

And we were informed by Al-Ḥasan Ibn ʿAlī Al-Jawharī, who said that he was informed by Muḥammad Ibn Al-ʿAbbās Al-Khazzāz, who said that he was informed by Abū Bakr ʿAbdullāh Ibn Muḥammad Ibn Ziyād Al-Naysabūrī, who said that he heard Abū Ibrāhīm Al-Mizanī saying that he was informed by ʿAlī Ibn Maʿbad, who said that he was informed by ʿUbaydullāh Ibn ʿAmr, who said:

---

[538] It is likely that Muḥammad Ibn Aḥmad Ibn ʿAbdullāh Ibn Warkān Al-ʿĀmirī is the person whose biography was given by Al-Dhahabī in *'Al-Mīzān'* (3/464) and he is the son of ʿAbdu'l-Jabbār Al-ʿĀmirī , but Ibn Warkan is not in his name. Regarding this last, Ibn Yoonus said, "He used to tell lies and he related a fabricated transcript.

The tradition was narrated by Ibn ʿAbdu'l-Barr in *'Jamiʿ Bayān Al-ʿIlm'* (2/131) from another source, on the authority of ʿAlī Ibn Maʿbad, but it includes someone whom I do not know.

"We were with Al-Aʿmash and he was asking Abū Hanīfah about certain matters and Abū Ḥanīfah was answering him. Al-Aʿmash said to him, 'From where did you get this?' He replied, 'You related to us such-and-such a ḥadīth on the authority of Ibrāhīm and you related to us such-and-such a ḥadīth on the authority of Al-Shaʿbī.' On this, Al-Aʿmash said, 'O assembly of jurists! You are the physicians and we are the apothecaries'."

And the wording of the ḥadīth is that of Al-Ṣaymarī.[539]

24. We were informed by Abū Muslim Jaʿfar Ibn Babī, Al-Faqīh, Al-Jīlī, who said that he was informed by Abū Bakr Muḥammad Ibn Ibrāhīm Ibn Al-Muqrī', in Aṣbāhan, who said that he was informed by Muḥammad Ibn Khālid Ibn Yazīd Al-Barzaʿī, who said that he heard ʿAṭiyyah Ibn Baqīyyah saying that his father said to him, "I was with Shuʿbah Ibn Al-Ḥajjāj and he said to me, 'O Abū Muḥammad! If a complex question came to you, whom would you ask about it?' I said to myself, 'This is a man whose mind impresses me.' Then I replied, 'O Abū Bastam! We would address it to you and to your companions, so that you might deliver a legal ruling for us.' He said, "A short while later, a man came to him and said, 'O Abū Bastam! A man struck another man on his skull and the man who was struck claimed that he had lost his sense of smell.' Shuʿbah then began to busy himself looking to right and left and so I indicated to the man that I insisted on a reply, upon which he turned towards me and said, 'O Abū Yaḥmad! What a great calamity to his family; nay, by Allāh, I do not have anything regarding it. But you may deliver a verdict.' I said, 'He asks you, and I will deliver a verdict?' He said, 'Because I have asked you.' So I said, 'I heard Al-Awzāʿī and Al-Zaydī saying, 'He should

[539] It is authentic due to the second chain of narrators.

completely crush mustard seeds and them sniff them, then if he sneezes, he has lied, but if he does not sneeze, then he has spoken the truth.'So I brought them and said, 'O jurist! By Allāh, a man who has lost his sense of smell will never sneeze'."[540]

This is the end of the letter of advice by Al-Khaṭīb.

All Praise and Thanks be to Allāh,
the Lord of the worlds.

[540] Its chain of narrators is weak.

'Aṭiyyah Ibn Baqīyyah was mentioned by Ibn Abū Ḥāṭim in *'Al-Jarḥ wa'l-Ta'dīl'* (1/3/381) and he said, "I wrote about him and his status was one of truthfulness, but there was some carelessness in him." He was also mentioned by Ibn Ḥibbān in *'Al-Thiqāt'* (8/528) and he said, "He makes mistakes and he narrates things that are *gharīb*; when he narrates on the authority of his father, his aḥādīth are respected, unlike the things that are *mudallasah*.

And the story is amazing and strange!!

And Allāh knows better the truth.

The verifier and explainer said, "This simple explanation and brief commentary was completed on the afternoon of Saturday, the 22nd day of the month of Dhū'l-Qa'dah 1415 AH. We ask Allāh, Most Glorified to grant us success, right guidance and a good conclusion.

The Original Manuscript Picture

الورقة الأولى والثانية من الجزء الأول

The Original Manuscript Picture

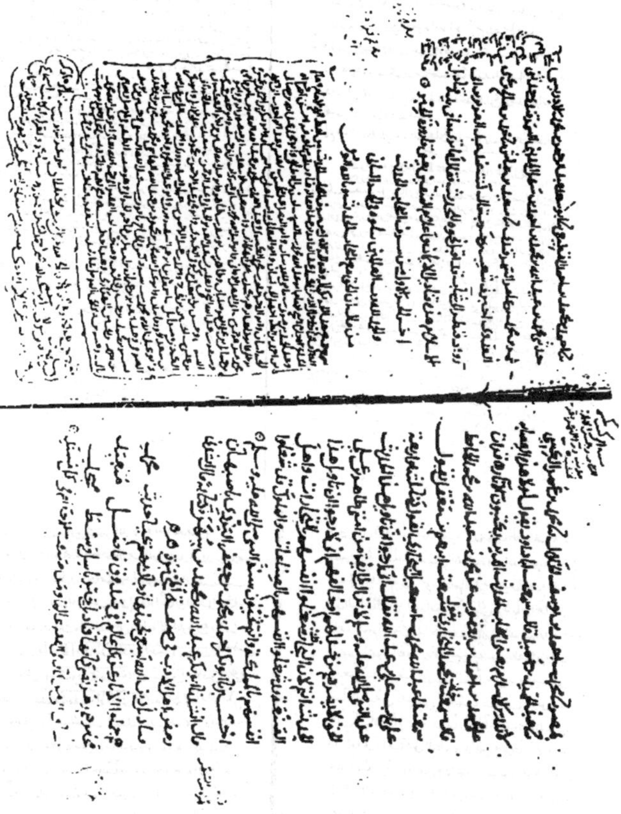

الورقة الأخيرة من الجزء الأول

The Original Manuscript Picture

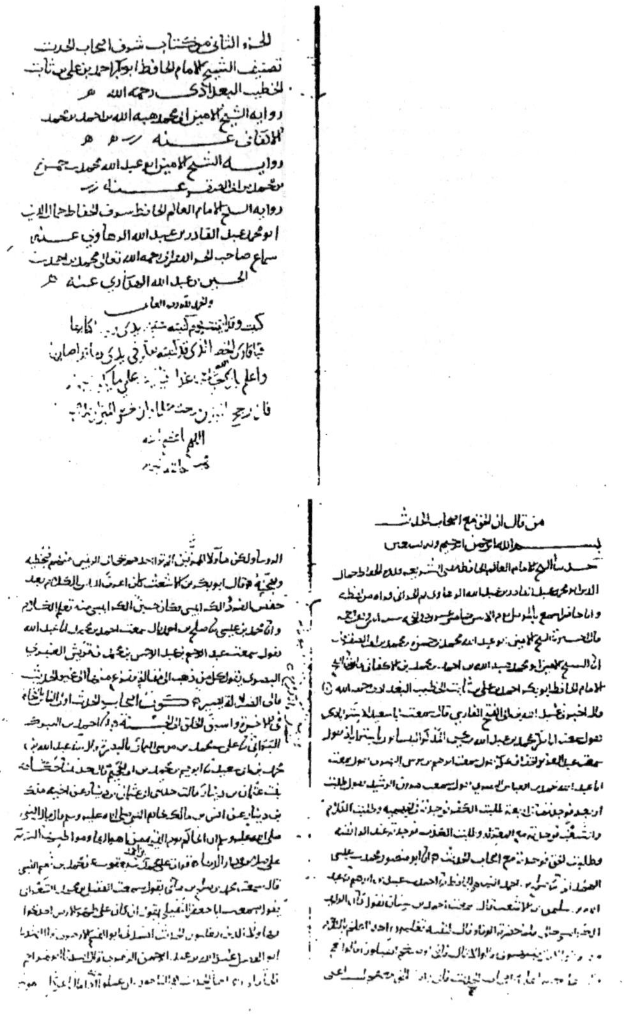
الجزء الثاني من كتاب شرف أصحاب الحديث
تصنيف الشيخ الإمام الحافظ أبو بكر أحمد بن علي بن ثابت
الخطيب البغدادي رحمه الله

الورقة الأولى والثانية من الجزء الثاني

The Original Manuscript Picture

الجزء الثالث من كتاب شرف أصحاب الحديث
تصنيف الشيخ الإمام الحافظ ابو بكر احمد بن علي بن ثابت
الخطيب البغدادي

بسم الله الرحمن الرحيم
ذكر ما رآه الصالحون في المنام لأصحاب الحديث من الحباء والإكرام

الورقة الأولى والثانية من الجزء الثالث

The Original Manuscript Picture

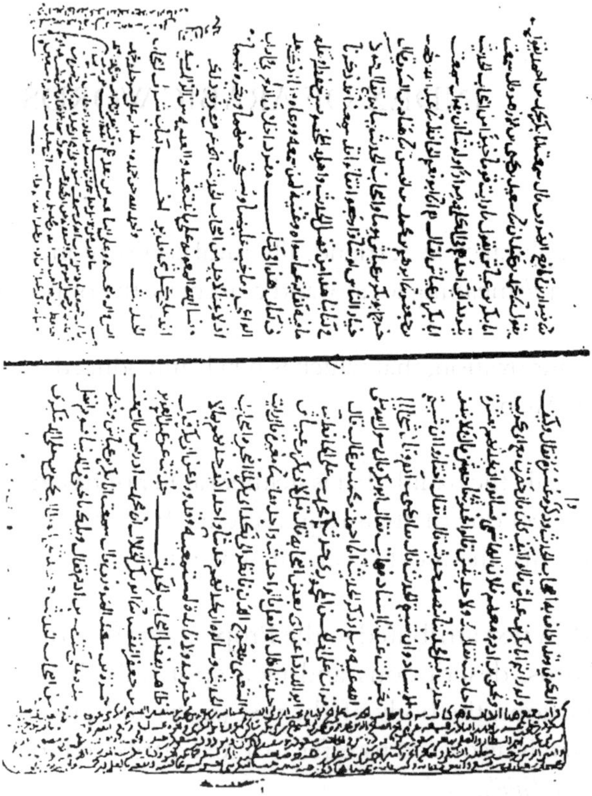

الورقة الأخيرة من الكتاب

INDEX OF ARABIC WORDS

Awliyāʾ: plural of *walī*; friend, ally, loyal companion. From the word *wilāyah* meaning loyalty and closeness, the opposite of enmity.

Bidʿah: innovation, that which is newly introduced into the religion of Allāh.

Ḍaʿīf: weak; the ḥadīth that is neither ṣaḥīḥ nor ḥasan because it fails to meet one of their requirements. It is of varying degrees of severity, the most severe of which being mawḍūʿ, fabricated.

Ḥadīth: A text attributed to the Prophet (ﷺ) describing his actions, words, descriptions and tacit approvals. It consists of two portions, the body of the text (*matn*) and the *isnād*. Rarely the term is also used to refer to a text attributed to a Companion or a *Tābiʿī*.

Ḥāfiẓ: pl. *ḥuffāẓ*. Ḥadīth Master, commonly referred to one who has memorised at least 100,000 ḥadīths.

Ḥasan: good, fair. A ḥadīth whose *isnād* is continuously linked of just, morally upright narrators but whose precision (*ḍabṭ*) falls short of the requirements of the ṣaḥīḥ ḥadīth; containing no irregularity (*shādh*) and no hidden defect (*ʿillah*). A ḥadīth can be ḥasan in and of itself, or contain a defect but still be ruled to be so due to supporting evidences.

Ḥudūd: limits, boundaries. The limits ordained by Allāh, prescribed punishments.

Iḥsān: beneficence, excellence. To worship Allāh as if one is seeing Him, and knowing that even though one sees Him not, He sees the servant.

Ikhlāṣ: sincerity, to strip oneself of worshiping any besides Allāh such that everything one does is performed only to draw closer to Him and for His pleasure. It is to purify ones actions from any but the Creator having a share in them, from any defect or self-desire. The one who has true *ikhlāṣ* (*mukhliṣ*) will be free of *riyāʾ*.

ʿIlm: knowledge.

Īmān: The firm belief, complete acknowledgement and acceptance of all that Allāh and His Messenger have commanded to have faith in, submitting to it both inwardly and outwardly. It is the acceptance and belief of the heart that includes the actions of the heart and body, therefore it encompasses the establishment of the whole religion. This is why the Imāms and Salaf used to say, 'Faith is the statement of the heart and tongue, action of the heart, tongue and limbs.' Hence it comprises statement, action and belief, it increases through obedience and decreases through disobedience. It includes the beliefs of faith, its morals and manners and the actions demanded by it.

Islām: submission, submitting to the will of Allāh through following His law as revealed upon the tongue of the Messenger (ﷺ).

Isnād: support. The chain of authorities on which a narration is based, linking the end narrator of a narration to the one it is attributed to, be it the Prophet (ﷺ) or anyone else, narrator by narrator.

Ittibāʿ: following, technically referring to following the Sunnah of the Prophet (ﷺ).

Jāhiliyyah: Pre-Islāmic Ignorance. Technically this refers to the condition of a people before the guidance of Allāh reaches them, or the state of a people that prevents them from accepting the guidance of Allāh.

Kalām: speech, discourse. Technically used to refer to dialectics and scholastic theology.

Kufr: denial, rejection, hiding, technically referring to disbelief. It can be major (removing a person from the fold of Islām) or minor (not removing a person from the fold of Islām).

Majhūl: unknown. A reference to a narrator from whom only one narrator narrates (*majhūl al-ʿain*) or whose state of precision (*ḍabṭ*) is unknown (*majhūl al-ḥāl*), such a narrator makes the *isnād ḍaʿīf.*

Matrūk: abandoned. A narrator who is accused of lying, or makes many mistakes, or makes mistakes in aḥādith that are agreed upon, or narrates from famous narrators that which those narrators do not know.

Munqaṭiʿ: that ḥadīth from which the narrator just before the Companion has been omitted from its *isnād.*

Mursal: disconnected. A ḥadīth whereby a *Tābiʿī* narrates directly from the Prophet (ﷺ) without mentioning the Companion. In the view of the majority of Scholars it is a sub-category of ḍaʿīf.

Muṣḥaf: text of the Qur'ān

Qadr: Divine Decree and Destiny.

Qur'ān: The actual Word of Allāh revealed to the Prophet (ﷺ) in the Arabic language through the medium of the Angel Gabriel and the greatest miracle bestowed him. It consists of 114 chapters commencing with al-Fātiḥah and ending with an-Nās.

Ṣāḥīḥ: correct, authentic. A ḥadith which has a continuously linked *isnād*, of just, morally upright and precise narrators; containing no irregularity (*shādh*) or hidden defect (*ʿillah*). Hence five conditions have to be met: the *isnād* being continuously linked; the justice (*ʿadl*) of the narrator; the precision (*ḍabṭ*) of the narrator; its not being *shādh*; and its not containing an *ʿillah*. The ḥadīth can be ṣaḥīḥ in and of itself, or it can contain a defect but still be ruled to be ṣaḥīḥ due to supporting evidences.

Salaf: predecessors. Technically used to refer to the best generations of Muslims, the first three generation: the *Ṣaḥābah*, the *Tābiʿūn* and the *Tabʿ Tābiʿūn* due to the ḥadīth, "The best of people are my generation, then the one that follows, then the one that follows."

Shādh: irregular, odd. A ḥadīth narrated by a trustworthy and precise narrator that contradicts the narrative of other narrators or the narration of one more trustworthy and precise than him, provided that a reconciliation is not possible.

Shirk: association, technically referring to directing a right that is due to Allāh Alone to another object of creation, either completely or partially. It can be major (removing a person from the fold of Islām) or minor (not removing a person from the fold of Islām).

Sunnah: way, path. The actions, words, descriptions, commands, prohibitions and tacit approvals of the Prophet (ﷺ).

Tābiʿūn: The generation following that of the Companions.

Tabʿ Tābiʿūn: The generation following that of the *Tābiʿūn.*

Tadlīs: deceit. An action of a narrator whereby he makes out that he heard something from a particular narrator what he did not hear or conceals the identity of the one he is narrating from. In order to do so, he will use terms that are vague such as 'such-and-such said' and 'on the authority of such-and-such.' The first type of *tadlīs* is blameworthy and constitutes a defect in the *isnād.* The second is dependant upon exactly what was done and the motives of the narrator, it can be blameworthy or not.

Taqwā: the basic meaning of which is setting a barrier between two things. This is why it is said that one *ittaqā* with his shield, i.e. he set it as a barrier between him and the one who wished him evil. Therefore it is as if the one who has taqwa (*muttaqī*) has used his following the commands of Allāh and avoiding His prohibitions as a barrier between himself and the Punishment. Hence he has preserved and fortified himself against the punishment of Allāh through his obeying Him.

Tawḥīḍ: unification, monotheism, the belief in the absolute Oneness of Allāh. It is to believe that Allāh Alone is the creator, nourisher, and sustainer of the worlds; it is to believe that Allāh Alone deserves to be worshipped; and it is to believe that He has unique and perfect Names and Attributes that far transcend anything that one can imagine.